GOD AND THE U

THE JUNGIAN CLASSICS SERIES

GOD AND THE UNCONSCIOUS

by

VICTOR WHITE
O.P., S.T.B.

with a foreword by

C. G. JUNG
and an introduction by

WILLIAM EVERSON

Spring Publications

First published in Great Britain in 1952
© Victor White 1952
Reissued as revised edition, 1982 under license by Spring
Publications, Inc.
Introduction by William Everson © 1982 by Spring
Publications, Inc.

Printed in the United States of America for Spring Publications,
Inc., P. O. Box 222069, Dallas, Texas 75222 by Braun-
Brumfield, Inc., Ann Arbor, Michigan

European agent: Spring, Postfach, 8800–Thalwil, Switzerland
Distributed also by Japan Spring Sha, Inc.; 31, Shichiku-
Momonomoto-Cho; Kitaku, Kyoto, 603, Japan

"Foreword to White's 'God and the Unconscious'," pp. 299–
310 of *The Collected Works of C. G. Jung*, trans. R. F. C. Hull,
Bollingen Series XX, Vol. 11: *Psychology and Religion: West and
East*. Copyright © 1958, 1969 by Princeton University Press.
Reprinted by permission of Princeton University Press.

Library of Congress Cataloging in Publication Data

White, Victor, 1902–1960.
   God and the unconscious.

   (The Jungian classics series ;   )
   Originally published: London : Harvill Press, 1952.
   Includes index.
   1. Psychology, Religious. 2. Jung, C. G. (Carl
Gustav), 1875–1961. I. Title. II. Series.
BL53.W52   1982   200'.1'9   82–19153
ISBN 0-88214-503-7

CONTENTS

		page
Introduction by William Everson		vii
Foreword by C. G. Jung		xv
Author's Preface		xxix
I.	The Twilight of the Gods	1
II.	The Gods Go A-Begging	13
III.	The Unconscious and God	23
IV.	Freud, Jung and God	41
V.	The Frontiers of Theology and Psychology	61
VI.	Aristotle, Aquinas and Man	81
VII.	Revelation and the Unconscious	107
VIII.	Psychotherapy and Ethics	141
IX.	The Analyst and the Confessor	163
X.	Devils and Complexes	175
XI.	Gnosis, Gnosticism and Faith	191
XII.	The Dying God	215
Acknowledgments		235
Index		237

INTRODUCTION

READING this book again after so many years, I was taken back to the autumn of 1955 when Victor White was a visiting lecturer at St. Albert's College, the Dominican House of Studies in Oakland, California. We were walking in the monastery garden, priest and lay brother, at a time of confusion and aridity in my spiritual life. Someone had placed his book in my hands as an introduction to a new way of addressing my problem. I was, however, as yet suspicious of depth psychology's pertinence to the spiritual life, preferring to suffer it out with St. John of the Cross, and it would be two years before this book would have its full impact on my life. Nevertheless, I read it with interest, and now I asked him about the *privatio boni*, the doctrine of the non-essentiality of evil as seen in the abiding tradition of the Church since St. Augustine, and which Jung opposed. Father White smiled and told me an anecdote regarding the difficulties besetting this immemorial problem.

It seems an old theologian was lecturing in the *studium* on the problem of evil, and noticed that one of the younger friars had fallen asleep. The old priest stopped his discourse and rapped on the lectern. "Brother John," he said sharply, "I have a question for you. Why does God permit evil?" The sleeper awoke with a start and stammered, "I . . . uh . . . Actually, Father, I knew that, but I have forgotten." The old priest looked about him in mock consternation. "This is indeed lamentable!" he exclaimed. "Here is a question men have wrestled with since the beginning of thought. Philosophers have wrenched their minds in the effort to solve it. Theologians have ransacked Scripture for some clue to its enigma. Mystics have stormed Heaven beseeching the Almighty for some glimmer of light on this impenetrable mystery. And in all this time, all this speculation and prayer, only two beings have ever claimed to know the answer: God and you. And you have forgotten!''

That was only a quarter-century ago but in retrospect it seems like another age, another epoch. Father White is no longer alive, and neither is Jung, and I am no longer a lay brother. It was during the Pontificate of Pius XII, who was very much alive, and very watchful. The Twenty-first Ecumenical Council, called Vatican II, was undreamed of. The Church pursued Her patient, immemorial way, undisturbed by innovation. Latin was the universal language of the liturgy. The ancient penitential practices were fervently performed. Confession, the Sacrament of Penance, as a conspicuous sign of loyal Catholic observance, was de rigueur. A rigid censorship over Catholic thought and expression prevailed. Truly, as Captain of the Bark of Peter, Pius XII ran a tight ship.

Into this cloistered atmosphere Victor White's little book wafted like an invigorating breeze. Though written by an Englishman addressing a European readership, its force was not lost upon the American Catholic intelligentsia. Assuredly no hurricane, its purpose was not to proclaim or revolutionize, but to enlighten and inspire, to reassure and confirm. This it did by inviting us into the fabled Unconscious, that bugbear of classic philosophical psychology. Moreover, it suggested an alternative to the uneasy modus vivendi between Catholic psychiatry and Freudian psychoanalysis, based on a moot distinction between *soul* and *psyche*, wherein the mentally distressed religionist placed his immortal soul in the sacred hands of his confessor, and his mortal psyche in the profane hands of his shrink. If the book was largely ignored by these professionals it was, for the Catholic literary community, the poets and writers no less than the teachers of literature and the humanities, a stimulus and an assurance. Indubitably orthodox in its Thomistic certitude, it gave us the courage to

liberate the imagination in the van of the intellect rather than
relegate it to the rear as camp follower or drudge.

The point is important, because the Catholic society this
book confronts today is a radically different world from the
one it was composed to engage, something that should be
borne in mind on opening its pages. The tight ship of Pius
XII is no more. Ancient formulas have been turned out and
the liturgy restored to the vernacular. There is now no Index
of Forbidden Books, no ecclesiastical censorship. The penitential practices are discontinued, and confession as an external sign of conformism is not practiced. Even in the sexual
sphere, sociologists find the practice of Catholics no longer at
variance with that of other Americans, attributing this to the
triumph of "the demographic power of the melting pot" over
ideology. Perhaps the most visible effect of the sexual revolution has been the renouncement of vows by hundreds of
priests and religious. Whether these innovations are all to the
good is debatable, but that they constitute the most radical
break with tradition in the history of the Church is generally
agreed.

Moreover, in the world at large, there has been a significant
shift in the climate of opinion since this book was published.
European thought in the fifties was dominated by the existentialism of Sartre and Camus, atheistic in emphasis. It was this
emphasis that led Victor White to open his book with
chapters devoted to the problem of atheism and its appropria-
tion of the function, if not the fixtures, of religion. These
chapters do not have quite the same relevance today, for a potent infusion of Oriental thought has eroded intellectual con-
ventions, leaving old-fashioned materialistic atheism somewhat passe. In its place scientific skepticism's search for
religious orientation finds a host in Buddhism's "no God-no
soul-no afterlife" equation to emerge, in my view, as the greatest threat to Christianity today. Which is not to deny its
positive aspects. I once heard Victor White remark that the

impact of Oriental thought on Catholicism in the twentieth century would be as marked as that of Aristotle in the thirteenth. But that was before Vatican II had arrived to draw Catholic concern from Sacramentalism to Social Action.

Although this book is addressed to the committed Catholic, what might be its appeal for the practicing Jungian, professional or lay? I would say the same now as then: the precision of its theological specification on issues close to psychological theory. This need is perennial, and the demand for clarity in a field fraught with pitfalls is obvious. The great appeal in Victor White's writing is a quality I can only describe as *sanity*. This sanity is the product of an intensely realized Thomism, though it is by no means the property of every Thomist. With Victor White you never get any feeling of logic-chopping, every opposition receiving the respect it deserves. There is, moreover, an English cultural equipoise that American Thomists, and American intellectuals generally, have never attained, almost a cultural substance, instilled or imbibed rather than consciously acquired. Below these, behind them and sustaining them, is the presence of a benignant humanity, always, for me, the mark of the man's sanctity.

Hence no single essay in this book is dated, though some of the issues have shifted in emphasis. Take the chapter on "The Analyst and the Confessor." Though no longer center stage, the distinction remains important, and Victor White's insightful study keeps its freshness through the niceness of its distinctions. The chapter "Aristotle, Aquinas and Jung" has increased in relevance precisely because of our anti-Aristotelian bias. Even as I was reading on "Devils and Complexes," a friend called to say he was leaving for a convocation of the Church of Satan in San Francisco, making the chapter seem quite up-to-date. In fact our vast interest in the occult today makes pertinent the perspective established in "Gnosis, Gnosticism and Faith." These instances are only suggestive of the fertility and sharpness of discernment Victor White brought to his reflections.

And so we arrive back where we began, at the painful subject of Victor White's dispute with Jung regarding the *privatio
boni.* Given the weight of tradition supporting the doctrine,
the burden of proof would seem to lie with Jung, but any
satisfactory appraisal of the prolonged controversy must wait
on the publication of Victor White's side of the correspondence. One thing does emerge from a perusal of Jung's letters:
at no time did he feel threatened or extended by the
arguments of his opponent. He was always the lion. Even
when Victor White went so far in temerity as to accuse him of
making "a public parade of splenetic shadow"—a clear invasion by the theologian of the psychologist's sovereign
ground—in reply the lion merely shifted his paw, almost
yawned. This Olympian superiority only deserted him once.
When an interviewer needled him by quoting White's stric-
tures, the mask slipped. "What Victor White writes about
assimilation of the shadow is not to be taken seriously. Being
a Catholic priest he is bound hand and foot to the doctrine of
his Church, and has to defend every syllogism." The master
protests too much. As published in his final book, *Soul and
Psyche,* Victor White's "The Integration of Evil" is a brilliant
Jungian-Thomistic synthesis. If not definitive, it may well
serve as prolegomenon to a larger work of that distinction.

Yet reading Jung's side of the correspondence one wonders,
"Why did Victor White persist? After it was apparent the two
were at an impasse, why did he keep pressing?" The answer,
of course, is that Jung's intransigence on this fundamental
theological issue placed in jeopardy White's brilliantly crafted
linkage between analytical psychology and Roman Catholicism. In Chapter IV of the present work, White explained
how Catholic psychiatry actually felt more comfortable with
the materialistic premises of Freud. "The fact is that the very
religiousness of Jung, is apt to scare off the religious-minded
as much as, or more than, the irreligious." The watchdogs of
the Vatican were only too suspicious of this muddying of the
waters of the Lord, and stood ready to pounce. White's acer-

bity in distinguishing Jung's professional psychological astuteness from his "naive" theological maunderings must be seen in this light. We will never know to what degree White's qualifications forestalled at least a cautionary admonition from the Vatican, though his efforts can't be dismissed. But its cost was brutal: the collapse of friendship and collaboration between an eminent psychologist and a top theologian.

Do Victor White's principled disagreements and occasional bluntness, so publicly expressed, lend credence to the charges of Laurens van der Post in *Jung and the Story of Our Time* that he, White, turned on his master with "unnecessary violence and reprehensible disregard of what he owed him both as a teacher and friend?" The charges boil down to three: the ingratitude of the pupil, the presumption of the amateur to the professional, and, in the case of White's supposed opposition to the Dogma of the Assumption, the myopia of the obscurantist. The first two charges must await the publication of Victor White's letters to Jung, but it is my guess he will emerge exonerated. Even from the glimpses one can get in the notes to Jung's letters, it is apparent that White was anything but ungrateful for the help he had been given. As to the charge of presumption, it is to be noted that in the field of theology their roles were reversed: White was the professional, and Jung was the amateur. Easiest to dismiss is the charge of opposing the Dogma of the Assumption. "White was among the foremost of Catholic intellectualists who pronounced the doctrine a religious scandal." On the contrary, what White did was write an article on "The Scandal of the Assumption," not protesting the dogma but meeting the objections of those who did! Given Jung's letter of approval to White (25 November 1950), van der Post's misattribution is astounding.

No, the painful dispute between Jung and White cannot be resolved by dismissing the priest as an ingrate. They were both big men. If Jung towered above him, it was because he was an original thinker and explorer of the psyche, whereas

White was essentially a scholar. Jung does not lose stature for being passionately wrong on a point of theological doctrine, but neither does White lose stature for standing up to the awesome presence of the founding father and refusing to equivocate on an issue of ultimate significance to the movement. No other figure comes to mind who took such a stand without retreat or apostasy. Both men loved each other, but loved Truth more. That is the core on which their relationship both prospered and foundered.

One of the most unfortunate consequences of their alienation was that Victor White was not at Jung's side when, in his closing years, he formulated his concept of the *psychoid*, the bedrock of his psychological edifice which remains the *terra incognita* of the Jungian world. This formulation undoubtedly came to Jung from his study of Meister Eckhart, that other great Dominican who in retrospect dominates the beginning of the fourteenth century as St. Thomas Aquinas dominates the thirteenth. In consultation with Victor White, Jung might have footed his way through the rarefied height of Eckhart's blitzkrieg theology to erect a microcosmic model of the *psychoid* based on the macrocosmic model of the *Ungrund*, Jacob Boehme's term for Eckhart's predication of the Godhead that lies beyond the Trinity. As it is, we have only Jung's provisional reflections on the subject, abetted by Ira Progoff's *Jung, Synchronicity and Human Destiny*. But twenty years after Jung's death, this last great subcontinent of the mind lies virtually uncharted.

In closing, there remains only to express my satisfaction at the reappearance of this book by my old friend and mentor who helped me through a bad place in my life by directing me to his own mentor, Carl Gustav Jung. It is with gratitude that I share in the destiny of this small masterpiece of the ongoing dialogue between Psychology and Religion.

William Everson
January 1981

FOREWORD

IT is now many years since I expressed a desire for co-
operation with the theologian, but I little knew—or
even dreamt—how or to what extent my wish was to be
fulfilled. This book, to which I have the honour of writing
an introduction, is the third major publication on the
theological side which has been written in a spirit of collaboration and mutual effort. In the fifty years of pioneer
work which now lie behind me I have experienced criticism,
just and unjust, in such abundance, that I know how to
value every attempt at positive co-operation. Criticism
from this side is constructive and therefore welcome.

Psychopathology and medical psychotherapy are, when
viewed superficially, far removed from the theologian's
particular field of interest; therefore it is to be expected that
no small amount of preliminary effort will be required to
establish a terminology comprehensible to both parties. To
make this possible certain fundamental realizations are
required on either side. Most important among these is the
appreciation of the fact that the object of mutual concern is
the psychically sick and suffering human being, who is as
much in need of consideration from the somatic or biological
side as from the spiritual or religious. The problem of
neurosis extends from the disturbed sphere of the instincts
to the ultimate questions and decisions of our whole *Weltanschauung*. Neurosis is no isolated, sharply defined phenomenon, it is a reaction of the *whole* human being. Here a
purely symptomatic therapy is obviously even more definitely
prohibited than in the case of purely somatic illnesses,
although these also invariably have a psychic component or
syndrome, even though they are not psychogenetic. Modern
medicine has just begun to take account of this fact which the
psychotherapists have been emphasizing for a long time. In
the same way, long years of experience have again and again

taught me that a therapy along purely biological lines does not suffice, but requires a spiritual completion. This becomes especially clear to the medical psychologist where the question of *dreams* is concerned, which, being statements of the unconscious, play no small part in the therapy. Whoever goes to work with an honest and critical attitude is bound to admit that the task of rightly understanding the dream is no small matter, but calls for careful reflection, leading far beyond purely biological points of view. The indubitable occurrence of archetypal motifs in dreams makes a thorough knowledge of the spiritual history of man indispensable for anyone making a serious attempt to understand dreams. The likeness between certain dream-motifs and mythologems is so striking that they may be regarded not merely as similar but even as identical. With this knowledge, however, not only is the dream raised to the higher level of the mythologem, but simultaneously the problems with which mythology confronts us are brought into connection with the psychical life of the individual. From the mythologem to the religious statement is only a step. But whereas the mythological figures appear as pale phantoms and relics of a long past age which has become strange to us, the religious statement represents an immediate 'numinous' experience. It is a *living mythologem*.

Here the empiricist's way of thinking and expressing himself gets him into difficulties with the theologian. The latter—when he is either making a dogma of the Gospel or 'demythologizing' it—rejects the idea of the myth, because it seems to him a depreciation of the religious testimonies, in whose supreme truth he believes. The empiricist, on the other hand, whose orientation is that of natural science, does not connect any idea of values with the concept 'myth'. He sees the myth as an 'expression of certain processes in the unconscious', which applies equally to the religious texts. He has no means of deciding whether the latter are 'truer' than the mythologem; for between the two he sees only one difference: the difference in living intensity. The so-called religious testimony is still 'numinous', a quality which the myth, on the other hand, has already lost to a great extent. The empiricist knows that rites and figures once 'sacred' have become obsolete and that new figures have become 'numinous'.

The theologian can reproach the empiricist and say that he does possess a means of deciding the question of truth, he merely does not wish to make use of it—referring to the truth of revelation. In all humility, the empiricist will then ask: Which? and where is the proof that one interpretation holds greater truth than another? Christians themselves do not appear to be at one on this point. While the latter are busy wrangling, the doctor is concerned with an urgent case and cannot wait for age-long schisms to be settled, but will unhesitatingly seize upon what is vital to the patient and therefore efficacious. He naturally cannot prescribe for his patient just any *Weltanschauung* assumed to be a living system; but, by dint of careful and persevering investigation, he must endeavour to discover where the sick person feels a healing, living quality, which can make him 'whole'. He cannot be concerned at first as to whether this so-called truth bears the official stamp of validity. If, however, the patient is thus able to rediscover himself and get on his feet again, then the question of consciously reconciling his individual realization —or whatever one may choose to call the new insight or life-giving experience—with the collectively valid opinions and convictions becomes a matter of vital importance. That which is only individual isolates, and the sick person will never be healed by becoming a mere individualist. He would still be neurotic, unrelated and estranged from his social group. Even Freud's exclusively 'personalistic' psychology of drives was obliged to come to terms, at least negatively, with the generally valid truths, the primordial *représentations collectives* of human society. Scientific materialism is by no means a private religious or philosophical concern, but a matter of *collective importance*, as we might well have realized from contemporary history. In view of the extraordinary significance of so-called general truths, a coming to terms between individual realizations and the social convictions becomes an urgent necessity. Just as the sick person in his individual distinctiveness must find a *modus vivendi* with society, it will be his urgent task to compare the views which he has acquired through exploring the unconscious with the general truths and to bring them into a mutual relation.

A great part of my life has been devoted to this work. Therefore it was clear to me from the outset that I should never be equal to this task alone. Although I am able to testify to the reality of the psychological facts, it is quite beyond my power to promote the necessary processes of assimilation which coming to terms with the *représentations collectives* requires. This calls for the co-operation of many, and above all of those who are the exponents of the general truths, namely the theologians. Apart from doctors, they are the only people who are professionally concerned with the human soul, with the exception perhaps of teachers. But the latter confine themselves to children, who as a rule only suffer from the problems of the age indirectly, *via* their parents or masters. Surely it would be valuable for the theologian to know what is happening in the psyche of the adult; and it must gradually be dawning on any responsible doctor what an incredibly important role the spiritual atmosphere plays in the psychic economy.

I must acknowledge with gratitude that the co-operation I had so long wished and hoped for has now become a reality. The present book bears witness to this, for it meets the pre-occupation of medical psychology half-way, not only with intellectual understanding, but also with good will. Only an uncritical optimism could expect such an encounter to be love at first sight. The *points de départ* are too far apart for this and the road to the meeting-place too long as well as too hard to hope for agreement as a matter of course. I do not presume to know what the theologian misunderstands or fails to understand in the empirical standpoint, for it is as much as I can do to learn to estimate his theological premises correctly. If I am not mistaken, however, one of the main difficulties lies in the fact that both appear to speak the same language, but that this language calls up in their minds two totally different fields of associations. Both can apparently use the same concept and are then bound to acknowledge, to their amazement, that they are speaking of two different things. Take, for example, the word 'God'. The theologian will naturally assume that the metaphysical *Ens Absolutum* is meant. The empiricist, on the contrary, does not dream of such a far-reaching assumption, which strikes him as downright impossible, but when he uses this word he just as naturally means a mere statement, at most an archetypal motif which preforms such statements. For him, 'God' can just as well mean Jahwe, Allah, Zeus, Shiva or Huizilopochtli. The divine attributes of almightiness, omniscience, eternity, etc., are to him statements which, symptomatically or as syndromes, more or less regularly accompany the archetype. He grants the divine image 'numinosity', a deeply stirring, emotional effect, which he accepts in the first place as a fact and sometimes tries to explain rationally in a more or less unsatisfactory way. As a psychiatrist, he is sufficiently hard-boiled to be deeply convinced of the relative character of such statements. As a scientist, his primary interest is the verification of actual psychic facts and their regular occurrence, to which he attaches incomparably greater importance than to abstract possibilities. His *religio* consists in establishing facts which can be observed and proved. He describes and circumscribes these in the same way as the mineralogist his mineral samples and the botanist his plants. He is aware that beyond provable facts he can know nothing and at best can only dream, and he considers it immoral to confuse a dream with knowledge. He does not deny what he has not experienced and cannot experience, but he will on no account assert anything which he does not think he can prove with facts. It is true that I have often been accused of merely dreaming of archetypes. I must, however, remind these too hasty critics that a comparative study of motifs existed long before I ever mentioned archetypes. The fact that archetypal motifs occur in the psyche of people who have never heard of mythology is common knowledge to anyone who has investigated the structure of schizophrenic delusions, if his eyes have not already been opened in this respect by the universal dissemination of certain mythologems. Ignorance and narrow-mindedness, even when the latter is political, have never been conclusive scientific arguments.[1]

I must be content to describe the standpoint, the faith, the struggle, hope and devotion of the empiricist, which together culminate in the discovery and verification of provable facts and their hypothetical interpretation. For the theological standpoint I refer you to the competent *exposé* by the author of this book.

When standpoints differ so widely, it is understandable that *in concreto* many and various clashes should occur, both of an important and unimportant nature. They are important above all where an encroachment on the part of one realm threatens the other. My criticism of the doctrine of the *privatio boni* is such a case. Here the theologian has a certain right to fear an intrusion on the part of the empiricist. This discussion has left its mark on the book, as the reader will see for himself. Therefore I feel at liberty to avail myself here of the right of free criticism, so generously offered me by the author, and to lay my standpoint before the reader.

I should never have dreamt of coming up against such an apparently remote problem as that of the *privatio boni* in my practical work. Fate would have it, however, that I had to treat a patient, a scholarly man, who had become involved in all manner of dubious and morally questionable practices. He turned out to be a fervent adherent of the *privatio boni*, because it fitted in admirably with his scheme: evil in itself is nothing, a mere shadow, a trifling and fleeting diminution of good, like a cloud passing over the sun. This man professed to be a believing Protestant and would therefore have had no reason to appeal to a *sententia communis* of the Catholic

---

1. The fact that the psyche is no *tabula rasa*, but brings with it just as instinctive conditions as the somatic life, naturally does not at all suit a Marxist philosophy. True the psyche can be crippled just like the body. But such a prospect would not be pleasing even to Marxism.

Church, had it not proved a welcome sedative for his peace of mind. This case originally induced me to come to terms with the *privatio boni* and its psychological aspect. To the empiricist, it is self-evident that the metaphysical aspect of such a doctrine does not come into question for himself, for he knows that he is only dealing with moral judgments and not with substances. We call a thing, *from a certain point of view*, good or bad, above or below, right or left, light or dark, etc. The thesis is then just as actual or real as the antithesis.[1] It would never occur to anyone—except under very special circumstances and for a definite purpose—to define cold as reduced heat, depth as reduced height, right as diminished left. With this kind of logic one could just as well call good a diminution of evil. The psychologist would, it is true, find this way of expressing it rather too pessimistic, but from a logical point of view he would have nothing to say against it. Instead of ninety-nine one might just as well say a hundred minus one, if it didn't seem too complicated. But should he, as a moral man, catch himself glossing over an immoral act by regarding it optimistically as a certain diminution of good, which alone is real, or as an 'accidental lack of perfection', he would immediately have to call himself to order. His better judgment would tell him: If your evil is actually only an unreal shadow of your good, then your so-called good is nothing but an unreal shadow of your real evil. If he does not reflect in this way he deceives himself and self-deception of this kind has dissociating effects which breed neurosis, such as for example feelings of inferiority, with all their well-known attendant phenomena.

For these reasons I have felt compelled to contest the validity of the *privatio boni* as far as concerns the empirical realm. On the same grounds I also criticize the dictum which is derived from the *privatio boni*, '*Omne bonum a Deo, omne*

---

1. A recent suggestion that evil should be looked upon as a 'decomposition' of good does not alter this in the least. A rotten egg is unfortunately just as real as a fresh one.

malum ab homine[1] , for then on the one hand man is deprived of the possibility of doing anything good, and on the other he is given the seductive power of doing evil. The only dignity which is left him is that of the fallen angel. The reader will see that I take this dictum literally.

Criticism can only be applied to psychic phenomena, i.e., to ideas and concepts, but not to metaphysical entities. The latter can only be confronted with each other. *Hence my criticism is valid only within the empirical realm*; in the metaphysical realm, on the other hand, good can be a substance and evil a μὴ ὄν. I know of no empirical fact which would come anywhere near such an assertion. Therefore at this point the empiricist must remain silent. Nevertheless, it is possible that there are—as is the case with other metaphysical statements, particularly the dogmas—archetypal factors in the background here, which have existed for an infinitely long time as psychically effective, pre-forming factors; and these would be accessible to empirical research. In other words, there might be a pre-conscious psychic tendency which, independently of time and place, continually causes similar statements, as in the case of mythologems, folklore motifs and the individual production of symbols. But apparently the existing empirical material—at least as far as I am concerned with it—permits no decisive conclusion which would point to an archetypal conditioning of the *privatio boni*.

Clear-cut *moral* distinctions are—unless I am mistaken—recent acquisitions of civilized man. Therefore they are still frequently so misty and uncertain; unlike other pairs of opposites which are indubitably of an archetypal nature and represent essential conditions for conscious realization, such as the platonic ταὐτὸν-θᾱτερον.

Like every empirical science, psychology also requires auxiliary concepts, hypotheses and models. But the theologian, as well as the philosopher, is apt to make the mistake

---

1.   The justice of this dictum strikes me as questionable, for Adam can hardly be held responsible for the wickedness of the serpent.

of taking them for metaphysical *a priori* assertions. The atom of which the physicist speaks is no metaphysical hypothesis, it is a *model*. Similarly, my concept of the archetype or of psychic energy is only an auxiliary idea, which can be exchanged at any time for a better formula. Seen from a philosophical standpoint, my empirical concepts would be logical monsters, and as a philosopher I should cut a sorry figure. Regarded theologically, my concept of the *anima*, for example, is pure gnosticism; therefore I am often classed among the gnostics. Moreover, the Individuation process develops a symbolism, whose nearest parallels are to be found in folklore, gnostic, alchemistic and other 'mystical' conceptions and—last, but not least—in those of shamanism. When materials of this kind are used for comparison, the reader is confronted with such a flood of 'exotic', 'far-fetched' proofs, that if he merely skims through a book instead of reading it, he can easily be overcome by the illusion that he is faced with a gnostic system. In reality, however, the Individuation process is a biological fact— simple or complicated according to circumstances—by means of which every living thing becomes that which it was destined to become from the very beginning. This process naturally expresses itself in man just as much psychically as somatically. On the psychic side it produces, for example, the well-known quaternity phenomena, whose parallels are to be found in mental asylums as well as in gnosticism and other *exoticis* and, last, but not least, in Christian allegory. Hence it is by no means a case of mystical speculations, but of clinical observations and their interpretation by means of comparison with analogous phenomena in other realms. It is not the daring phantasy of the expert in comparative anatomy that can be held responsible when he throws light on the fact that the human skeleton is closely related to that of certain African anthropoids, of which the layman has never even heard.

It is certainly remarkable that my critics, with few exceptions, ignore the fact that, as a scientist, I proceed from empirical facts which every one is at liberty to verify.

On the other hand, they criticize me as if I were a philosopher, or a gnostic who claims supernatural knowledge. As a philosopher and speculating heretic I am naturally easy prey. This is probably the reason why people prefer to ignore the facts which I have discovered and proved, or to deny them without scruple. But it is the facts that are of primary importance to me and not a provisional terminology or attempts at theoretical reflections. The fact that archetypes exist is not dismissed by saying that there are no inborn representations. I have never maintained that the archetype in itself is an image, but have expressly pointed out that I regard it as a *modus* without definite content.

In view of these many and various misunderstandings, I set a particularly high value on the real understanding shown by the author, whose *point de départ* is diametrically opposed to that of natural science. He has successfully endeavoured to feel his way into the empiricist's way of thinking as far as possible, and if he has not always entirely succeeded in his attempt, I am the last person to blame him, for I am convinced that, involuntarily, I am guilty of many an offence against the theological way of thinking. Discrepancies of this kind can only be settled by means of lengthy discussions, but they have a good side: not only do two apparently incompatible spheres come into contact, but they also mutually animate and fertilize each other. This requires a great deal of good will on either side. Here I can give the author unstinted praise. He has dealt with the opposite standpoint with the utmost fairness, which is most valuable to me, and at the same time he has illustrated the theological standpoint in a highly instructive way. The medical psychotherapist cannot in the long run afford to overlook the existence of religious systems of healing—if one may so describe religion in a certain respect—any more than the theologian, in so far as he has the *cura animarum* at heart, can afford to ignore the experience of medical psychology.

In the practical field of individual treatment it seems to me that no serious difficulties should arise. These may first be expected where the discussion begins between individual experience and the general truths. In the individual case this necessity usually occurs only after a certain length of time, if at all. In practical therapy, cases are not rare in which the whole treatment takes place on the personal plane, without any inner experiences that are definite enough to call at all urgently for any coming to terms with general convictions. In so far as the patient remains firmly within the frame of his traditional faith, he will, even if he is moved or perhaps shattered by an archetypal dream, translate his experience into the views of his faith. This operation strikes the empiricist (if he happens to be a fanatic of the truth) as questionable, but it can be harmless or even lead to a satisfactory issue, in so far as it is *legitimate* for this type of man. I try to impress on my pupils not to treat their patients as if they were all alike: the population consists of different historical layers. There are people who, psychologically, might just as well have lived in the year 5000 B.C., *i.e.*, who can still successfully solve their conflicts as people did 7000 years ago. There are countless barbarians and men of antiquity in Europe and in all civilized countries and a great number of medieval Christians. On the other hand, there are relatively few who have reached the degree of consciousness which is possible in our time. We must also reckon with the fact that a few of us belong to the third or fourth millennium A.D. and are consequently anachronistic. It is therefore psychologically quite 'legitimate' when a medieval man solves his conflict today on a thirteenth-century level and treats his shadow as the incarnate devil. For such a man any other way would be unnatural and wrong, for his belief is that of the thirteenth-century Christian. For the man who belongs by temperament, *i.e.*, psychologically, to the twentieth-century certain considerations are of importance which would never enter the head of the medieval human specimen. How strong the spirit of the Middle Ages still is in our world can be seen, among other signs, by the fact that such a simple truth as the psychic quality of metaphysical figures will not enter people's heads. This is by no means a matter of intelligence and education or of *Weltanschauung,* for the materialist also cannot perceive to what extent, for example, God is a psychic entity which nothing can deprive of its reality, not insisting on a definite name, but willing to be called reason, energy, matter and even ego.

The fact that there are different historical layers must be carefully taken into consideration by the psychotherapist and at the same time the possibility of a latent capacity for further development, which should, nevertheless, hardly be taken for granted.

Just as the reasonable, *i.e.,* 'rationalistic' point of view is satisfying to the man of the eighteenth century, the psychological standpoint appeals much more to the man of the twentieth century. The most threadbare rationalism means more to the former than the best psychological explanation, for he is incapable of thinking psychologically and can only operate with rational concepts, which must on no account savour of metaphysics, for the latter are taboo. He will at once suspect the psychologist of mysticism, for in his eyes a rational concept can be neither metaphysical nor psychological. Resistances against the psychological standpoint, which looks upon psychic processes as facts, are, I fear, altogether of an anachronistic nature, including the prejudice of 'psychologism', which does not understand the empirical nature of the psyche either. For the man of the twentieth century this is a matter of the highest importance and the very foundation of his reality, for he has recognized once and for all that no world exists without an observer and consequently no truth, for there would be nobody to register it. The one and only immediate guarantor of reality is the observer. Even physics, the most unpsychological of all sciences—oddly enough just physics—comes up against the observer at the decisive point. This knowledge sets its stamp on our century.

It would be an anachronism, *i.e.,* a regression, for the man of the twentieth century to solve his conflicts 'rationalistically' or metaphysically, therefore, *tant bien que mal,* he has built up for himself a psychology, because it is impossible for him to get along without it. The theologian as well as the somatic doctor will do well to take this fact earnestly into account, if he does not wish to run the risk of losing touch with his time. It is no easy matter for the psycho-somatic practitioner to see his long familiar somatic clinical pictures and their etiology in the unusual light of psychology, and in the same way it will be no mean task for the theologian to adjust his thinking to the new fact, *i.e.*, that of the existence of the psyche and particularly of the unconscious, in order that he also may be able to reach the man of the twentieth century. No art, science or institution which is concerned with the human being will be able to avoid the effect of the development which the psychologists and physicists have let loose, even if they oppose it with the most stubborn prejudices.

Father White's book has the merit of being the first theological work from the Catholic side which deals as deeply with the far-reaching effects of the new empirical knowledge in the realm of the *représentations collectives* and makes a serious attempt to integrate it. Although the book is addressed in the first place to the theologian, the psychologist and particularly the medical psychotherapist will be able to glean from it a rich harvest of knowledge.

C. G. JUNG

May, 1952.

AUTHOR'S PREFACE

SEVERAL years ago I was invited to write a book on God and the Unconscious. My elaborate plans for a fairly comprehensive treatise which would cover the whole ground psychologically, historically, philosophically and theologically, proved altogether too ambitious for my capacities and opportunities. Other occupations left little time or inclination to undertake a fraction of the research and reflection which the task required. Moreover, it gradually transpired that others more competent had done, or were doing, much that I had set out to do. Albert Béguin's *L'Art romantique et le rêve* dispensed me from the need for research into the origin and early developments of the idea of the unconscious. Much that I had proposed to write was already written, and with a thoroughness I could not emulate, by the group of Swiss Catholic *savants* who produced *Rätsel der Seele*. The need I had felt for an objective and methodical general survey of Jung's psychology, with particular regard to its religious implications, was admirably met, first by a Protestant pastor, then by a Catholic priest. The reader is asked to supply the deficiencies of the present volume in this respect from their useful and complementary works, Hans Schaer's *Religion and the Cure of Souls in Jung's Psychology* and Josef Goldbrunner's *Individuation*. The latter's booklet, *Heiligkeit und Gesundheit*, also took many words out of my mouth.

So, with no great regrets, the original enterprise was abandoned, but not my interest in the subject. On many occasions I have been called upon to write or speak on some subject touching the relationship of depth-psychology and religion: the bulk of the present volume comprises revised versions of a number of these essays and addresses. Although each item is fairly complete in itself, and indeed was originally intended to be such, I venture to believe that together they form a reasonably consecutive unity.

But if this can be said for their subject-matter, I am painfully aware that as much cannot be claimed for their manner. The reader will have the impression that the several sections of this book address quite different sets of readers, and his surmise will in fact be quite correct. The worker on the borderlands of religion and psychology must be bilingual, and there is no dictionary which will supply the exact equivalents of the two languages he must employ. His work will bring him into contact with two peoples who know remarkably little about one another, who have seldom shared one another's experiences, whose respective upbringing and ways of thought render mutual understanding extremely difficult. There is a difference, not easy to bridge, between the world of the empirical psychologist, accustomed to scientific training and method, and that of the trained theologian or philosopher whose mental processes, though no less disciplined, operate in quite different fashion. Even when the two languages have been mastered, the task of the interpreter has hardly begun. Possibilities of misunderstanding still abound. The philosopher or theologian tends to read 'explanations' into the provisional postulates and working hypotheses of the empirical scientist, entities into his categories of classification, even moral codes into his statistically established 'laws', unwarrantable trespasses into his own domain in the scientist's generalized 'theories'. Nor are scientific workers always so self-critical as to be wholly guiltless of provoking such interpretations. They, on their side, tend to be impatient with meticulous linguistic analyses, with inferences and deductions which seem incapable of sustaining conclusions far remote from direct observation, which cannot be verified by methods to which they are accustomed, and which nevertheless amazingly lay claim to permanent and universal validity. Moreover, it is not only with the experts on both sides, professional theologians or psychologists, that the worker on these frontiers must converse. On the one hand there are, besides professional theologians, interested believers and churchgoers, and these are not all of one tradition or denomination: one or two of the papers which follow were originally intended only for groups of fellow-Catholics, more for those of all denominations or none. On the other side there are those who, without being professional psychologists, have come to the subject wholly from the psychological side, whether through reading and reflection or through personal experience of psychological analysis. Some of the items in this volume were originally addressed to groups in the U.S.A., one to an international conference of *savants* in Switzerland. Others were broadcast by the B.B.C., to whomsoever, by accident or design, happened to tune in.

The result is an inevitable unevenness of style and approach. Although every effort has been made to take as little as possible for granted in the technicalities either of religion or of analytical psychology, and as far as possible to cut out repetitions and to provide connecting links between the several items, it has been found neither possible nor desirable to iron out the unevenness entirely. It is hoped that psychologists may find it of some interest to listen in to the domestic chat of Catholics, and churchgoers generally, to become acquainted with the sort of talk that goes on among some psychologists; the 'general reader', it is hoped, will be more enlightened by such personal addresses than by airy abstractions and generalities which touch nobody in particular.

The first two sections do, however, call for a more especial apology. They were to have been the introductory chapters of the abandoned treatise. There can be no denying that they are altogether too weighty an overture to the *miscellanea* that now take its place. I have, nevertheless, thought it well to retain them with very little modification. If they stimulate more questions than the remainder of the volume succeeds in answering, or even attempts to answer, that is perhaps no very great loss. The questions themselves remain, and it may be of some value at least to formulate them.

The third item, 'The Unconscious and God', is made up of notes for lectures given in America in 1948 and at Oxford in 1949. The basis of the fourth and fifth is a pamphlet published by the Guild of Pastoral Psychology in 1942: to the fourth has been added material from scripts of talks broadcast by the European Service of the B.B.C. in 1952; the bulk of the fifth, while retaining matter from the 1942 pamphlet, has been specially written for this book. The sixth and seventh were read at the Eranos Tagung, Ascona, Switzerland, in 1947, and were published in the *Eranos Jahrbuch* for that year; the seventh had also been published in *Dominican Studies* and, in French translation, in *L'Année théologique*: both have been slightly revised for this volume. 'Psychotherapy and Ethics' is a revision of a paper read to the Oxford branch of the Newman Association in 1945, and subsequently published in *Blackfriars* and as a separate pamphlet. The 'Analyst and the Confessor' appeared in 1948 in the American weekly, *Commonweal*. 'Devils and Complexes' was read to the Aquinas Societies of Oxford and London in 1950 and 1952. 'Gnosis, Gnosticism and Faith' was read to the Analytical Psychology Club of New York in 1948, and was subsequently published in England by the Guild of Pastoral Psychology. 'The Dying God' comprises two talks broadcast on the Third Programme of the B.B.C., following upon three talks on ethnological aspects of the same subject from Professor Henry Frankfort, during November 1951.

To these I am privileged to add, as an appendix, a translation of an important article by my good and learned friend, Father Gebhard Frei, Professor of Comparative Religion and Psychology at Schöneck-bei-Beckenried, Switzerland. It is, perhaps, the most important contribution that has yet been made to discussions on the frontiers of theology and depth-psychology; to the value of Dr Frei's own observations and reflections is added that of the extracts from his correspondence with Dr Jung; these should clarify several widespread misunderstandings. This article first appeared in German in *Gloria Dei* in 1947; the fuller version which we here translate appeared in *Annalen der philosophischen Gesellschaft Innerschweiz und Ostschweiz* in 1948. Readers uninitiated into technical Jungian terminology will find in it succinct explanations of most of Jung's principal concepts. My warmest thanks are due to the author for allowing its incorporation in this volume.

They are due no less to Professor C. G. Jung for his long-standing offer to contribute a foreword. At the time of my writing his foreword is unwritten, and I have thought it well to leave him with the last word, and free to make any criticisms and reservations which may seem fit to him. (His foreword will not, of course, be subject to the ecclesiastical *imprimatur* obtained for the rest of the book.) My indebtedness to him in other respects should be to some extent apparent from my text; though what I owe to his personal friendship, our frank discussions, my direct acquaintance with his kindness, his genuineness and—above all—his astonishing humility, can never be expressed. My expressions of disagreement or misgivings about some of his views and approaches in no way reduce my indebtedness and gratitude.

My thanks are also due to the editors and publishers who have permitted inclusion of material in this volume. My debt to other writers, living and dead, will be manifest from text and footnotes. Many great names will be found there, from Aristotle and Aquinas to Freud; may their names not have been taken in vain by any avoidable misrepresentation of their thought! A still greater debt is, however, due to those who in direct human encounter, personal or professional, kindly or hostile, have enabled me to know whatever I do of the human psyche, mine and theirs. My publishers deserve more than thanks for their patience and co-operation. The defects of this book are to be attributed to my own unconsciousness; in such uncharted territory, where opportunities for illusion, misunderstanding and prejudice are so considerable, they are bound to be many. My gratitude will extend to every reader who has the kindness to point them out.

VICTOR WHITE, O.P.

Oxford, March 1952.

I

THE TWILIGHT OF THE GODS

THE pews were empty, the creeds were outworn; the gods, it was supposed, were dead. Dead; not just, as had often happened before, transformed or displaced by newer gods: as Zeus had unmanned and displaced Kronos and cast him into the underworld, as Teutonic and Celtic deities had become gnomes and fairies in Christianized Europe. 'The God is dead, Long live the God' was no new cry in human history; it was, as Frazer showed, the very secret of the Golden Bough of Nemi and its countless parallels all over the globe.

And indeed, gods must die that men may live and grow. Image-breaking is no less part and parcel of human life and history than image-making; it is also no less part and parcel of man's religion, and no less essential to it. For the fixed image evokes the fixed stare, the fixed loyalty which may blind man's vision to the claims of further and wider loyalties, and so paralyze the human spirit and crush its inherent will to advance and to venture. The ancient sympathetic magic which slew to fertilize, whose bloody rites of the dying and rising god enacted the natural processes of the seed which must likewise die if it is to be fruitful and to multiply, may have been a blind alley in the progress of agriculture. But its working on human culture, on the mind of man himself, is not lightly to be estimated. Already in the Hellenistic Mysteries the ancient nature cults are consciously recognized and practised as outward and visible signs and means of an inward mental transformation. The painful recognition of the clay feet of old idols is indispensable to human growth; it is also indispensable to the emergence of more appropriate figures for human awe, devotion and service. This is the inexorable law of growth both in the individual and the

I

group; it is an inexorable law of religion itself. The evolving, elusive Deity of Professor Alexander and many a modern thinker—the Deity which is a Fox of Heaven for ever out-pacing the pursuit of the human hounds—is an illogical monstrosity to the traditional metaphysician and theologian. To the former it is an outrage to attribute the characteristics of change and decay to the Transcendent and the Absolute; to the latter it is perverse to invert the roles of the pursuing God of Love and sin-laden, fleeing Man.

But what may be false as a predicate of Deity is true of human *images* of Deity; and indeed the metaphysical and theological absurdity represents what metaphysician and theologian must alike recognize to be psychological fact. Every succeeding human *imago* of God must dissolve and elude man's grasp if man himself is not to be (as the Jewish psalmist foretold) petrified into the likeness of his own idols, and if the image itself is not to come between man and what-ever the image would represent. The lesson of anthro-pology and the history of human culture is also the lesson of religion itself; not only of the protean metamorphoses of the myths and the mysteries, but no less of the image-prohibition of the Old Testament, of the image-shedding of the Vedanta and of Yoga, of the *Nada* of St John of the Cross, of the cry of God-forsakenness on Golgotha. Even the cultured apostate Julian echoes the 'pale Galilean': 'O Helios, thou hast forsaken me'.[1] The mystic and the ascetic, the theologian and the philosopher, can lament no more than the humanist historian of human culture the passing of forms of the Formless.

But while the mutation of forms is one thing, and a very ancient and indispensable thing, the passing away of *all* forms, and of the very Formless itself, is quite another, and—in appearance at least—something quite new; even though perhaps to contemporaries of bygone twilights of the gods it was less obvious than to the subsequent historian that the oncoming, overpowering darkness was but the shadow of an

---

1. Ammianus Marcellinus, xxv. 3 (quoted by H. Rahner, *Griechische Mythen in christlicher Deutung*, p. 127).

approaching dawn; the death the prelude to resurrection, or, more prosaically, the decay of religion the preparation for religious revival.

But the twilight of the gods which we have witnessed in the past few centuries, and of which we see the fulfilment in our own time, is unique in many respects. At first it was felt, even widely welcomed, as something final and definitive. God was dead and done with—or very soon would be—dead ignominiously and almost imperceptibly, and never to be replaced. He was slain, moreover, not by other and more powerful divinities, but by the triumphant march of science, by man's own all-conquering brain; his own head emancipating him from the delusions and superstitions which had enslaved his heart. The situation, as it is widely apprehended, is too familiar to require any detailed exposition. 'Every schoolboy knows' that Kant or somebody had disproved the alleged proofs of God's existence—he knows it with a certainty hardly paralleled in ages of faith, but he little knows on what grounds, or in what way, or that it was only to replace a 'true' God by a 'practical' Categorical Imperative. The pure thought of the philosophers having destroyed all *reason* for God's existence, anthropology, comparative religion, Biblical criticism and the physical sciences were held to have shattered all grounds for *faith* in him. The story needs not to be retold.

But then came psychology, and ironically enough, psychotherapy, to drive the last nails in the coffin of Divinity. As Professor Raymond Cattell (in a book to which we shall have further occasion to refer) succinctly put it: 'The psychologists have jostled each other to be the first in routing the shattered remnants of religious forces from the battlefield of human thought. The situation is considered to be . . . that since the physical sciences have shown how illusory religious notions are, psychological science will show through what flaws in the human mind the illusion is created and sustained.'[1] In particular, depth-psychology, led by Freudian

1. Raymond B. Cattell, *Psychology and the Religious Quest* (Nelson Discussion Books), p. 60.

psycho-analysis, is credited with singular success in this iconoclastic achievement. It is believed to have demonstrated that gods and demons are but 'projections of the unconscious', which in their turn are understood to be delusional personifications of unconscious complexes, illusory by-products of the conflict between our inward instinctual drives and the demands of our environment. Freud himself is well known to have proclaimed that religion is the universal neurosis of humanity: nay, it is 'more than an obsessional neurosis'.[1] Dr Theodore Schroeder. expressed what has become a widely-held opinion when he wrote: 'All religion in its beginning is a mere misrepresentation of sex-ecstasy, and the religion of to-day is only the essentially unchanged evolutionary product of psycho-sexual perversion.'[2] More recently and more ambitiously a Professor of the Sorbonne has produced a complete 'Pathological Theogony'—an exposition of the origin of belief in the supernatural in terms of human lunacy.[3] With a wealth of clinical material he presents and classifies the syndromes (*i.e.*, the distinguishing symptoms) of the various mental diseases, and shows in turn their close correspondence to men's traditional beliefs concerning, and behaviour towards, gods and demons. Although

---

1. Sigmund Freud, *The Future of an Illusion* (1928), p. 80.
2. T. Schroeder, *American Journal of Religious Psychology*, vol. vi., quoted by R. H. Thouless, *An Introduction to the Psychology of Religion*, p. 128.
3. Georges Dumas, *Le Surnaturel et les dieux d'après les maladies mentales: Essai de théogonie pathologique* (Presses universitaires de France, 1946). It is not our purpose to disparage this book as a whole: it contains much valuable data and is an important contribution to the problem of the classification of psychoses. But the value of these data as a contribution to 'theogony' must depend upon—*inter alia*—the manner in which psychosis itself is understood, a question which the author expressly ignores. The tacit implication of the book is that 'the supernatural' is an alien and hostile element peculiar to the psychotic, and that this fact somehow invalidates religion and shows the unreality of that with which it is concerned. And yet the fact that men sometimes drown is no argument against ships—still less against the reality of the sea or of the respect which is due to it.

he is careful to point out at the outset that such purely symptomological pathology ignores causation (and so really 'explains' nothing), and although he reminds us of the risks inherent in attempting to account for the 'normal' in terms of the 'abnormal', such unexciting notes of scientific caution are less impressive to the untrained reader than the powerful, reiterated suggestion that it is of the more or less latent insanity in humankind that God and gods, saviours and devils, creeds and cults, are begotten and nourished.

To our parents—perhaps also to ourselves in our youth—it seemed a famous victory, this triumph of the human mind over nature, and not least its triumph over its own hallucinations. The salvation of man by man, not through religion but from religion, was an inspiring theme indeed. The conquest of human want and misery through human science seemed but a matter of time. Many even of those who still clung to the external forms of traditional religion could little doubt it in their heart of hearts.

Myths, the more they are inspiring, and especially in the dark, bewildering hours between crucifixion and resurrection, die hard. But to-day we can be much less sure of what value to put upon the substitution of man's scientific brain for his mysterious God or gods. Even his old demons seemed less potent and less destructive. There is darkness over the earth. Science itself seems to have shown that its own former clarities were a delusion: the more man knows, the more he finds remains unknown. The enlightened sceptic whose self-sufficient science was to have guided us yesterday is the benighted dogmatist of to-day. 'The notion of the complete self-sufficiency of any item of finite knowledge,' writes Professor Whitehead, 'is the fundamental error of dogmatism. Every such item derives its truth, and its very meaning, from its unanalysed relevance to the background which is the unbounded Universe. Not even the simplest notion of arithmetic escapes this inevitable condition for existence. Every scrap of our knowledge derives its meaning from the fact that we are factors in the universe, and are dependent on the universe for every detail of our experience. The thorough sceptic is a dogmatist. He enjoys the delusion of complete futility. Wherever there is the sense of self-sufficient completion, there is the germ of vicious dogmatism. There is no entity which enjoys an isolated self-sufficiency in existence. In other words, finitude is not self-supporting.'[1] So once again, *omnia abeunt in mysterium*; or at best, as Whitehead goes on to show, all is dissolved into algebraic 'patterns'—for, 'Alas, arithmetic totters'.[2] The brightest certainties of everyday experience, no less than of yesterday's science, dissolve into the chaotic and the unintelligible before our eyes. Time and Space, Mass and Energy, Waves and Corpuscles, organic and inorganic matter merge into one another and into the unknown and the unknowable, as did the alchemist's *materia prima* in amorphous *solutio* and *putrefactio*. But even for the most disinterested alchemist, this painful confusion and disorder was but a step, however terrifying and perilous, to the new integration and order of the Philosopher's Stone: the corruption of the familiar world of distinguishable sense-perceptions was but a prelude to the generation of an Elixir of Life. The hopefulness of the alchemist of long ago, and of the optimistic evolutionist of yesterday, are alike negated by Boltzmann's general theory of the laws of nature, which is to the effect that 'every order has an inherent tendency to disorder, but not vice-versa'.[3] The most advanced physicists of our time summon us to prepare for a *sacrificium intellectus* unparalleled in the previous history of humanity; a sacrifice of that very intellect which we had supposed was to enlighten us and save us. The new physics and the new astronomy do not merely summon us to an unprecedented asceticism of intellectual abnegation, they positively force upon us the darkest night both of sense and understanding.[4]

---

1. A. N. Whitehead, *Essays in Science and Philosophy* (New York, 1947), pp. 101, 102.
2. From letters of Frege to Bertrand Russell, quoted by Whitehead, *ibid.*
3. *cf.* E. Schroedinger, 'Der Geist der Naturwissenschaft', *Eranos Jahrbuch*, 1946, p. 518.
4. *cf.* F. Dessauer, *Eranos Jahrbuch*, 1946, pp. 325 ff.

While our commonplace certainties dissolve into incomprehensible and terrifying enigmas, the more familiar, more
comforting mysteries of bygone days are mysterious no more.
The sacred is no longer secret: the veil of the Temple is rent
in twain from top to bottom. What we had supposed to be
awesome mysteries are exposed to the gaze of everybody in
all their seeming triviality of 'complexes' and 'projections'
and 'misunderstood sex-ecstasy'. The tombs are opened: in
the frustration and guilt of epidemic neurosis and the terror
of psychosis we are haunted by the sins of our forefathers,
and by the intractability of our inherited dispositions to the
needs and the burdens of the present. Our triumph over
nature is looking like a Pyrrhic victory which has immeasurably increased our servitude.

Perhaps we could pass all this by (many still manage to
pass it by) if this dissolution of our old familiar world, this
annihilation of our hopes, could remain only in the brains
of scientists and in learned, unintelligible books which we
need never read. But their complicated algebraic formulas
express cataclysmic facts and prospects for which even the
crude language of old apocalypses is hardly adequate.
Einstein's equation of Mass and Energy does not just remain
on paper, nor only make darkness of the mental light by
which we had walked: it is a formula for earthquake, which
threatens to take away the very ground on which we tread,
and deprive us of our most elemental security. 'If some
physicist were to realize the brightest dream of his kind,
and teach us to unlock the energy within the atom, the whole
race of man would live under the threat of sudden destruction, through the malevolence of some cynic, the inadver-
tence of some optimist, or the benevolence of some
pessimist.'[1] Professor McDougall's nightmare of 1931 became fact twelve years later. Human *hubris* had reversed
the creation-story of Genesis not merely on paper but in
fact; man's own ingenuity had begun to reduce matter back

---

1. William McDougall, 'World Chaos: The Responsibility of
   Science as Cause and Cure.' Lectures before the University
   of Manchester, in *Religion and Sciences of Life* (1934), p. 198.

to force, cosmos to chaos. The official code-name for the explosion of the first atom-bomb in the New Mexican desert was 'Operation Trinity'.[1]

But not only have the fruits of the victory of the sciences turned sour; many, even among creedless scientists, have grown alarmed at the results of the defeat of religion itself; the outcome to be anticipated from 'the slow religious and moral disillusionment of the average citizen.'[2] Professor Cattell's pre-war booklet, from which these words are taken, rested on assumptions and reached conclusions which differ considerably from those of this writer—though the differences may be found on examination to be sometimes more terminological than real. But it was to be admired for its sterling candour and courage; it made no attempt to belittle the dangers, even from a purely human and social standpoint, of the experiment in godlessness to which the mass of Western man is now committed. We must here neglect his impressive collection of evidence, and content ourselves with a few of his shrewd generalizations concerning the social outcome of the cultural struggle:

> For the pure-bred scientist the conduct of the resolute invaders requires no justification or apology. He sees a false ideology laid waste and a race of crabbed and timid intellects replaced by an enlightened people of nobler mental stature. A single-minded devotion to truth, no matter into what emotional difficulties it leads its followers, is, in his opinion, the most important value in life.

> Men of affairs, on the other hand, who are concerned with how the world behaves rather than with any abstract pursuit of truth by the few, are aware that a heavy devastation has been wrought, and that a heavy price in human happiness remains to be paid. The fact is beginning to dawn even upon the victors. . . . Psychologist and social scientist lose their militant attitude to religion when they realize that all their forces may well be needed to re-establish some order in the city they have so successfully besieged. The intellectual world is full of 'post-war'

---

1. *Science News No.* 2 (Penguin Books), p. 103.
2. R. B. Cattell, *op. cit.*, p. 50.

problems from this enormous cultural conflict, but perhaps the everyday world is even more distressingly aware of imminent emotional famines and pestilences arising from the intellectual readjustment.

For though the acute mental conflict may first have raged only in the minds of intelligent and educated people, the consequences are going to affect all lives. Changes from religious belief are going to mean changes in social and economic organization. Individuals who will not suffer conflicts in their own minds will sooner or later find themselves in bloody physical conflicts between opposing groups irrationally bound to incompatible ideas. Boredom and misuse of energy, vacillating loyalties, false goals, fruitless conflicts and despair are the demons fated to torture a generation which has not clearly and consciously thought out the process of readjustment occasioned by this conflict. Not the least of the present social dangers is a disintegration of the system of order and morality, formerly sustained directly or indirectly by religious belief.[1]

These words, written before the Second World War, have been amply confirmed by subsequent history. But Professor Cattell went on very rightly to deplore a fashionable and facile 'return to religion' if that was to imply a surrender of truth and an escape from the hard historic destiny which modern science has bequeathed to us:

No scientist worthy of the name will follow any of these escapes to religion, no matter how great his sympathy with a society in torment or individuals in extremities. For he holds the search for truth to be the noblest aim— and as for human suffering, he knows that no people have ever been permanently happy or successful by cherishing an illusion. He recognizes in such pragmatic arguments as that men will return to religion in their troubles an argument equally applicable to drink and drugs. He has more respect for the proud unreason of the religious man, like Macmurray, who cries, 'It is high treason to say you believe in God because it is helpful to believe in Him'.

Stoically to follow science into its bleak altitudes is the only course left to us. But who knows if we penetrate by

1. *op. cit.*, pp. 42, 43.

holding on to scientific methods more patiently, and further than many of our too rash fellow-scientists have done, we may yet reach something as valuable as all that was lost with religion?[1]

Professor McDougall, in the lecture we have already quoted, contended that the remedy for the 'world-chaos' caused by science was not less science but more; and especially the pursuit of the sciences of life (psychology and biology) which the physical sciences of 'dead matter' had disastrously outpaced. Professor Cattell's book is dedicated to Professor McDougall and is inspired by the same belief. He maintains that the psychologists, in their endeavour to show how religious 'illusion is created and sustained', have not been too scientific (as some critics would maintain), but have not been scientific enough. They 'have failed to follow reason enough. Instead they have persisted conservatively in a dull habit of destructive analysis of religion. It is amazing that none of these psychologists has perceived, as he helped clear the ground of the litter of broken religious dogma, that his own science marked out clearly the foundations of a new and nobler structure of scientifically founded religion.'[2]

It is no part of the purpose of this present volume to examine in detail or to criticize Professor Cattell's own stimulating and thoughtful effort to show 'how the last of the sciences is performing the miracle of transferring religion from the mean and cramping foundation of dogmatic superstition to the basis of limitless growth found in science'. His ingenious conception of the 'Theopsyche' is perhaps *too* clever; a fact which he himself acknowledges when, with characteristic courage, he puts the crucial question, 'What shall we teach our children?' and admits with equally characteristic candour that he 'is uncomfortably aware that this book is too technical to help many people, sadly lost in the ruins of religion'.[3] The most brilliant theory about religion, or the most would-be scientific substitute for

1. *op. cit.*, p. 49.
2. *op. cit.*, pp. 60, 61.
3. *op. cit.*, p. 183.

religion, is actually unscientific if it disregards the proved characteristics of that 'unconscious' to which psychology, with a powerful display of evidence, ascribes many of its ingredients. As C. G. Jung has said:

. . . our age has a blindness without parallel. We think we have only to declare an acknowledged form of faith to be incorrect or invalid, to become psychologically free of all the traditional effects of the Christian or Judaic religion. We believe in enlightenment, as if an intellectual change of opinion had somehow a deeper influence on emotional processes, or indeed upon the unconscious! We entirely forget that the religion of the last two thousand years is a psychological attitude, a definite form of adaptation to inner and outer experience, which moulds a definite form of civilization; it has thereby created an atmosphere which remains wholly uninfluenced by any intellectual disavowal. The intellectual change is, of course, symptomatically important as a hint of coming possibilities, but the deeper levels of the psyche continue for a long time to operate in the former attitude, in accordance with psychic inertia. In this way the unconscious has preserved paganism alive. The ease with which the classic spirit springs again into life can be observed in the Renaissance. The readiness with which the older primitive spirit reappears can be seen in our own time, even better perhaps than in any other historically known epoch.[1]

Indeed, we are compelled to raise the question: Are the gods really dead after all? Or have the psychologists only changed their name? These questions must be faced before we admit too readily their claims to have shown how the 'religious illusion is created and sustained'.

---

1. C. G. Jung, *Psychological Types* (1938), p. 230.

II

THE GODS GO A-BEGGING

DEPTH-PSYCHOLOGISTS themselves have convinced us that a dream, or a spontaneous, dreamy phantasy, can tell us more of what is happening below the surface of the human mind than any amount of intellectual analyses or statistics. One such phantasy is related in Dr Halliday Sutherland's otherwise matter-of-fact account of his *Lapland Journey*. It is worth recounting here, not because it is rare, but contrariwise because it is characteristic, and has the advantage—as against the quantities of similar material which is locked away in private case-histories—of having already appeared in print.

Dr Sutherland relates how, during a long, monotonous and tiring sleigh-journey through the Lapland forests, the forest became enchanted, peopled by fairies and goblins and princesses and talking trees, both good and bad. Such experiences are no marvel to the psychologist who is familiar with the fashion in which, once our waking 'modern' attention is relaxed, more primitive ways of viewing our surroundings take its place. 'Since time immemorial Nature has always been animated (*beseelt*); now for the first time we are living in a Nature deprived of both spirits and gods (*in einer entseelten und entgötterten Natur*)'.[1]

But, to return to Dr Sutherland's daydream, this is one of the things that happened:

> Beyond the lane, and at the far end of a straight road, was a large oblong building of great height.... When our sledge came in sight the door opened, and three black-cowled figures descended the steps and stood in the snow, each with his hands clasped and his head bowed in an attitude that was too obsequious.

---

1. C. G. Jung, *Aufsätze zur Zeitgeschichte*, p. 106.

'They seem to be expecting you,' said a Tree.

'I know nothing about them.'

'All the dead religions of the world are kept there. Each has a room to itself. The three attendants were supposed to look after them. Of course that was impossible, and it's a long time since any of them have visited the upper rooms—but you will see for yourself.'

'It would take years to inspect that place.'

'Years! It would take centuries, but one day all these religions are going to explode and the place will be blown up.'

'How can dead religions explode?'

'Because they are not quite dead. Even in the upper rooms they are smouldering.'

'I had every reason to be alarmed, especially as Little Bread Eater[1] was making straight for the door and I was now almost within hailing distance of the three black-cowled figures, obsequiously waiting. The animal must also have seen them, because suddenly he swerved and galloped away to the right. In an instant the Three knew they had been tricked. Gone was their obsequious attitude as they rushed across the snow to intercept the sledge. . . . Little Bread Eater was going "hell for leather", and the sledge passed the point of interception before the Three had reached it, but not before they were so close that I saw, under the cowls—the heads of skeletons.[2]

Dr Sutherland tells us that to find that forest we must follow the directions of the great explorers of fairyland, we must be ourselves 'physically tired, a little sad, and very poor'. He himself has little trust that professional psychologists can be of assistance, for he adds: 'If you have no belief in fairies and are very rich you may take this story to a psycho-analyst and ask for his interpretation. . . . In that event I give you . . . a fair warning that his interpretation will be written in Latin, Sanscrit, Hebrew or in some other language not easily read by The Servants, about whose morals we are so much more concerned than about our own.'

The justice of the doctor's comment on the myopic

---

1. The reindeer.
2. Halliday Sutherland, *Lapland Journey* (1938), pp. 148 ff.

rationalizations of his psychiatric colleagues is no more our
concern than is the comment of his phantasy on the clerical
skeletons whose too obsequious attentions to Ego have caused
them to neglect the religious dynamite of which they are
supposed to be the custodians. All that concerns us here is
to note the presence in the modern psyche of both its religious
and explosive character. Spontaneous phantasies of import
similar to that of Dr Sutherland's are by no means exceptional these days. To *establish* this would be impossible
without access to thousands of dossiers of case-histories in the
safe-keeping of analysts, and a quantity of space for the
presentation and examination of the material which would
far exceed the scope of this essay. But to *illustrate* it by a few
facts and documents which are public property should not
be beyond our powers.

One such document is provided by that very remarkable
book, *A Life of One's Own* by 'Joanna Field'.[1] It is a book
well worth reading on its own account, and few could read it
without profit. Here is recorded the frank and courageous
self-analysis of an enlightened woman psychologist, previously confident of her emancipation from every form of
superstition or religious belief. She tells us of the shock and
astonishment with which she discovered, quite early in her
interior explorations, the unmistakably 'religious' character
of her free associations, their crude and almost savage
primitiveness, and the immense power which they had
evidently exercised on her supposedly free and autonomous
thinking and behaviour. Such experiences are by no means
unique, and few analysts would perhaps deny the frequency
with which specifically 'religious' images and attitudes
appear in the material of their most sceptical and 'emanci-
pated' patients. Truly, they will differ widely in their
estimate of their value and importance in their patients'
lives; and still more in the interpretations which they put
upon them. More often than not, perhaps, they will regard
them as nothing but manifestations of regressive trends, and

1. London: Chatto and Windus; re-issued in Pelican Books
(1952).

substitutes for biologically conditioned functions and attitudes. But their existence and their power are seldom to be disposed of so easily.

This should hardly surprise even the inexpert layman, nor should it be difficult for him to surmise how inevitably the breakdown of religious belief and practice must engender new and acute problems for mankind and profound disturbances in men's relations to their environment and to one another. For there is no reason whatever to suppose that the psycho-physical constitution of man to-day differs very widely from that of his fathers. We have only to consider the immensity and intensity of the libido—the psychic energy—which our forebears, not many generations ago, have poured into or extracted from their religion, which they have given to their gods or attributed to them: the love, the hate, the passion, the devotion, the wrath, the fear, the wonder, the beauty, the joy, the horror, the cruelty, the ecstasy, the self-denial, the inspiration, the thought, the intelligence, the power, the weakness, the tears, the laughter, the guilt, the repentance. How much of all this can find conscious and directed expression in human life when the gods have gone? Let us suppose, if only as a possible hypothesis, that the law of the conservation of energy holds some validity in the human psyche as well as in the physical universe: let us suppose, in other words, that none of this psychic energy has been lost or can be annihilated. The evidence is certainly strong which leads many psychologists to hold that the psychic forces which are not consciously accepted and directed will not on that account cease to exist or to be active, but will become unconscious and affect our thought and behaviour none the less; that they will form autonomous complexes of psychic contents, which, as likely as not, will either disturb our conscious attitudes and endeavours by introjection, or be projected on to our neighbours and our environment. If this hypothesis is true we shall find that we cannot, for instance, evade the character of omnipotence which our fathers attributed to divine beings. But, being deprived of divine beings, we shall find that, willy-nilly, we are in practice attributing omnipotence to a State, a Leader, a Party, a relation, a neighbour, or that we ourselves are behaving as if we were God almighty, or are the victims of inscrutable forces within, against which our conscious wills and endeavours are powerless. Jung goes so far as to assert that 'whenever the Spirit of God is excluded from human consideration, an unconscious substitute takes its place.'[1] And again, 'The gods have become diseases; not Zeus but the solar plexus now rules Olympus and causes the oddities of the professional office hour, or disturbs the brain of the politician and journalist who then unwittingly release mental epidemics. . . . When God is not recognized, selfish desires develop, and out of this selfishness comes illness.'[2]

The Second World War did much to make even the average citizen aware of the fearful vengeance which is wreaked on earth when the human spirit clears the skies of its gods and the underworld of its demons. He has seen in his newspapers and on the screen how irrational forces are unleashed which are more antagonistic to sweet reasonableness, and even to utilitarian self-interest, than he had thought possible. What shocked and astounded us at Belsen and Buchenwald was less their shaming inhumanity, than their manifestation of stark, ruthless, primitive devilry. They were inexplicable merely in terms of cynical, utilitarian power-politics. There was no use, no reason, not even a bad reason, in keeping thousands of people just alive, when they could have been so easily slain or just left to die, merely for their torture and affliction. Could it be that gods and demons, heavens and hells, are ineradicable from the nooks and crannies of the human mind, and that if the human mind is deprived of its heaven above and its hell beneath, then it must make its heaven and corresponding hell on earth? Can it be that the ancients were right in their persistent belief that immortality was the distinctive attribute of divinity? —that though the gods could metamorphose or be replaced,

---

1. C. G. Jung, 'Der Geist der Psychologie', *Eranos Jahrbuch*, 1946, p. 400.
2. C. G. Jung, *The Secret of the Golden Flower*, pp. 112, 113.

they could never finally die? For however crudely, however anthropomorphically, however subject to human passions and vicissitudes, the gods of Olympus were pictured, they were yet always the Deathless and Immortal ones. And in Northern lands, although there was a twilight of the gods of Asgard, it was a twilight only which heralded the on-slaught of the cold Fimbul-Winter; and the final hecatomb in Valhalla left Surtur in possession and made way for the Kingdom of Heaven of Gimle the Blest.[1]

The symptoms of the concentration camps were blatant and—being those of the 'other fellow', and of the enemy at that—were easily recognizable. But it is not readily to be supposed that they were symptoms of a purely German disease, rather than the peculiarly virulent and spectacular manifestations of a widespread and typical modern *malaise*; the new disease of unconscious religion which becomes epidemic when man is filched of his gods. More commonly the symptoms are less undisguised, more private and intimate agonies known only to a few, and whose nature is suspected by still fewer who have themselves travelled into the depths of the human psyche and faced the 'perils of the soul'. Yet how often are we spontaneously betrayed into employing the language of 'religion' as though it alone were adequate to describe political, social, domestic and personal up-heavals! We have seen even Professor Cattell write of 'the *demons* fated to torture a generation which has not clearly and consciously thought out the process of readjustment occasioned by this conflict'. And do we perhaps speak more wisely than we know when we employ the language of adoration in affairs of love and even of politics? Romanticism already made gods and goddesses of human partners; it was inevitable that thereafter they could become devils and their homes hells. Clergymen and moralists assure us that the alarming increase of divorce, the breakdown of countless homes and the prevailing misery in many more, the chaotic 'Sexual Behaviour of the Modern Male' revealed in the

---

1. *cf.* K. Boult, *Asgard and the Norse Heroes*, chap. xvi.

Kinsey Report: that all these are the outcome of our loss of the sense of the sanctity of marriage, of sexuality and of the home. There is an undeniable but superficial sense in which that is true. But the deeper levels revealed in the analyst's consulting room show that these catastrophes are more often to be attributed to the fact that unconsciously marriage has been regarded as *too* sacred rather than otherwise, and hence required to bear a weight too heavy for it, and which in other days carried *it*. Sex is expected to provide a mystical union, the partner a divinity, the home a heaven —each, in short, is required to provide a substitute for religion and to be saddled with a task to which each is of its nature unequal.

It is the analytical psychology school of C. G. Jung which has given most express recognition to the theory that 'many neuroses are caused by the fact that people blind themselves to their own religious promptings because of a childish passion for rational enlightenment'.[1] But every school of depth-psychology has been compelled to face the same set of *facts* in the etiology of neurosis. From the beginning, Alfred Adler broke with Freud owing to the preponderating role he found in the power-complex; to this Adler himself expressly gave the name of 'God-almightiness', and it is indeed difficult to understand it otherwise than as an unconscious identification with, or hankering after, divine power. 'Ye shall be as God' was, we are told, the tempter's original bait. To succumb to that temptation is not in itself pathological; it is pathological only in the measure in which it is unconscious. But unconscious and pathological it inevitably becomes so soon as 'God' is dismissed from consciousness. The language of religion will talk of the 'wrath of God' when he is neglected or scorned; the language of psychology can say only that the law of compensation demands that if the God-imago be repressed or ignored it must react negatively on the health and consciousness of the subject.

---

1. C. G. Jung, *Modern Man in Search of a Soul*, p. 77.

It is still more significant that the later Freudians have
themselves been increasingly compelled to pay attention to
factors in mental disorder which—however they may be
clothed in 'scientific' language—are essentially 'religious'.
Freud himself explored far 'beyond the pleasure principle',
and it is well known that the later developments of psycho-
analysis and its derivatives have travelled far from the early
simplicities. By way of 'sado-masochism' they have been
compelled to lay increasing emphasis on the functions of
what Freud called the 'super-ego'. According to Dr Karen
Horney (admittedly a 'heretic' to rigid Freudian orthodoxy)
these 'play a universal and central role in neuroses'.[1] The
story of this development is related in Professor Flugel's
Man, Morals and Society. It is difficult to read this book
without seeing that the components of the 'super-ego' are
mainly nothing but repressed (or at least rejected)—and
therefore unconscious, irrational and damaging—religion.
More will be said of this book in a later section; meanwhile
it must suffice to record that it gives ample justification to
Jung's assertion that 'Freud's idea of the super-ego is a
furtive attempt to smuggle in the time-honoured image of
Jehovah in the dress of psychological theory'. Jung adds that,
'When one does things like that it is better to say so openly:
for my part, I prefer to call things by the names under which
they have always been known'.[2] But the autistic thinking of
many psycho-analysts hardly permits such realistic respect
for history and common speech: even Professor Flugel must
assume (for he cannot possibly prove) that 'god' is a projection of the super-ego rather than allow that the super-ego
might be an unconscious introjection of 'God' (or at least of
certain divine images and attributes). We need not here
inquire whether to this assumption is to be credited his
very pessimistic prognosis of the therapeutic value of psycho-
analysis. It is not, however, easy to deny that Freudian
psycho-analysis, so far from having analysed away the
religious 'illusion', has been increasingly confronted by it

1. Karen Horney, *New Ways in Psychoanalysis*, p. 233.
2. C. G. Jung, *op. cit.*, p. 141.

and that in the 'super-ego' it has come up against the most complicated and intractable, as well as a 'universal and central', factor in the afflictions of the mind of modern man.

Yet so late as 1938 Freud himself, though with less of the dogmatic assurance of earlier years, still suspected that his researches might lead 'to a result that reduces religion to the status of a neurosis of mankind and explain its grandiose powers in the same way as we should a neurotic obsession in our individual patients.'[1] How far psycho-analysis may be said to 'explain' even individual neuroses is an open question to which we shall again have occasion to allude. But it may be asserted with some confidence that the expectation that depth-psychology would dispose of gods and demons for us has been gravely disappointed.

The gods are dead indeed—at least to the consciousness of masses of Western men and women. Even among those who still pay them the lip-service of conventional acknowledgment, they are seldom realized as decisive, active powers in the formation of human life and behaviour.

But although they are dead, they will not lie down. And it is depth-psychology itself which is exposing them again in all their potency—indeed in all their naked primitiveness and explosiveness as inescapable factors in the fashioning of human health and happiness, misery and destiny. Paradoxically, in the very fact of treating them as 'projections' or contents of the unconscious, it has revealed their ineluctable and all-pervasive power. Scientifically labelled and filed, the gods all the more persistently go a-begging for our attention, and that with a claim more imperious than such as can usually be heard in logical 'arguments for the existence of God'. For, as Jung has said, 'If I know that God is a mighty activity in my soul, at once I must concern myself with him; he can then become even unpleasantly important, and in practical ways, too'. We are far from rid of him by calling him a psychological content or a mental disease, but it does affect us profoundly whether or not we so describe

---

1.   S. Freud, *Moses and Monotheism*, p. 91.

him. As Jung continues, 'It is not a matter of unconcern whether one calls something a "mania" or a "God". To serve a mania is detestable and undignified: to serve a God is . . . rich in possibilities because it means yielding to a higher, invisible and spiritual being'.[1]

But is this association of God with the unconscious in any way admissible? What, anyway, is meant by 'the unconscious', and how did the very idea of an unconscious come about? Why such diametrically opposed evaluations of religion in Freud and Jung? These questions we must now briefly examine.

---

1.   C. G. Jung, *Secret of the Golden Flower*, p. 112.

III

THE UNCONSCIOUS AND GOD

ALREADY in 1902 William James could write:
I cannot but think that the most important step forward
that has occurred in psychology since I have been a student
of that science is the discovery first made in 1886 that . . .
there is not only the consciousness of the ordinary field,
with its usual centre and margin, but an addition thereto
in the shape of a set of memories, thoughts and feelings,
which are extramarginal and outside of the primary
consciousness altogether, but yet must be classed as conscious facts of some sort, able to reveal their presence by
unmistakeable signs. I call this the most important step
forward because, unlike the other advances which psychology has made, this discovery has revealed to us an entirely
unsuspected peculiarity in the constitution of human
nature.[1]

Jung goes so far as to say that by the discovery of the
unconscious 'the old psychology was thrown out of the saddle
and as much revolutionized as classical physics by the discovery of radioactivity' and he compares it in importance
to the discovery of numbers and their properties.[2] Yet it
may well be asked what facts or phenomena were then 'discovered' that had not been familiar from time immemorial.
Dreams, automatisms of various sorts, the influence of
'forgotten' experience or unacknowledged desires upon
conduct, alternating personalities, the phenomena of trance,
abnormal and paranormal psychological phenomena of

---

1. William James, *Varieties of Religious Experience*, p. 233 (35th
   impression, 1925). The date 1886 refers to the year of the
   publication of F. H. W. Myers's theory of 'subliminal
   consciousness'.
2. C. G. Jung, 'Der Geist der Psychologie', *Eranos Jahrbuch*,
   1946, p. 241.

many kinds: none of these was new in human experience. Nor was it any novelty to attempt to correlate and account for them in various ways. Gods and demons, influences celestial and terrestrial, hereditary dispositions, the *karma* of previous lives or the experience and acquired inclinations of the individual, bodily 'humours' or environment: to any or all of these and to many other factors had such phenomena for centuries been ascribed.[1] What was certainly new, in the latter part of the nineteenth century, was the deliberate application of experimental method to the study of such phenomena. Comparatively new also—and it is this that here concerns us—was the conception and name of *the unconscious* or 'subliminal self' as the agent or source to which these phenomena were to be attributed, or at least as the collective noun to be employed to cover them.

Comparatively new though it is, this concept has rapidly become an important and indispensable item in modern man's stock of thought-forms and categories. We can hardly read any book, not only about psychology, but about art or morality or politics or any manner of human behaviour, without stumbling constantly upon it. It has become practically impossible to carry on any sort of conversation, to discuss our own experiences and ills, or even to gossip about our neighbour, without employing it frequently, if not as a noun then at least in its adjectival or adverbal forms. For the psychologists themselves it has become—despite the protests of a few behaviourists—an indispensable term of reference.

Truly, not all psychologists are easy about this state of affairs. Some will be found to complain—and with ample reason—that ' "The unconscious" . . . is becoming too ready a resource in psychological difficulties'.[2] Many more will complain with N. Ach: 'As a rule this concept is never defined in the works which employ it. More often than not the reader is obliged step by step to make his own picture of

---

1. See *infra*, 'Revelation and the Unconscious'.
2. C. K. Ogden, *The ABC of Psychology* (Pelican Books), p. 17.

what each author understands by it'.[1] This comes as something of a surprise to the layman who has been led to suppose that 'the unconscious' has been not only discovered but thoroughly explored and explained, and that in its turn it has provided a definite and defined 'explanation' of the phenomena attributed to it.

The very association of God with the unconscious may still strike many as bordering on the bizarre if not the blasphemous. This may be due in part to our inheritance of dominantly intellectual pictures of God: an exclusively transcendent God in the Highest who has nothing to do with the lowest. But still more must it be attributed to the restricted views of the unconscious to which the popularization of Freud has given currency. We have come to think of the unconscious as nothing but an alleged refuse-bin of the mind, a receptacle into which all noxious material is hastily repressed, and on which decent people keep the lid firmly shut.

It is well known how this conception of the unconscious came about. The work of Charcot at Paris had revealed the important role which repression—the unconscious dismissal from the mind of experiences, emotions and ideas which it has failed to assimilate—played in bringing about mental and emotional disorder. This had manifested itself mainly in the utterances and behaviour of patients suffering from hysteria while under hypnosis, and it was hoped that hypnotic suggestion would also supply lasting cure. It is also well known how Charcot's pupil, Sigmund Freud, came to question the therapeutic value and desirability of hypnotic suggestion, and, still more importantly, the need and value of hypnosis for diagnostic purposes. The dreams of natural sleep, he found, supplied the same information, and proved to be 'the royal road to the unconscious'. Discussion of these dreams with the patient in the fully conscious state seemed to be more therapeutically efficacious, and more respectful

1. N. Ach, 'Über den Begriff des Unbewussten in der Psychologie der Gegenwart', *Zeitschrift für Psychologie*, 1933, p. 223.

for the patient's individuality and independence, than hypnotic suggestion: thus was born what Freud's first patient called the 'talking cure', and what Freud himself called 'psycho-analysis'.[1]

Similar conclusions about the importance of repression in psychoneurosis and psychosis were being reached in Switzerland by Bleuler, and more especially by the word-association tests of his pupil, C. G. Jung. To the latter was due also the name and concept of the 'complex'. Already at the beginning of the nineteenth century, 'Herbart's psychology extended beyond the realm of the conscious to that of the unconscious',[2] and had been occupied with the mutual attraction and repulsion of 'ideas'; it had even reached the conclusion that, 'an idea that has suffered inhibition (or repression, *Druck*) does not thereby cease to exist. It merely joins the vast company of ideas that have gone from consciousness, but may return —either through a weakening of opposite ideas or by co-operation with an ally'.[3] Some such conception had been implicit in all association-psychology since Aristotle's *De Memoria et Reminiscentia*, and it had not been until the time of Descartes that the field of psychology had been confined to that of consciousness.

Such considerations, while they dispose of popular beliefs that Freud first 'discovered' a hitherto wholly unknown and unsuspected region of the mind, do not in any way minimize the revolutionary importance of his actual achievements. As Professor Flugel says, 'Freud's theories [as against Herbart's] had the immense advantage of being based on years of laborious and systematic investigation of individual cases. . . . With Herbart the opposition seems to be on the whole an intellectual one: with Freud it depends upon an opposition in the field of desire; certain desires are incompatible with other dominant tendencies of the personality, and for this reason are banished to the unconscious'.[4]

---

1. J. C. Flugel, *A Hundred Years of Psychology*, IV, xiii, pp. 279 ff.
2. J. C. Flugel, *op. cit.*, p. 18.
3. *ibid.*   4. *op. cit.*, p. 19.

It was a short step from the discovery that this 'banishment' or repression was at the root of much mental disorder to the assumption, tacit or expressed, that it was the *only* root, and that repression, thus understood, would account for *all* unconscious contents. If this assumption were correct, then the psyche would indeed be a closed system, all of whose contents could be mechanistically explained in terms of the individual's life-history, and at least theoretically analysable until there was no 'unconscious' left. On this assumption also, 'God' would be nothing but a projection of banished desires or repressed fears, and this, though with some caution and reservation, was the view of Freud himself in *Totem and Taboo* and *The Future of an Illusion*. Yet the very assumptions on which was based this critique of religious beliefs as illusory had to be abandoned in the light of empirical data, first by Jung, then by Freud himself. For it is idle to minimize the revolutionary importance of Freud's recognition in his later works of 'the archaic heritage of mankind [which] includes not only archaic dispositions but also ideational contents, memory traces of the experience of former generations'.[1]

(For it cannot easily be maintained that 'The whole structure of Freudian metapsychology is unaffected by his

---

1. S. Freud, *Moses and Monotheism*, p. 159, *cf. Outline of Psychoanalysis*, p. 28. Dr Edward Glover in his 'Freud and Jung' (*Horizon*, Oct. 1948, pp. 249 ff.) plays down the importance of this recognition, oblivious that the whole argument of *Moses and Monotheism* stands or falls with it. Truly enough, Freud stated on p. 208 that he did 'not think much is to be gained by introducing the concept of a "collective unconscious" ' (in the manner of Jung), but this was because 'the content of the unconscious is collective anyhow, a general possession of mankind'. In fact Jung's hypothesis of 'inherited dispositions to reaction' is very much more cautious than Freud's, and keeps safely at bay the bugbear of the inheritance of acquired characteristics which Freud feared. No Jungian has maintained inherited symbols or images, and it is merely a truism that 'symbols are re-created in the course of individual development', as (according to Dr. Glover) 'many Freudian analysts prefer to think'.

incursion into the region of phylogenetic speculation'[1]—
quite apart from his recognition of paranormal phenomena,[2]
inexplicable in terms of the past history either of the individual or the race. In any case, Freud moulded history
to fit his theories;[3] as an 'explanation' it was of *ignotum per
ignotius*. But whatever is to be thought of his 'speculation',
he had the honesty and courage to recognize the *facts* which
undermined the earlier structure, especially in so far as it
had been the basis of his critique of religion. The closed
system of the optimistic early days of psycho-analysis is not
merely cracked, it has burst wide open. The presuppositions
of *The Future of an Illusion* are shown to have been themselves
an illusion).

Under the word 'Unconscious', the *Encyclopædia Britannica*
offers two separate articles; there is one on 'Unconscious
(Philosophical)' and another on 'Unconscious (Psychological)'. The division is arbitrary, and although the scientific
and clinical investigations of Freud and those who have
followed him appear to have been quite independent of
previous investigation and reflection in somewhat more
'philosophical' circles, it will be germane to our own inquiry
to recall briefly some of the work that had been done.

A century ago there was nothing very unusual, in many
philosophical, literary, and even some medical circles, in
juxtaposing—nay, in almost identifying—God and 'the
unconscious'. In 1848 appeared the very remarkable book
called *Psyche* by Carl Gustav Carus. He was in his time a
man of some note, Court Physician to the King of Saxony,
a painter of some distinction and, to judge from the versatility

---

1. Edward Glover, *op. cit.*, p. 251.
2. See *infra*, pp. 117, 118.
3. 'I am not an ethnologist, but a psycho-analyst. It was my
   good right to select from ethnological data what would
   serve me for my analytical work. The writings of the highly
   gifted Robertson Smith provided me with valuable points
   of contact. . . . I cannot say the same of the work of his
   opponents'. (*Moses and Monotheism*, p. 207).

of his writings, a man of many parts. He had been led to psychology from the study of comparative anatomy. His *Psyche* has not yet been translated into English. Though it seems to have made some stir in its time, there are many factors which may account for its subsequent neglect. Apart from the more limited views of the unconscious which were to result from the work of Freud and other psychopathologists some fifty years later, as we have seen, the slenderness of the evidence which Carus adduced to support his theories could hardly commend them to the rigidly scientific mind. Only in our own day is the evidence being supplied.

We cannot here attempt even a summary of Carus's entire book; it must suffice us to mention some relevant highlights among its conclusions. The book's main theme is epitomized in its opening words: 'The key to the under-standing of conscious life can be found only in the realm of the unconscious'. Its aim—which, we are told, should also be the aim of human life and growth—is the '*Bewusstwer-dung des Unbewussten*'—the making conscious of the un-conscious. Carus then proceeded to criticize the academic psychology of his time which confined its attention to con-scious mentation: 'the psychological inquirers of antiquity, from Aristotle on,' he wrote, 'even though they were less informed about organic processes, went further on the true way than the moderns.' Aristotle and Aquinas, in particular, are accorded special praise for their insistence on psycho-somatic unity and their realization of the non-conscious sources of mental events. The psyche is not only, or even chiefly, conscious; consciousness is the instrument, rather than the subject-matter of psychology.

It is astonishing to read Carl Gustav Carus to-day and to see how he anticipated many of the conclusions of Carl Gustav Jung, though without the latter's accumulation of empirical data to support them. He was not, however, a psychopathologist, and we naturally find him more con-cerned with the positive 'participation' of consciousness in the unconscious than with such manifestations as projection, introjection, complex-formation and functional disorder.

But Carus quite expressly postulates a supra-personal unconscious, and we cannot fail to recognize Jung's 'archetypes' in what Carus called *Urbilder*. Presently his picture of the unconscious begins to emerge: it is sketched mainly in a series of sharp contrasts with consciousness as we know it. The realm of consciousness is invariably individual, ego-centred: the realm of unconsciousness is supra-individual. The unconscious is ceaselessly operative, it is untiring and sleepless (and in this respect also, godlike): unlike consciousness it is unfettered by the categories of space and time: it is both epimethean and promethean. It is the source of consciousness itself, and the source of all *Können*—all power and possibility. By definition unknown and unknowable to consciousness, it can be known only by its effects as perceived by consciousness. It is itself unfathomable, immeasurable, infinite.

Such affirmations may strike us as arbitrary and fanciful; but we are here concerned only with some of Carus's conclusions, rather than with the observations and arguments he used to support them. It may be admitted that they afford a meagre foundation for so vast a superstructure. They consist mainly of particular specimens of the intelligence and teleology of unconscious manifestations of life, human, animal or plant—for Carus the supreme and irrefutable proof of the existence of a (to us) unconscious mind. It is more to our present purpose to notice that the attributes of the unconscious as Carus sees them are precisely the attributes which tradition has ascribed to gods or God, and Carus himself more than hints at the similarity: 'The basis of all life,' he says, 'is the Divine (*das Göttliche*), which *for us* cannot be fully grasped on the analogy of a human intelligence, but only as what *to us* is purely unconscious'.[1] Already for Schelling, all nature was '*ein bewusstloses Denken*'—an unconscious Thinking—and for Carus himself, in one of his other books, 'the unconscious is the subjective expression

---

1. Christoph Bernoulli, *Die Psychologie des C. G. Carus* (Jena, 1925).

for that which we know objectively under the name of "Nature",[1] and this in turn is a partial revelation of, a participation in, the divine Mind. Early in his *Psyche*, the unconscious is called 'the creative activity of the Divine'; towards the end of the book it is hardly distinguishable from God himself. But by then Carus has distinguished a relative and absolute unconscious. It is of the latter that he writes that it is the task of the human mind 'to pursue the Divine within us in its unfolding out of the unconscious to consciousness'. He is, however, no pantheist: divine immanence, he insists, is itself unintelligible unless God is also utterly transcendent. 'The highest aspiration of the conscious mind, the attainment of God,' he says, 'can be approached only by its submission to the deepest depths of what to us is purely unconscious.'

Some twenty years later appeared Eduard von Hartmann's *Philosophy of the Unconscious*, a book which, notwithstanding its bulk and weight, has run into several editions, both in the German original and in the English translation. Here indeed the concept of the unconscious is so refined as to lose almost every connection with human psychology. Von Hartmann indeed sharply distinguishes his 'unconscious' from what he supposed to be 'the God of the theists', but this only on the odd supposition that 'the God of the theists' was alleged to possess consciousness in his own restricted sense of a subject-object distinction produced by 'brain and ganglia'. But it is hardly distinguishable from the 'God' of the traditional natural theology of, for example, St Thomas Aquinas. Von Hartmann himself, a Prussian officer who had turned to Idealist philosophy, described it as the 'all-unity' which 'embraces the Cosmos, and is at last revealed as that which has formed the core of all great philosophies, the Substance of Spinoza, the Absolute Ego of Fichte, Schelling's Absolute Subject-Object, the Absolute Idea of Plato and Hegel, Schopenhauer's Will, etc'.[2]

---

1. C. G. Carus, *Natur und Idee*, p. 12.
2. Ed. von Hartmann, *The Philosophy of the Unconscious*, tr. Coupland, Vol. I, pp. 3, 4.

These speculations of Carus and von Hartmann had not dropped out of the blue. Herbart and Schelling have already been mentioned as forerunners of the conception of the unconscious, but its history goes still further back, and is intimately connected with the whole history of European culture. Much had happened since the Middle Ages when dreams and their like were attributed to God and spirits and many other mundane, supramundane and inframundane influences. Faith and reason had been divorced: God and even angels might still be acknowledged, but in practice it was hardly supposed any longer, even by believers, that they were constantly operative in conditioning human thought and behaviour. If they were invoked at all, it was on special occasions only. Psychology, especially since Descartes, had become exclusively concerned with consciousness, and increasingly isolated from the larger context of the entirety of life, still more so from the cosmos as a whole. The *cogito*—the awareness of our own consciousness—became not only the sole concern of psychology, but also the unique basis for all philosophy. The movement tended, not (as is usually said) to the glorification of Man, but to that of the conscious Ego—a part only of man, but one which is increasingly considered to be omnicompetent. The movement reaches its climax in the eighteenth century—*le siècle sans étonnement*—and supremely in the Enlightenment. Man is now the master of his own thought, and his thought an exact copy of 'external reality'.

Then came the reaction. It is an ineluctable psychological law that over-valuation of consciousness brings forth an over-compensation from the unconscious, and so it came to pass in the latter part of the 'century of Reason'. From the Enlightenment came its diametric opposite, Romanticism; and from Romanticism, itself an upsurge from the neglected unconscious, came first the activity and imagery, then the idea and the name itself, of the unconscious.

The story is brilliantly told, and with a wealth of fascinating material, by Albert Béguin in his *L'Art romantique et le rêve*. His story is confined to Germany and France, but it is doubtless paralleled in England. The difference between Pope and Dryden on the one side, and Keats, Coleridge, Shelley and Blake on the other, is not just of style or taste, but of *Weltanschauung* and dominant values. It is true that, as the Enlightenment in England never attained the extravagances of the Encyclopædists and the *Philosophes*, so neither was the reaction quite so extreme as on the Continent. But in England, too, the bright day of the age of reason was succeeded by the inbreak of a dim world of moonlight and mists, ruins and dreaminess, aching hearts and hemlock-numbed senses:

> I saw pale kings and princes too,
>   Pale warriors, death-pale were they all:
> They cried—'La belle dame sans merci
>   Hath thee in thrall!'

She had indeed. Like almost every line of Keats, this describes a dreamland, far away from the world of daytime consciousness. Coleridge will deliberately quench normal consciousness with opium to produce *The Ancient Mariner* and produce an artificial dream-world: in his prose works he practically deifies the untrammelled, uncontrolled Imagination. For Blake the unfettered Imagination *is* the Mind of God, the Kingdom of Heaven.

But on the Continent, Béguin shows, the Romantic reaction started much more violently: at first with a preoccupation with death, and with an almost obsessional advocacy of suicide, understood as the way to the total extinction of consciousness. But then the movement settled down to preoccupation with the images of the Night, the Underworld, the Dream. Already in the eighteenth century we find among the Romantics a dawning recognition of the dream as contributing to human wholeness. In its last decade G. C. Lichtenberg is writing, 'The dream is a life which, joined to the rest of our existence, becomes what we call *vie humaine*'. Elsewhere he has this startling piece of autobiography: 'I know by experience that dreams lead to self-knowledge. . . . I dream every night of my mother, and I find my mother in everything'. Even before that, Hamann had written, 'Self-knowledge means a descent into hell, the subterranean region of the mind, but that is the way to deification'.[1]

Quite early in the nineteenth century, according to Béguin, the word 'the unconscious' with the definite article (*l'incon-scient, das Unbewusste*) is used to describe this subterranean region, and it soon gains general currency in Romantic circles. Béguin clearly summarizes the situation when he writes, 'Romanticism revives several ancient myths, that of the universal unity and the *Anima Mundi*; and it also creates several more: that of the Night, which is the Guardian of the Treasure, that of the Unconscious as the sanctuary of our hallowed communing with the Supreme Reality, and that of the Dream which transfigures perception, and in which every image becomes a symbol, and all language becomes mystery'.[2]

It is not difficult to see how this Romantic mythology filled the vacuum left by the enthronement of Reason and the breakdown of Faith; but it was not the only revolt which the Enlightenment produced. Reaction set in among philosophers themselves, and this reaction also was to contribute to the conception of the unconscious. Leibniz attacked the basic postulate of Locke's *Essay on Human Understanding*—the postulate of the equation of Mind and Idea with actual perception—and produced his *petites perceptions*. On account of this Leibniz has been claimed as the father of the concept of the unconscious; but he did not himself work out the implications very far.[3] Kant also was to write of 'ideas we have without being cognisant of them', but again without much further elaboration; only later was von Hartmann to argue that Kant's whole *Critique of the Practical Reason*, if not also the Transcendental Categories,

---

1. Quoted by A. Béguin, *L'Art romantique et le rêve* (Marseilles, 1937), pp. 38, 103.
2. *op. cit.*, p. 98.
3. J. C. Flugel, *op. cit.*, p. 18, *cf.* A. Wilwoll in *Rätsel der Seele* (Olten, 1946), p. 33, ff.

presupposes an unconscious Mind.[1] Not until we come to Schelling do we find the unconscious as a central philosophical conception. In Schopenhauer this stream of thought is joined by another, flowing from the Hindu and Buddhist metaphysicians who were for the first time becoming known in Europe.

It need hardly be said that this philosophy of the unconscious had little to do with Dreams, the Night, and all the other paraphernalia of literary Romanticism; rather had it grown out of reflection on conscious processes themselves. But the result was similar, both in fact and in terminology; and the two streams may be said to meet in Carus and von Hartmann.

This sketchy historical account will hardly solve the problem of the relationship of 'God and the Unconscious', nor enable us to state very exactly what the problem is, or even if there be any such problem. But it may assist to widen the context in which it is nowadays usually discussed. For it is clearly impossible to say anything very definite or conclusive about 'God and the Unconscious' until there is some agreement about the meaning of our terms. And, while it should be agreed that 'God' is undefinable, agreement on the definition of the unconscious is notoriously lacking. There is indeed general agreement that, with the exception of few besides the Behaviourists (for whom the concept of consciousness is equally obnoxious), 'the present-day psychologist is compelled to postulate an unconscious psychic life whether he likes it or not. Apart from the reality of the unconscious, any explanation of the regular processes of conscious phenomena is simply impossible'.[2] There is fairly general agreement also that this postulate is demanded by (1) the phenomena of involuntary mentation (particularly, but not only, of dreams), and (2) the seeming purposiveness

---

1. Ed. von Hartmann, *op. cit.*, 20.

2. N. Ach, *op. et loc. cit.*

of non-conscious biological functioning.[1] But there is little agreement as to what the content or boundaries of this unconscious may be. At one extreme we find Dr Ernest Jones proclaiming the simple, early orthodox Freudian view that 'the unconscious is the result of repression' and describing its contents as consisting exclusively of what is 'repressed, conative, instinctive, infantile, unreasoning and predominantly sexual'.[2] At the other extreme we find his Jungian opposite number in England, the late Dr H. G. Baynes, out-Junging Jung in the sweeping assertion that 'the unconscious is merely a term which comprises everything which exists, that has existed, or that could exist, beyond the range of this individual consciousness'.[3]

Enough has already been said to indicate that Dr Jones's narrow definition fails to satisfy many of the needs to meet which an unconscious is postulated at all. We have also seen that Freud himself, in his later works, abandoned the theory that repression could account for all the phenomena attributed to the unconscious; indeed he so broadened his concept of repression itself as to render it useless for supplying a causal 'explanation'. The evidence is at least strong that the early pscyho-analysts mistook a part for the whole; the shallows which they so valuably discovered and examined for a whole mighty ocean which lay beyond. But where Dr Jones errs by defect, Dr Baynes errs by a needless excess.

But there are two points that we may assert with some confidence. The first is, that the boundaries of the unconscious, understood as the source of biological purposiveness

---

1. E. Spiess, *Rätsel der Seele*, p. iv, *cf. The Personality of Man* by G. N. M. Tyrrell (Pelican Books), ch. i, 'The Subliminal Self and the Unconscious'.

2. Ernest Jones, *Psycho-analysis*, p. 123; *cf.* p. 121: 'The existence of the unconscious is the result of repression'.

3. H. G. Baynes, *Analytical Psychology and the English Mind*, p. 156. In fairness it should be remarked that the paper from which this utterance is taken was composed for a 'private meeting'; there are many less indefinite definitions and descriptions of the unconscious in this volume of collected papers.

and undirected mentation (including dreams) have yet to be discovered and are probably undiscoverable. The unconscious is at best a postulate, known (as is God, according to Aquinas), only by its phenomenal effects. It is primarily a negative concept for what is *not* conscious; and however valuable, and indeed indispensable, it is as a postulate, or working hypothesis, it can positively 'explain' precisely nothing at all. Of his own conception of the unconscious, Freud in his last major work acknowledges 'that it is not properly a theory at all, but a first attempt at a stock-taking of the facts of our observation . . . it keeps as close as possible to those facts and *does not seek to explain them*'.[1] The 'unconscious' is for Jung a *Grenzbegriff*,[2] a 'boundary concept', to describe that into which, by definition, our consciousness cannot penetrate, but which yet often behaves as if endowed with consciousness, and often intelligence and purposeful volition. We may recall that the term *Grenzbegriff* was employed by Kant to describe the concept of God.

The second point we may note is that this postulate is employed precisely, though not exclusively, to account for phenomena which in ancient and medieval times were attributed to God or gods, to angels or demons—alongside, of course, physical or biological factors. Then, the purposiveness of irrational life was precisely a ground for the affirmation of an intelligent God—as in Aquinas's 'fifth way' to establish the reality of God. Dreams, involuntary phantasy, inspiration, parapsychological phenomena, and the rest now ascribed to the 'unconscious', were then regularly ascribed, as well as to bodily humours and environmental factors, to God or gods, demons or angels.

To this we shall return in other contexts. Here we have confined ourselves to a brief historical survey of ideas that have been held, and are still held, concerning 'the unconscious'. Before concluding, we may turn to some still earlier observations concerning God and what we should now call

---

1. S. Freud, *Outline of Psycho-analysis*, p. 21, italics ours.
2. C. G. Jung, *Psychological Types*, p. 613.

the unconscious—to the early Christian writer Tertullian at the turn of the second and third centuries.

Tertullian is celebrated for having coined the phrase: *anima naturaliter christiana*—the soul or psyche is naturally Christian. It is, however, less well known how that phrase was occasioned, and what Tertullian meant by it. It first occurs almost casually in his long *Apologia* for Christianity against pagan and sceptical criticism, but it was in his *De Testimonio Animæ* that he develops the theme. In this little book we find him grappling with the same problem as that which besets us to-day: the problem of finding some common ground, some common speech, between the believer and the unbeliever. The difficulty lies in this (Tertullian points out), that there is no common authority, no common scripture or corpus of writing, which the believing Christian and the unbeliever alike accept as a starting-point for thought and discussion. The sceptical, educated pagan precisely denies or doubts, even if he does not deride, the fundamental assumptions of Christian belief and thought. Tertullian finds the answer to this problem in what he calls the *testimonium animæ*—the witness of the phenomena of the human soul, be it Christian or not. The common ground is to be found, not indeed in any external scripture, but within the human soul itself. He argues that if only men will look into their own souls, there they will find all the presuppositions of Christianity which the cultured and sophisticated consciousness doubts or denies. They will not find indeed Christianity itself: Christians, he recalls, are made such by grace and baptism, not born such by nature. But they will find all that with which Christ's salvation, and the Christian Scriptures and Church, have to do: God and demons, sin and guilt, heaven and hell, conflict and immortality. He shows how the involuntary and spontaneous speech and behaviour even of the most sceptical mind—its uncontrolled and unpremeditated phantasies, prayers, curses and feelings —persist in testifying to its belief in these things, even in spite of doubts and denials of consciousness. Stated in the language of to-day, his appeal is precisely to the spontaneous, automatic expressions of the unconscious as against the sophistications of the spoiled and 'educated' conscious ego. 'Stand forth, O Soul,' he writes, 'stand forth and give thy witness. But I call thee not as when, fashioned in schools, trained in libraries, glutted in academies, thou belchest forth thy "wisdom". I address thee, simple and unspoiled, uncultured and untaught, such as they have thee who have thee only. I want thine inexperience, since in thy learning and experience, no one any more feels confidence. . . . I require of thee, not what thou hast acquired in thy lifetime, but what thou bringest with thee into life. . . . If you would have faith in God and Nature, first you must have faith in your own soul, and so believe in your own self. . . . Man is one name belonging to every nation upon earth: in them all there is one soul, though many tongues. Every country has its own language, yet the subjects of which the untutored soul speaks are the same everywhere. . . . Look into the soul, and you will find that God is everywhere, and the goodness of God is everywhere. Demons too are everywhere and the cursing of demons everywhere: all the world over is this witness of the Soul. There is not a soul of man anywhere that does not, by its own natural light, proclaim those very things we (Christians) are derided for believing'.[1]

---

1. Slightly adapted from the translation of *The Writings of Tertullian*, Ante-Nicene Library, Vol. I, pp. 37 ff.

IV

FREUD, JUNG AND GOD

I N their respective attitudes to religion there is a notorious
cleavage between Freud and Jung, one which has
progressively widened and deepened. Even before the publication of *Moses and Monotheism*, Roland Dalbiez could write
with truth: 'Ever since *Totem and Taboo* and *The Future of an
Illusion* Freud's attitude towards religious beliefs has steadily
become increasingly hostile'.[1] Already in 1907 he had
assimilated religious belief and practice to obsessional
neurosis; from that position he has never withdrawn. On
the contrary, in *Moses and Monotheism* this theory is repeated
and elaborated; and the fancifulness of the pseudo-historical
scaffolding with which he there sought to support it testifies
to the lengths to which he was prepared to go to maintain
what had become an unshakable *idée fixe*.

Freud's critique of religion, perhaps reflected indirectly,
perhaps thoroughly misunderstood and distorted, is part of
our modern heritage. Believers or unbelievers, we can hardly
have escaped its impact. Comparatively few can have
studied, tested or examined it for themselves, but it can
be all the more impressive for that. This was no case of a
specialist trespassing outside his own field to express opinions
on subjects about which he is no authority. When Freud
said religion was a neurosis, he was presumably talking about
what he knew, for he was a pioneer discoverer of causes and
cures of neurosis.

An obsession of humanity or not, religion was certainly
something like an obsession with Freud himself. The subject
seems to have fascinated him: in his writings he could never

---

1. R. Dalbiez, *La Méthode psychoanalytique et la doctrine freudienne*
    (1936), I, pp. 614 ff.

leave it alone for very long. Perhaps it is ungracious to subject Freud's writings to his own technique of psycho-analytic investigation, yet it is difficult to avoid doing so; and we begin to suspect that his anxious, sometimes tortuous, theorising about religion tells us more about Freud than religion. But that is hardly our business; we must consider what he says on its own merits, rather than his personal motives for saying it.

His first important utterance on the subject occurs in *Totem and Taboo* in 1907. He then wrote, 'Psycho-analytic investigation of the individual teaches with especial emphasis that god is in every case modelled after the father, and that our personal relation to god is dependent on our personal relation to our physical father. . . . If Psycho-analysis deserves any consideration at all, then the share of the father in the idea of a god must be very important, quite aside from all the other origins and meanings of god upon which psycho-analysis can throw no light'.[1] Here there is at least a note of caution: a recognition that there is more to the matter than comes within the competence of psycho-analysis. Most ethnologists, as well as many psychologists, will probably disagree that 'god is in every case modelled after the father'; they will insist that Mother and Daughter goddesses, and even divine Sons, appear to be much older and more wide-spread in human religion, and that Father-gods appear comparatively late.[2] But, as Freud was to say later: 'I am not an ethnologist, but a psycho-analyst. . . . It is my good right to select from ethnological data what would serve me for my analytical work.'[3] That is fair and frank enough. But will such ingenuous selection bear the weight to be built upon it?

How much was to be built appeared in 1926, in *The Future of an Illusion*. The illusion of course was religion: its future was that it had not much of a future, because, it was

---

1. *Totem and Taboo* (Pelican edn.), p. 196.
2. See G. Van der Leeuw; *Religion, its Essence and Manifestation*. pp. 91 ff, 178 ff etc.
3. *Moses and Monotheism*, p. 207.

implied, psycho-analysis would eventually show it to be an illusion. When we ask Freud what he means by religion, his answer is as clear as it is surprising: 'I take my stand by this,' he forewarns us, 'Religion consists of certain dogmas, assertions about facts or conditions of . . . reality, which tell one something that one has not oneself discovered, and which claim that one should give them credence.'[1] Now, on any hypothesis, this is unsatisfactory as a definition of religion. It is far too broad: on Freud's own admission it would apply equally well to a geography book: but there is the difference that the assertions of the geography book are verifiable by methods which Freud will recognize as valid: assertions about God are not. But the definition is also far too narrow. However important or otherwise may be creeds or dogmas *for* religion, it is surprising that an empiricist who had met religion of any sort could suppose it *consists* of them—and (apparently) nothing else. But that is constantly the layman's trap in reading Freud: it is not so much that he must learn a strange and difficult jargon, as that familiar words like 'religion', as well as 'sex' and 'incest', are given an unfamiliar extent of meaning until little is left that means quite what it seems to say. But having confined religion to dogmas and assertions, the task of showing God to be an illusory rationalization of unconscious wishes is greatly simplified.

But we have also to notice that Freud had his own private meaning for the word 'illusion' as well. We read with some astonishment that 'an illusion is not necessarily an error . . . it need not be necessarily false . . . unrealizable or incompatible with reality'.[2] In Freud's private vocabulary any belief, true or false, is an illusion 'when wish-fulfilment is a prominent factor in its motivation'. And if we ask him what wish-fulfilment is, it is the response to a basic psychological demand and need. Freed from Freud's novel and unconventional language, it all adds up (so far) to commonplace

---

1. *The Future of an Illusion*, p. 43.

2. *ibid*, p. 54.

platitudes. Religious teachers themselves have always supposed that they were meeting inner needs and demands of the soul.

Undoubtedly Freud himself believed religious belief to be not only an illusion in his peculiar sense of the word, but also untrue. Chapter Five of *The Future of an Illusion* is wholly devoted to an attempted refutation of the truth-value of religious statements; but the arguments, such as they are, have nothing to do with the findings of psycho-analysis, or indeed with anything about which Freud could claim to speak with greater authority than anybody else. They seldom rise above the level of the popular tracts of Victorian rationalism. So far as psycho-analysis is concerned, the untruth of religion is assumed, not proved. The findings of psycho-analysis will claim no more than to show how the illusion was brought about.

What then were the findings of psycho-analysis about religion? Most of *The Future of an Illusion* is an elaboration of the theory already quoted from *Totem and Taboo*, eked out with some more highly tendentious speculation about primeval hordes and parricides. God, in short, is 'at bottom an exalted father', a phantasy substitute for the actual, and never wholly satisfactory, parent: a projection to compensate for an infantile sense of helplessness. There is little in that (apart from the language) that is strikingly new. Jews and Christians for thousands of years have cheerfully sung the psalm-verse: 'When my father and mother forsake me, the Lord taketh me up.' 'Our Father who art in heaven' would be meaningless to us had we no knowledge or experience of fathers who are on earth, nor of their children's relationships to them. It is neither new nor startling that, genetically, religious relationships—or for that matter any human relationships—grow out of parental relationships (call them infantile sexuality if you must); nor is it to be wondered at that subsequent relationships are largely conditioned by these original ones. What is odd is the point of view, and the conclusion that it is therefore all abnormal and neurotic. Oaks grow from acorns, but we do not ordinarily think of an oak as a 'substitute' for an acorn or as a 'displacement' of an acorn which has been compelled to grow into something else because an unkindly environment has prevented its remaining an acorn. But we should remember that psycho-analysis was born and nurtured in the climate of Victorian science, with its concentration on past mechanistic causes, at the expense of consideration in terms of function, dynamism, finality.

Freud's presentation of psycho-analysis assumes atheism, it does not even claim to prove it. Several Freudians, among whom Dalbiez and Pfister are prominent, have set out to disengage Freud's psychology from his metapsychological theories and prejudices. In England we have had the remarkable effort of Mr. B. G. Sanders to re-present Freud's psychology on the supposition that there is a God, instead of on the supposition that there is not.[1] Mr Sanders is prepared provisionally to swallow Freud's psychology hook, line and sinker, and to show what follows from the elimination of Freud's atheism. But meanwhile the sufficiency of Freud's theories and methods has been radically criticized by psychologists themselves on their own ground. Once we question the sufficiency of the repression-theory to account for all unconscious contents, and are ready to detect function and purpose, as well as historic causation, in their manifestations, Freud's account of the genesis of religious belief is found to be at best partial and lop-sided.

And yet, perhaps, it is by no means valueless. If religion is found to be withering in Western man and society, is not this largely due to the fact that it has often become over-intellectualized, uprooted from its lowly origins in elemental, instinctive human needs and experience? Nor, perhaps, is Freud's conception of religion as a universal *neurosis* entirely without truth and value—once we have understood his terminology. We must remember that for him, not only religion, but dreams, unbidden phantasies, slips of the tongue and pen—everything short of an unrealizable ideal of

---

1. B. G. Sanders, *Christianity after Freud* (Bles, 1949).

complete consciousness is somehow abnormal and pathological.[1] But theology will also confirm that religion, in the
sense of creeds and external cults, arises from man's relative
unconsciousness, from his incomprehension of—and disharmony with—the creative mind behind the universe, and
from his own inner conflicts and divisions. Such religion, in
theological language, is the result of man's fall from original
innocence and integrity, his remoteness on this earth from
Divine vision. There is no religion in the beginning of the
Bible[2]—in Paradise—and there is none in the heavenly
City at the end: 'I saw no temple therein; for the Lord God
Almighty and the Lamb are the temple of it.'[3] Freud was
surely right in sensing that religion as we know it was somehow a sign of some radical irregularity and incompleteness
in man; but unduly optimistic in supposing it could be
psycho-analysed away. Theology has perhaps been more
realistic in insisting that this irregularity must be accepted
together with all its consequences; more in line with the
findings of depth-psychology itself in trying to keep it constantly before our consciousness if it is to be finally overcome.

Jung moved steadily away from the position which in his
earlier days he shared with Freud into a diametrically
opposite attitude, even though, at least in his published
writings, it cannot be said that he has reached any very
definite position regarding what he would call the transcendental and metaphysical (as distinct from the purely
pragmatic) validity of religious representations. Within the
framework of purely empirical psychology he would not be
justified in doing so; but this has not prevented ironical
critics from charging him with abandoning the physician's
coat for the professor's gown, and the professor's gown for
the clergyman's surplice, if not the robes of the magician,
the prophet, the mystagogue. We do indeed find him increasingly preoccupied with the psychological significance

1. *cf.* Freud's *Psychopathology of Everyday Life, passim.*
2. *cf.* Genesis, iv, 26.
3. Apocalypse (Revelation), xxi, 22.

of religious symbols and their efficacy or inefficacy in varying psychological types and historical epochs. It seems that, whereas for Freud religion is a symptom of psychological disease, for Jung the *absence* of religion is at the root of all adult psychological disease. 'During the past thirty years,' Jung wrote in 1932, 'people from all the civilized countries of the earth have consulted me. . . . Among all my patients in the second half of life—that is to say, over thirty-five—there has not been one whose problem in the last resort was not that of finding a religious outlook on life. It is safe to say that every one of them fell ill because he had lost that which the living religions of every age have given to their followers, and none of them has been really healed who did not regain this religious outlook.' Jung adds some words which must serve as justification for our venturing to treat of the matter at all. 'Here then the clergyman stands before a vast horizon. But it would seem as if no one had noticed it. . . . It is indeed high time for the clergyman and the psychotherapist to join forces to meet this great spiritual task' (namely, to 'cope with the urgent psychic tasks of our age').[1]

At first sight it seems odd that those few churchmen, clerical or lay, who have given any serious attention at all to the psychotherapeutic needs of our age, should have shown a marked predilection for the approach of Freud and Adler rather than that of Jung. As Jung himself has remarked: 'The fact that many clergymen seek support or practical help from Freud's theory of sexuality or Adler's theory of power is astonishing, inasmuch as both these theories are hostile to spiritual values, being, as I have said, psychology without the psyche. They are rational methods of treatment which actually hinder the realization of meaningful experience. By far the larger number of psychotherapists are disciples of Freud or Adler. This means that the greater number of patients are necessarily alienated from a spiritual standpoint . . . a fact which cannot be a matter of indifference to one who has the realization of

---

1. *Modern Man in Search of a Soul*, pp. 264 ff, p. 259.

spiritual values much at heart.'[1] Yet perhaps Jung's astonishment is itself somewhat naïve. The fact is that the very 'religiousness' of Jung is apt to scare off the religious-minded, as much as, or even more than, the irreligious. Freud's underlying philosophy may be materialistic, mechanistic, deterministic, openly atheistic. Adler's conception of human nature may be of all the most cynical perversion of the divine image.[2] But one can always (it is contended) distinguish between the false philosophy and the valid empirical technique. One can analyse *ad infinitum* in the manner of Freud or Adler without ever intruding on the holy ground; one may even, if so disposed, but with doubtful consistency, adorn one's analysis with some pious preachments of one's own for the patient's edification—oblivious that the very fact that the patient is suffering a neurosis is an indication that his religion is itself involved in the dislocation, and that no adjustments of it *ab extra* on the conscious level alone can enable it to fulfil its rôle of transcendent and integrating function.

Rudolf Allers in *The Successful Error* has argued, as against Dalbiez, Maritain and a fairly wide consensus of Catholic psychotherapists, that no such distinction can be made

---

1. *op. cit.*, p. 263.

2. Theologically considered, Adler's diagnosis of the condition of fallen man goes deeper than Freud's. Freud stops at the *malum poenæ* ('the evil we undergo') which is the immediate outcome of the Fall and which Western theology since St Augustine calls *concupiscentia inordinata*, the disorder of desire, which is at the root of all human ills. Adler takes us further to that *malum culpæ* (the 'evil we do') which, by sundering the grace-relationship with God, is the cause of this *concupiscentia* itself and of the conflicts and disintegration which follow upon it. This latter the theologians call *superbia*— the self-assertion of the individual ego over against the Absolute, and, as a consequence, over against the community and the exigencies of integral human nature itself. As to the manner in which Jung includes the Freud-Adler antithesis in a higher and integrating synthesis, see especially the first of his *Two Essays in Analytical Psychology*.

between Freudian philosophical theory and clinical practice. Whilst many of Allers' premisses seem highly disputable, and the much-shifting ground from which he levels his attack quite bewildering, it is difficult to disagree with this conclusion. But to wean from Freud is not to win for Jung, and the fact remains that Jungian theory and technique are apt to cause the deepest misgivings by reason of the very religious aura which they assume. And it may be agreed that, if it is difficult to divest Freud of the professor's gown, it is quite impossible to divest Jung of his surplice. Both in theory and in practice, Jung's realm of the psychological merges into the purely 'spiritual'; it becomes quite impossible to draw a hard and fast line between them; and in the last analysis—if not long before—the psychological must so merge if real 'cure'—let alone 'integration'—is to be effected.

To those for whom the religious realm is a closely-guarded holy of holies, into which none but the accredited priest may enter, this very fact is apt to appear highly disturbing. Yet a fact it is, and the path marked out by his dream-sequence has proved to many a patient to be a kind of interior religious pilgrimage which leads progressively to something very like a religious conversion. Sometimes a deep and successful analysis is more like a religious retreat than most religious retreats, because it makes deeper and more particularized and more exacting demands, because it is less stereotyped, less conventional, more moving, more personal, more imperative. Compared with much pulpit eloquence and ecclesiastical ceremonial, a dream may be a poor thing; 'a poor thing, but mine own'. For the neurotic and the religionless it may be the only thing.

It is important to realize that the contradictory evaluations of religion which we find in Freud and Jung are not merely accidental or temperamental. They are logical consequences of the differences in the interpretation of psychological data which originally separated the two men. The grounds of Jung's break with Freud were anything but trivial or secondary. Those grounds were many, but they were closely

connected, and their implications were far-reaching. First
came the qualifications and amplifications which, notably
in *The Psychology of the Unconscious* and in the first of the *Two
Essays*, Jung brought to Freud's theory of sexuality as the
basic and dominant psychological factor. It was true that
Freud himself had already considerably expanded his
original conception of sexuality; but Jung reached the
conclusion that nothing could be sufficiently comprehensive
to account for the empirical psychological phenomena short
of an abstract conception of absolute, undifferentiated,
unspecified, formless energy. To this he gave the name of
libido, deliberately retaining Freud's word, but indefinitely
enlarging its meaning. The sexual is only one of the countless
forms which this *libido* may assume, however important—
and ontogenetically primary—it may be.

This difference between Jung and Freud may seem at first
sight to be purely academic, indeed, merely a matter of
names. But, however little Jung himself at first may have
realized it, it meant at the very outset that psychology and
religion could no longer follow their several paths without
some merging. Indeed, it is clear from the opening chapters
of *The Psychology of the Unconscious* that Jung was led to this
conception of undifferentiated energy by the fact that he
was constantly presented by his patients with symbols which
comparative religion showed to be universal symbols among
mankind for the creative and undifferentiated Divinity.
Jung himself saw this clearly; but seems to have been content
at that time to regard God as a phantasy concretization of his
libido instead of drawing the conclusion that his *libido* is
actually realized only in God, or that in its manifold manifestations it indicates an innate aspiration—a *naturale
desiderium*—for God. As we shall see, he was still very shy of
religion: he was also very shy of metaphysics. Perhaps it was
just as well. He has always been very sensitive to the charge
of being a metaphysician, but it can hardly be denied that in
positing an undifferentiated *libido* he was, in spite of himself,
asserting that the psychological data were unaccountable
except on a postulate which was as metaphysical as could

be.[1] Yet for traditional metaphysics formless energy is synonymous with *actus purus*, and *actus purus* (under one name or another) is, as natural theologians have pointed out, what men call God.[2]

Had this been put to Jung in those days, he would probably have said that his *libido* was not so undifferentiated as all that, and that anyhow such conclusions were outside his competence. Whether or not the concept of a purely psychic, but otherwise undifferentiated, *libido* can be logically maintained so long as we confess ignorance of where the bounds of the psyche are to be set (an ignorance which Jung repeatedly and emphatically acknowledged,[3]) is an interesting and important point which cannot be pursued here. The fact that the central psychological standard of reference was transferred from sexuality, itself centred in the incest-wish, to an unspecified *élan vital*, made inevitable a complete revaluation of the psychological function of religion. Jung, in *The Psychology of the Unconscious* (1912) following on *Die Bedeutung des Vaters* (1909) in no way

---

1. This is not said in disparagement. In resting psychology on a conception that transcends empirical psychological observation (for *libido* is observable only in particularized forms and manifestations) Jung, in effect, complies with the Aristotelian doctrine that no science can demonstrate its own ultimate principles, but must relinquish this task to a superordinated science.

2. That is to say, formless *energeia*, if it *exists as such*, is none other than God. Jung's 'undifferentiated *libido*' is confessedly no more than an abstraction from differentiated forms of *libido*. It stands in a similar relationship to *actus purus* as does *ens communissimum* to *ens realissimum*. Within the strict limits of empirical psychology *libido* is simply (as is 'energy' in physics), 'an abstraction that expresses dynamic relations and rests upon a theoretic postulate confirmed by experience'. (J. Jacobi, *The Psychology of C. G. Jung*, p. 30).

3. e.g., *Two Essays in Analytical Psychology*, p. 188, cf. p. 226: 'There is no certainty at all as to whether an unconscious content belongs, or does not belong, to the self. It cannot be determined *a priori* whether it pertains to me, to others, or to both'.

repudiated Freud's account of the psychogenesis of the
Man-God relationship—which, as we have noted, is even
for Freud in his more sober moods only a partial account.
On the contrary, Jung accepted, elaborated and deepened it.
'The religious instinct,' he wrote, 'feeds upon the incestuous
libido of the infantile period. In the principal forms of religion
which now exist, the father-transference seems to be at least
the moulding influence. . . . Religious activity (is com-
pounded of) those impulses which in childhood are withdrawn from incestuous application through the intervention
of the incest barrier and which, especially at the time of
puberty as a result of affluxes of *libido* coming from the still
incompletely employed sexuality, are aroused to their own
particular activity. . . .'[1] The whole book, as is indicated
more clearly by the original title, *Wandlungen und Symbole
der Libido*, was in fact devoted to showing how the undifferentiated *libido*, originally in the infantile state wholly
absorbed in the parental relationship, is by religious symbols, rites and beliefs, weaned from the parents and transformed into creative and atoning power. An immense
erudition, covering the myths and religions of widely
differing levels of culture, re-enacted in the case-histories of
contemporary and often quite 'non-religious' patients, is
brought to bear to support and illustrate this general thesis;
but perhaps nowhere does Jung succeed in establishing his
conception more satisfactorily than in his recurrent studies
in this book of the unique significance from the psychotherapeutic standpoint of the teaching, life, death and
resurrection of Jesus of Nazareth.

But it cannot be said that, during this transitional period
of his thought, Jung's conscious and explicit attitude towards
religion was much more favourable than that of Freud. That
attitude was not altogether very clear, nor even very consistent; certainly there does not seem to have been any very
definite realization of the implications of his own premises.
On the one hand, there was a quite extraordinary insight into

---

1. *The Psychology of the Unconscious*, p. 38.

what religion should do for man and what it had achieved in the past; but on the other, there was still pretty full agreement with Freud that religion is a regressive and illusory activity. At this late date, there is no particular point in subjecting Jung's earlier pronouncements on the value and validity of religion to close scrutiny, nor yet the ideal of 'moral autonomy' which he opposed to it in those days.[1] Two ultimately incompatible ideas seem to intertwine in *The Psychology of the Unconscious*; on the one hand, an acute awareness, based on the empirical data, that religion is not only psychologically valuable but also irreplaceable; on the other, an idea, which we may trace rather to the assumptions of pre-1914 humanistic optimism, and perhaps also to exaggerated hopes that psychological analysis would exhaust unconscious contents, that all religious activities, representations and origins, by being subjected to analytical investigation, and so rendered fully conscious and rationally explained, could thereby be spirited away, leaving man the ultimate master of his own soul, supreme, autonomous and godless.

But in point of fact, Jung's differences with Freud were to lead to a revaluation of religion, and particularly of Christianity, far more radical than Jung could then see. The substitution of the word 'undifferentiated *libido*' for 'sexuality' necessarily involves a complete inversion of evaluation. It may make no objective difference whether we call *mana* transmuted infantile sexuality, or infantile sexuality potential *mana*—but it makes a world of difference to our standards of appraisal. In Freud, if we do not gravely misread him, the centre of interest is in the ultimate *cause* of all manifestations of the psyche, which cause is conceived to be the sexual incest-wish. Everything else is interpreted solely in this purely etiological context, and the etiological centre of interest is identified with the axiological. Psycho-analysis was born and nurtured in the medical clinic, and it need not be wondered at that the same principles of mechanistic cause and effect which were considered adequate for the

---

1. *op. cit.*, pp. 142-145, 307 (note 42).

diagnosis and cure of the diseases of the body were considered adequate for the diagnosis and cure of the diseases of the soul. In Freudian theory the reduction of the disease to its cause, discovering it to consciousness and evoking the appropriate abreaction, were all that was required. The *cause* was all that mattered to the analyst, and the ultimate cause was infantile sexuality. All else is a more or less satisfactory substitute, be it art, culture, science, neurosis, psychosis, religion, but rather especially religion. Some substitutes work; others fail. But whether they be regressions or sublimations, all are really substitutes for the real thing, and the real thing is the prohibited incest.

I hope this is not a gross caricature of the early Freud. Alfred Adler had already parted from the psycho-analytical community on this issue. Adler had been a socialist, and from the socialists he had learned that it was vastly more important to know what societies became and what they might become than to know where they came from. So far, so good; teleology, finality, purpose, the *causa causarum*, was reinstated, and to that extent psychology was delivered from the crushing limitations of mere mechanism. Direction rather than origin became the dominant concern of the psycho-therapist; drives rather than desires were consequently the material in his patients which most interested him. Had Adler learned no more than that from socialism, all might have been well. Unfortunately, as Jung was to show, his finality was far too narrowly conceived; the principles of class-struggle applied to the individual in the form of the Will to Power were, by themselves, as insufficient to account for all the data as was sexuality.[1] But for Jung also the important thing is not the acorn but the oak; the important thing for the patient to know is not what he had been but what he could and should become. Reductive analysis is valuable only as subordinated to a prospective synthesis; the discovery of causes only in so far as they make possible the realization of ends. The whole viewpoint is changed

---

1. See the first of the *Two Essays in Analytical Psychology*.

from a mere looking backward to a looking forward.[1] The way is thus opened for a view of religion, for instance, set from a totally different standpoint. It becomes possible to view religion no more as a tolerated but regressive substitute for the forbidden incest, but as the fine flower and fruit of psychic energy liberated from its confinement to infantile incestuous channels.

But Jung did not stop there. His analytic experience, confirmed and illuminated by the study of comparative mythology, compelled him to revolutionize Freud's incest theory itself. The whole story cannot be told here; but it may be fairly summed up by saying that Jung was led to the conclusion that the data which Freud had interpreted as indicating an incestuous wish were not ultimately incestuous at all. Impregnation of the mother for its own sake, or motivated by the pleasure principle, was not the ultimate object of the *libido* at all; what was really desired was the return to the womb—rebirth.[2] The incest-wish is no longer the ultimate 'thing symbolized'; it is itself the symbol of a yet more fundamental need and desire. Hence it could be that manifest sexuality is itself symbolic; it is in fact only one form of life-urge bigger than itself. Freud, in effect, is turned upside down by Jung, in much the same way as Hegel had been turned upside down by Marx. Freud's data are accepted and indeed amplified; but their significance is inverted. Fire-making rites are no longer seen as thinly disguised imitations of, or substitutes for, sexual intercourse; sexual intercourse is the fitting model for the psychological trans-formations symbolized and realized in fire-making rites. Examples are multiplied indefinitely throughout the length of *The Psychology of the Unconscious*. The incubation of the *mystes* in the cave, the plunging of the neophyte in the font, are not sorry substitutes for incestuous penetration of the mother; the union with the mother is the shadow of inward rebirth and baptismal regeneration into life more abundant. (The

---

1. All this is excellently summarized by Jacobi, *op. cit.*, pp. 66, 84.
2. *cf. The Psychology of the Unconscious*, p. 138.

Western rite for the blessing of the Font at Easter, with its frank and undisguised fertility symbolism, is but one indication of how Jung's theory is no novelty, but a return to what to the Christian Church has been a commonplace.)

For what does it mean, this longing for the womb and rebirth? 'How can a man be born when he is old? Can he enter a second time into his mother's womb and be born?' So asked Nicodemus with Freudian-like literalness. To which Christ replied, 'Except a man be born of water and of the spirit, he cannot enter into the Kingdom of God. That which is born of the flesh is flesh; and that which is born of the *pneuma* is *pneuma*. Marvel not that I said unto thee, Ye must be born again. The *pneuma* bloweth (*pnei*) where it listeth, and thou hearest the sound thereof, but canst not tell whence it cometh or whither it goeth; so is everyone that is born of the *pneuma*'.[1] Thus, as Jung comments, 'the *libido* becomes spiritualized in an imperceptible manner. The power which "always wishes evil" thus creates a spiritual life. In religion this course is raised to a system.'[2]

Here we are brought to Jung's most distinctive contribution to psychology and psychotherapy; to which he was led by experience with his patients, and to which the way was opened by the substitution of *libido* for sexuality. The ontogenesis of the psyche is a 're-echo' of a phylogenesis; the contents of the unconscious are not limited by the acquisitions of the individual's lifetime; behind them lie dormant the experiences of the race; it includes collective as well as personal elements. Behind submerged 'memories' of events in the individual's lifetime lies a racial heritage manifested in archetypal figures. Behind the particularized physical mother's womb lies the archetypal womb of the Great Mother of all living; behind the physical father the archetypal Father, behind the child the '*puer æternus*'; behind the particular manifestation of the procreative sexual *libido* lies the universal creative and re-creative Spirit. The second

---

1. John iii, 4-8.
2. *Psychology of the Unconscious*, p. 139.

of all these pairs appears now, not as a phantasy-substitute for the first; but rather does the first appear as a particular manifestation and symbol of the second. The way is now open to us, for instance, no longer to conceive of God as a substitute for the physical father, but rather the physical father as the infant's first substitute for God, the genetically prior bearer of the image of the All-Father. God is less a Big Father than the physical father a little god. Clearly we are not far from St Paul's 'Father . . .' from whom all fatherhood (*patria*) in heaven and in earth is named.[1]

This is only one example—but it is a fundamental one—of the manner in which the findings of analytical psychology have opened up vistas into a vast territory which the theologian cannot fail to recognize as closely resembling his own, however differently the psychologist and the theologian may respectively regard it. Jung has in fact, and even in spite of himself, given a point to Tertullian's *anima naturaliter christiana* such as has never been exhibited with such clearness before. An immense field for confrontation, comparison and correlation is opened out. A theologian who reads Jung's works, or who studies case-histories conducted under Jungian inspiration, finds himself at once in a strangely familiar world; familiar in its contents and features, but strange in its angle of approach. It is impossible for him, for instance, not to recognize in the undifferentiated *libido* of Jung something very like the *naturale desiderium* of Aquinas; in the figures of the archetypal Mother, symbols of the undifferentiated Divine *Ousia*; in her 'terrible' and 'benign' aspects, the First and Second Eve. But even more striking still than these static symbols is the manner of the integrating or redemptive process itself as it is observed to take place in an analysis conducted along Jungian lines—so remarkable indeed, and so inexplicable on a purely mechanistic hypothesis, that Jung so far departs from Freud's assumptions as to call in question the competence of the causality-principle to explain many phenomena of the

---

1. Ephesians iii, 14.

psychology of the unconscious at all.[1] Whether the 'syn-chronistic' principle which he would oppose to that of causality is indeed a principle which excludes causality, rather than a salutary re-enlargement of it beyond the narrow confines to which positivistic assumptions have restricted it, is, perhaps, highly questionable. But it would seem to be certain that any deep and successful analysis involves a response to the 'leadership' (the word is Jung's) of manifestations of the unconscious which are closely parallel to, even if not sometimes actually a vehicle of, the redemptive functioning of faith and grace as known to Christian experience and studied in Christian theology.[2]

All this is, of course, very suspect to those who have been trained in the mechanistic traditions of the old schools of science—it was clearly very suspect to Jung himself for many years. In spite of the lessons of more recent developments in physics, it is still not easy to admit mysteries and imponder-ables into science, and risk the overthrow of cogent and comprehensible systems—even at the cost of disregarding manifest facts. Those critics whose writings suggest that they are more solicitous for the tidiness of the psychiatrist's own mind than the health and happiness of their patients, will doubtless continue to dub Jung an unscientific mystic and mystifier; certainly Jung's later excursions into the more exotic byways of superstition and magic will do nothing to appease them. But Jung's work is hardly less disturbing to the professed theist and religious believer, even to a zealot for his creed or for his church. Perhaps even these have long ago ceased to think of God, and good and evil spirits, as ever

1. *The Secret of the Golden Flower* ('In Memory of R. Wilhelm') p. 142. *cf.* Jung's preface to Wilhelm's edition of the *I Ching*, and the full development of this theory in his contribution to *Naturerklärung und Psyche* (Zürich, Rascher, 1952).

2. *Two Essays*, p. 169: *cf. Secret of the Golden Flower*, p. 126. Compare St Paul's transcendence of the inner conflict of the laws of life and of reason through the response of faith to grace *e.g.* in Romans, vii. 5 ff. *Cf.* 'Coué and St Paul' by William Temple (late Archbishop of Canterbury) in *Essays in Christian Politics*, pp. 131 seq.

active influences in their own life and conduct; almost un-wittingly they may have so 'objectified' them, so relegated them to the 'supernatural', confined them to Sundays, that it has never occurred to them that their ceaseless activities could and should become empirically observable—and a challenge to searching self-examination.

For it would be grossly misleading to quote Jung as an apologist for religion as he commonly finds it among us Europeans to-day, and it is rather as a challenge than as an apology that his work should be viewed. Doubtless there is much in his own published writings that has been, and will be, challenged—both by the theologian on one side, and by the scientist and the psychiatrist on the other. He himself would have it so, and that we take nothing on faith from him. His own challenge to the unprejudiced sceptic and unbeliever is obvious enough. His challenge to the professed believer is perhaps more subtle—but no less serious. It is comparatively easy for the man of religion to dismiss Freud, who never took religion very seriously anyhow, and whose psycho-analysis can be labelled as 'science' and outside the concern of ulti-mate beliefs and values. Jung insists that such a dichotomy is impossible: that consciously or unconsciously religion affects everything in our lives. Whether we belong to any denomina-tion or none, he challenges us to become more conscious, more responsible, more adult in our religion—or irreligion—if we would not destroy ourselves and our fellows. Western man fools himself when he thinks he has outgrown religion and has no need of God—as he is learning in the bitter Nemesis to his pretensions to self-sufficiency. But he *has* outgrown an infantile religiosity which is no more than an escape-mechanism, an outer and theoretic compensation for inner godlessness in practice. When the salt has lost its savour, it is indeed good for nothing but to be trodden down by men.

V

THE FRONTIERS OF THEOLOGY
AND PSYCHOLOGY

JUNG's psychology, perhaps more than any other psychology, thus brings modern science to the very frontiers of
the realm traditionally held by theology. More exactly,
it brings the methods of empirical science into the heart-
lands of that territory—the territory of the human soul. Nor
is this invasion only a purely theoretic reconnaissance of
the theologian's ancient domain, for not only does the
theoretical psychologist claim to inspect this territory of the
systematic theologian, but also the practical psychotherapist
(and the word means precisely 'curate of souls') increasingly
takes over many of the functions formerly performed by the
practical pastor. The worries and anxieties, the moral
problems and conflicts, the obsessive sense of guilt and
frustration, the hunger for guidance and assurance—all
these and many other problems which our grandparents
took to the confessional, the rectory or the manse—are now
far more often taken to the consulting-room of the physician
and the psychologist. It would be profitable to examine the
reasons for this; inquiries have been set on foot which yield
startling, if not altogether regrettable, results.[1] Here we must
be content to record the unquestionable fact. Those who
seek help from psychologists rather than from the clergy
are by no means only those who have no clergy to go to, or
who own no Christian faith or denominational allegiance;
sometimes they are devout and regular churchgoers. Indeed,
it is very often the clergy who send them, sometimes consciously and deliberately, perhaps more often unconsciously

---

1. See C. G. Jung, 'Psychotherapists or the Clergy', *Modern
Man in Search of a Soul*, pp. 260 ff.

and involuntarily. Many pastors of souls and religious writers would perhaps be surprised to know how often the very prescriptions and advice they have tendered in the exercise of their own 'cure of souls' are the overt or latent 'complaint' when sheep of their flock become the psychologist's patients. 'The fact is not unknown that certain strict religious retreats and mission-sermons among Catholics, and a certain sort of sin-sodden training among Protestants, lead not to the Kingdom of God—but to the psychiatrist's consulting-room.'[1]

Those who seek the psychotherapist's aid are sometimes disappointed, and it is from these that the clergy are especially likely to hear more. More especially are they likely to hear the denunciations and appeals of those among their flock who may be passing through a phase of negative transference on the analyst; and if the priest or pastor does not understand what is happening, he may not only do considerable harm to the patient, but find his own worst suspicions of psychology powerfully reinforced.

But there are many more who have found, with the analyst's help, the release and health which they sought, and which they failed to find from the official representatives of religion or from their own religious practices. In common with others, who would never have thought of seeking aid from that quarter, they have found, not indeed that their troubles could be removed like some bad tooth, but that with the aid of analytical psychology they could find insight, understanding, freedom and ability to deal with them, which previously they lacked. The result has been remarkably like the religious conversions and renewals of which they may have read, and so, too, have the actual experiences and processes by which the goal has been attained. The symbols which they have confronted in their dreams and phantasies have had much in common with those of religious initiations and other rites, and have been all the more impressive and effective because they have not been super-

---

1. C. G. Jung, *Psychologie und Alchemie*, p. 37.

imposed from without but have arisen from within, and have come, not just as the expression of the beliefs of a group, as a traditional and collective pattern, but as closely inter-mingled with their own most personal and private experiences and problems. Those who have even begun to experience such release and salvation from whatever had previously tortured them, can give very little weight to the misgivings of theologians or the warnings of some of their pastors. In their attainment of light and insight they are likely to echo the man in the Gospel, 'If he be a sinner, I know not: one thing I know, that whereas I was blind, now I see.' (John ix, 25).

Yet it is not surprising that the very 'religiousness' of Jung's psychology has alarmed many of the religious-minded hardly less than it has alarmed the sceptic. A theoretical dichotomy between religion and practical psycho-therapy, even at the cost of fostering conflict and schizo-phrenia, seems to the more timid preferable to the risks of admitting the psychotherapist into the holy precincts of religion itself, or to the still more painful risks of luring the pastor of souls away from the security of his textbook lore to face the realities of the human psyche in the raw— beginning (as he must) with his own. The belief that spiritual and mental disorder are independent of each other saves a great deal of trouble to the specialists in the treatment of both, and a misapplication of the venerable distinction between the 'natural' and the 'supernatural' supplies a ready rationalization to justify the convenience. But the belief is as untenable in the light of the traditional theo-logical principle that 'grace perfects nature' as it has been shown to be unsound and disastrous therapeutically. But neither are the risks wholly illusory, so long at least as the res-pective roles of theologian and psychologist, of pastor and psychotherapist, are not clearly distinguished and co-ordi-nated. The psychologist who abandons empirical psychology for the role of amateur preacher, moralizer and dogmatizer is unhappily not unknown; nor is the clergyman who 'preaches psychology' and virtually abandons the ministry of Word and Sacraments[1]: each is a menace to religion and psychology alike. If the two roles are to unite in harmonious collaboration, they must first be clearly distinguished, and the specialist in each must learn what the other is about.

It is not to be expected that the task of mutual understanding between the theologian and the Jungian psychologist will be found an altogether easy one; and it is not only the theologian who may find it difficult to do justice to Jung's work. Jung's psychology is not primarily a theory but a *praxis*; the theory has grown out of, and is only incidental to, the *Heilsweg*, the therapeutic art, the way of liberation and healing, which can never be quite identical in any two cases. Hence, as one of his leading collaborators has said: 'Theoretic conceptions and explanations are adequate only up to a certain point for the comprehension of Jung's system, for in order to understand it completely one must have experienced its vital workings within oneself'.[2] It is therefore perhaps pardonable that most theologians who have given any attention to depth-psychology at all still appear to be too busy catching up with Freud to have noticed the 'Copernican revolution' (the phrase is Schaer's) which Jung has introduced. Freud, they find, is eminently tidier and more systematic, and to that extent more congenial to their own scholastic ways of thinking. Thomist theologians particularly must find much in common in Aquinas and Freud,[3] and while much of this common ground is axiomatic for Jungians also, there are very understandable reasons which

---

1. See H. Guntrip, *Psychology for Ministers and Social Workers* (1949) chapters i and ii, for some excellent practical observations on this point. We would not assert that the roles of priest or clergyman and of therapist cannot be combined in the same individual (there is evidence not only that they are successfully so combined, but also that there are cases of neurosis among religious people which only a priest-psychologist can touch), but it is essential that the two roles are not confused in his own mind and practice.

2. Jolan Jacobi, *The Psychology of C. G. Jung*, p. 59.

3. *e.g.*, A. Plé, O.P., *Saint Thomas d'Aquin et la Psychologie des Profondeurs*, *Le Supplément de La Vie Spirituelle*, Nov. 1951. Translated and amplified in *Dominican Studies*, 1952.

have made it difficult for theologians and philosophers to take Jung's work seriously.

The obstacles to understanding are considerable, and should not be minimized. Jung himself has repudiated every claim to have constructed a complete and water-tight system. 'It is my firm conviction,' he has written, 'that the time for an all-inclusive theory, taking in and presenting all the contents, processes and phenomena of the psyche from one central viewpoint, has not come by a long way; I regard my theories as suggestions and attempts at the formulation of a new scientific conception of psychology based in the first place upon immediate experience with human beings.'[1] He sees his work as that of a pioneer, and for that reason deems it unnecessary to chart territory already surveyed by other workers. The lack of 'one central viewpoint' is particularly perplexing to the theologian, but not only to the theologian. Jung's psychology has grown out of psychopathology, and although it has now become much more than that, the influence of this preoccupation with the abnormal and the erratic is still very marked. This should not be forgotten by the reader of Jung's works who is perplexed by what must seem to him (especially if he be a Catholic) Jung's excessive interest in, and sympathy for, the more erratic and eccentric manifestations of religion also. Jung's whole approach to religion in his published writings, even when all allowances have been made for his empiricism, must often seem somewhat one-sided. At the beginning of his *Psychology and Religion* he describes religion as 'a careful and scrupulous observation of what Rudolf Otto aptly terms the "numinosum", that is, a dynamic existence or effect, not caused by an arbitrary act of will'.[2] But in line with Schleiermacher and Otto, the emphasis is on the primitive experience of the 'numinosum', inasmuch as 'it seizes and controls the human subject', and is 'an involuntary condition of the subject', rather than on the character and quality of the 'careful

---

1. 'Foreword' to J. Jacobi, *The Psychology of C. G. Jung*.
2. C. G. Jung, *Psychology and Religion*, p. 4.

and scrupulous observation'. To many this will seem the raw and shapeless material of religion, rather than religion itself: a material which is equally capable of assuming the form of magic or any manner of superstition, if not also of lunacy. This stress on the primitive experience (*Urerfahrung*) in religion is needful to the extent that it has been neglected elsewhere, and may rightly be considered to be the psychological root of the whole matter, yet it could give a very unbalanced view of human religion as a whole as it presents itself even to the inspection of factual psychological and anthropological inquiry. Schaer does not contradict Jung, but nevertheless restores a necessary balance, when he insists that 'religion consists not in merely experiencing the supra-personal forces of the soul as such, but in adopting—psychically—an active attitude'.[1] Yet even Schaer fails us in clearly distinguishing a developed religious and worshipful active attitude, involving rational and voluntary decision (let alone one that is distinctively Christian), from that of the magician or the gnostic, or even the poet. Here, it might be thought, the theologian should have much of a constructive character to offer to the analytical psychologist in the elucidation of his own material, and within his own legitimate field of inquiry.

In the article which we are privileged to print as an appendix, Professor Frei draws attention to other points at issue between the theologian and the analytical psychologist. Among these, Jung's personal distrust of inferential thinking indeed presents a serious difficulty, one which, however, does not seem inseparable from his empirical work, but rather attributable to metapsychological assumptions and the repercussions of the Kantian influences apparent in his earlier writings.[2] Closely allied to this is the difficulty which the theologian, together with other critics, may find in Jung's conception of 'psychological truth'. He

---

1. Hans Schaer, *Religion and the Cure of Souls in Jung's Psychology*, p. 100.

2. Notably in some of the notes to the original edition of *The Psychology of the Unconscious*.

may well be inclined to sympathize with Flugel when he writes, 'In becoming a psychologist Freud has not been willing to sacrifice the general criteria of truth observed by other sciences, while Jung on his part has become so enthralled by the psychological significance of religious dogma and symbolism that he seems to some extent to have lost interest in these criteria'.[1] But Jung is justified in contending that these other criteria are not his business, and that the only 'truths' with which he is competent to deal are the psychological facts which come under his observation. Yet among these facts must surely be counted the psyche's deep yearning for true *judgment* concerning facts, whether attributed to faith or reason. If Freud was mistaken in reducing religion to a matter of intellectual assertions, we cannot push the 'rational element' in religion into the background altogether.[2] The 'truth' of religion does indeed lie outside the competence of the empirical psychologist as such, and the practising psychotherapist must necessarily confine himself to the manner in which it works. Jung deserves the praise rather than the blame of both theologian and scientist for his rigid and constant insistence upon this principle. He does not deserve to be labelled (as by Flugel) a philosophical

---

1. J. C. Flugel, *Man, Morals and Society: A Psycho-analytical Study* (Duckworth, 1945), p. 267.
2. Without some appeal to extra-psychological criteria, it would seem impossible for the psychologist to distinguish hallucinations from 'real' perceptions. Flugel (*op. et loc. cit.*) is justified in his note drawing attention to the ambiguities in the term 'psychological truth'. A Thomist will be more accustomed to distinguish 'material truth' (Flugel's 'mere existence of mental states or processes') from 'formal truth' (to be had only in judgment) and both from estimates of functional value. On the 'rational element' in religion from the psychological standpoint, see R. H. Thouless, *An Introduction to the Psychology of Religion*, Chapter VI. Its presence among even primitive peoples has been noted by many anthropological field-workers, *e.g.*, by P. Radin, *Die religiöse Erfahrung der Naturvölker* (Zürich, Rhein-Verlag, 1951).

pragmatist for this scientific integrity. Yet it must always be found to be itself a psychological fact that a religion which is not 'true'—or at least apprehended as 'true'—does not even 'work'. It is here, we would suggest, that the theologian could offer his services in a positive and constructive fashion, rather than with a suspicious resentment at the psychologist's intrusion on his own territory.

For this intrusion should not of itself disturb or surprise a theologian who has been trained in the traditional school as represented, for instance, by St Thomas Aquinas. For him it is almost axiomatic that the different human sciences and disciplines are to be distinguished, not necessarily by different subject-matter or fields of inquiry ('material objects' as the schoolmen called them), but by the different ways (*rationes cognoscibiles*) in which the subject-matter can be rendered knowable by and to the human mind. It is no scandal to him (Aquinas had shown the contrary in the very first page of his *Summa*) that the selfsame 'God' whom the believer acknowledges by faith in revelation, could also be the legitimate object of purely rational inquiry, even by the unbelieving investigator. The viewpoint and method of the theologian who tries to 'understand what he believes', and of the empiricist or rational thinker who tries to draw the consequences from what he observes, will differ widely; so also may their conclusions. If they should appear to conflict, loyalty to truth will require of each that he should verify and check his own processes, and attempt to understand those of the other, and to see where misunderstandings and mistakes may have arisen.

Nor will a Thomist theologian be unfamiliar with the idea that the selfsame 'soul' or 'psyche' which is his professional concern may also be the subject of empirical observation and scientific inquiry. Aquinas himself conducted just such an inquiry, commenting upon and developing Aristotle's *De Anima*. This inquiry was based on observation of fact no less than is that of more modern psychologies. But its methods and treatment of observed facts differed considerably. Where modern scientific method proceeds by way of generalization, postulate, hypothesis, law, prediction or—and notably in the instance of Jung's psychology—the correlation of phenomena in terms of function, the psychology of Aristotle and Aquinas proceeded mainly by way of inference. The next section in this book will suggest that this ancient psychology (though commonly despised and misunderstood as an obsolete faculty-psychology with no basis in experience) still has much of importance and value to offer those who follow purely empirical methods. Here it is enough to point out that a Thomist theologian should have no objection to the scientific examination of the workings of the human soul from standpoints other than his own. On the contrary, he may not unreasonably expect that it will enrich his understanding of the material in his own field of inquiry, and hope that he himself may be able, from his own theological standpoint, to contribute to the work of the empirical psychologist. St Thomas himself will tell him that every science must be met on its own ground, and understood only in the light of its own premises and observations.

The way, then, is open to an unprejudiced interchange of ideas and experiences; an interchange whose importance the theologian, the priest and the preacher should be very ready to recognize. It is his own experience that contemporary religious scepticism is due less to a widespread belief that the Gospels and creeds are positively untrue, than to the widespread feeling that they are irrelevant. It is precisely that *relevance* of faith and practice to the needs and workings of the human psyche that Jung's psychology appears to have rediscovered, and to be subjecting to methodical study. It does not claim to sow, still less to explain or explain away, the Gospel seed; but it does inform us about its effects in the soil that receives it, and upon the soil's condition which enables the seed to live or die. (*cf.* Matt. xiii, 4-8).

But it is not to be expected that the encounter between the theologian and the analytical psychologist will be without difficulties which may make considerable demands on the patience of both. Each may cover the same territory, yet each must realize that the other approaches it from a different, sometimes an opposite, point of view, which he must endeavour to understand and appreciate. A Christian may, for instance, experience a momentary and involuntary impatience when he finds a chapter-heading in one of Jung's books entitled, 'Christ as Symbol of the Self': it may strike him as literally preposterous, for to him it will seem self-evident that it is rather Jung's concept of 'the Self' that is a symbol—or perhaps only an unsatisfactory and elusive cipher —of Christ. But he has to remember that what is considered to be symbolic of what is largely a matter of the conscious standpoint, and of what is first apprehended in consciousness. Each party has to make the due allowances for the position of the 'observer', his own and the other's, and to keep a check on its influence throughout the treatment of the same facts. Where for instance Jung, starting from the situation of present-day secularized science, considers that the medieval alchemists were unconscious heretics, and unconsciously inconsistent in claiming to be good Catholics and esoteric redeemers of matter at the same time, a Catholic will be more prone to suppose that it was not the alchemists who joined together incompatibles, but the moderns who have rent asunder what God had joined together, and that it is *our* consciousness which is at fault in sundering them. He will accept with eager gratitude all the facts which Jung records in his invaluable books on alchemy, yet often incline to dissent from some of their interpretations and evaluations. When we come to discuss matters more strictly close to theology, possibilities of mutual misunderstanding must be expected to increase.

As yet, too few theologians have given much attention to the task to which these developments in psychology challenge them. The pioneer work of the Methodist, Dr Scott Frayn, *Revelation and the Unconscious*, cleared away much débris, and offered several ideas which might stimulate many who could not give unqualified assent to all his views. Dr Hans Schaer's *Religion und Seele in der Psychologie C. G. Jung's*, which we have just quoted, was another contribution from a Protestant standpoint, which gave an admirably objective and unbiased presentation of the religious implications of Jung's psychology, and reserved to the end the author's own personal opinions. From Catholic sources we have had Father Josef Goldbrunner's *Heiligkeit und Gesundheit*, a gem of simple, practical wisdom, but with no scientific pretensions. The same author's *Individuation* is a more considerable work; so also is that of Professor Frei and his colleagues in *Rätsel der Seele*. Professor Frei's essay at the end of this present volume should straighten out once and for all what has proved one of the most considerable tangles which confronts the theologically-minded student of Jung, namely his conception of the 'Self' in its religious aspects. The distinction of the 'God-imago' of the psychologists from 'God-in-himself' should satisfy the most exacting and cautious theologian, for, on his account also, God infinitely transcends every image, concept or name that can be used of him. Nor should he be disturbed if analytical psychology offers at least a partial explanation of the origin and formation of such images and conceptions in terms of psychological processes. For so long as we must confess—as Jung confesses—that the psyche itself is an entity (or, more exactly, a postulate) 'beyond science',[1] whose contents are inexhausted, and probably inexhaustible, and whose boundaries have not been discovered, it is clear that an endopsychic explanation cannot be exhaustive or final. The 'archetypes' explain no more so long as we must acknowledge, as Jung acknowledges, that no empirically verifiable hypothesis can account for their ultimate origin.[2] In general, it must be said that, while empirical psychology can observe and correlate the raw material of psychological data, and to some small extent account for their proximate origins and general tendencies, it is incapable of challenging whatever claims may be made by the theologian or the philosopher

---

1. *Two Essays in Analytical Psychology*, p. 268.

2. *op. cit.*, pp. 71 ff. They are in any case only categories of experience—like the species of the botanist—and in no sense causal explanations, as Jung has explained in *Der Geist der Psychologie*.

to account for their ultimate cause and ground, or their final and all-governing purpose and direction.

In a letter written to a theologian in 1945, Jung stated as follows his own view of the respective positions of the psychologist and the theologian, and of the importance of their encounter:

You have rendered justice to my empirical and practical standpoint throughout. I consider this a very meritorious act, since most of my philosophically or theologically minded readers overlook my empiricism completely. I never allow myself to make statements about the divine entity, since this would be a transgression beyond the limit of science. It would therefore be unfair to criticize my opinions as if they were a philosophical system. . . . When you want to talk to scientists you cannot begin with a religious creed. You have to show the facts and let them draw their own conclusions. You also cannot say that man's goal is actually realized in God, but you must again show facts demonstrating in what the goal is realized. What you can show in this respect is the symbol of the *self*, a well defined psychological phenomenon, which anybody may call God; but the scientists cannot prove it to be God. As a scientist I must give a wide berth to anything dogmatic or metaphysical, since it is not the scientist's task to preach the Gospel. But it is precisely what the theologian has to say, namely, that the dogma is the hitherto most perfect answer to, and formulation of, the most relevant items in the objective psyche, and that God has worked all these things in man's soul. . . .

Thus when I said that God is a complex, I meant to say: Whatever he is, he is *at least* a very tangible complex. You may say he is an illusion, but he is *at least* a psychological fact. I certainly never intended to say: He is *nothing else* but a complex. Naturally, when my books got into the hands of readers outside my psychiatric sphere, they read them with very different eyes. Hence many mistakes. . . .

It is so much a matter of to-whom-you-talk. My public does not consist of theologians, but of worldly, educated people of our day. When you talk of God, they do not know of *what* you talk, since such ideas have been dismissed long ago as nebulous phantasies. I show facts to them, and not metaphysical assertions which they cannot grasp. If I were talking to peasants, I certainly would talk about God, since I know that they know of what I am talking. But it is *of the highest importance* that the educated and 'enlightened' public should know religious truth as a thing living in the human soul. . . . People must be taught to see where they come in, otherwise you never bridge the gulf between the educated mind and the world of dogmatic ideas, which they comprehend nowhere and which more-over offend their reason.

In the same letter, Jung recalled how his work with his patients had compelled him to give attention to doctrines and symbols concerning the Trinity, how inadequate was his equipment, 'supported only by my experience, and with practically nothing on the theological side'. It is inevitable that in his resultant essay, 'Zur Psychologie der Trinitätsidee'[1] there is much which must raise theological eyebrows. On the one hand there is a realistic approach to the subject in terms of human experience which has hardly been matched since the *De Trinitate* of St Augustine; a vivid realization of what the docrine has meant, or should have meant, in the history of human culture and in the development of the mind of Western man. On the basis of experience with the human psyche alone, we find Jung unwittingly at grips with the most abstruse and recondite points of Trinitarian theology —such as the a-logical and 'non-natural' character of the 'procession' of the Third Person and the impossibility of giving him any distinctive name.[2] On the other hand, the theologian will detect confusion of the timeless 'generation' of the Second Person with Incarnation, with his 'sending' and human birth in time, a confusion which is nevertheless reminiscent of some of the earliest Christian fathers. He will be still more perplexed in missing any clear recognition of the more obvious fact that any doctrine of the Trinity—

---

1. *Eranos Jahrbuch*, Band VIII, 1940-41.
2. These points are treated by Aquinas, *Summa Theologica* I, 27 and 36.

however much it is itself a psychological fact, and to be
elucidated only in terms of human experience and psychology—essentially consists of assertions *about* God, and *not* of
assertions *about* man. It may seem to him, too, that Jung,
while venturing boldly into theological intricacies, misses
much of what (whether consciously or unconsciously, and
as against polytheism or an undifferentiated monism), the
worship of the Trinity means even psychologically to a simple
Christian. Jung sees how much was at stake psychologically
in the heated Trinitarian controversies of earlier Christian
centuries, and why (to the amazement of modern historians)
they were carried on with such passion. Yet so determined is
he to see this psychological relevance in terms only of psychological functions, that the primary value of the Athanasian
doctrine as a prototype of personal, and particularly of
parental, relationship seems quite to escape him. Nor, perhaps, does he show adequate realization of the importance of
the doctrine in the psychology of religion itself. Without
dissenting from all that Jung has to say about the psychological immanence of God and his 'relativity' to the human
psyche, and while admiring his scientific integrity in refusing
any affirmations about divine transcendence, we would urge
that the fact that men make these affirmations of God's transcendence is a psychological fact of immense importance and
influence, which the empirical therapist can ignore only at
his peril. God, as acknowledged by the Christian psyche itself,
is more 'transcendental' than the most 'transcendentalist' of
the world-religions and philosophies, not excluding speculations on the 'Parabrahman' of Vedanta and the 'One' of
Plotinus. In the Trinity, the reflecting Christian finds the
Absolute itself transcended in the union of the Absolute and
the Relative,[1] and in this he finds the supreme 'reconciling
symbol', which sanctifies relationship itself, and meets the
paradox in all religion in its perennial search to satisfy the
thirst for the Absolute by entering into relationship with it.

---

1. *cf.* Cardinal de Vio Cajetan, *Commentarium in Summa Theol.*
    I, 39, 7.

In Jung's essay on the Trinity the theologian (and again, not the theologian alone) will also be confronted with what has proved to be a most obstinate point of difference and mutual incomprehension between Jung, together with most of his school, and even the most sympathetic of his critics, especially among Catholics. Jung repudiates the traditional definition of evil as the absence of appropriate good from a subject which is itself relatively good, and maintains that this conception of evil as a 'privation' is false to the empirical facts and psychologically harmful. Regarding evil as having (apparently) some positive existence and reality of its own, Jung logically enough requires the admission of evil, not only into the 'self', the human totality, but also into the Godhead itself; in his essay on the psychology of the doctrine of the Trinity, this leads him to favour a Divine Quaternity, with a fourth and 'evil' hypostasis, in a fashion which orthodox Christians must find quite inadmissible. This is not the place for definitive judgment on a discussion which is still in progress, but so far with inconclusive and nugatory results. It must suffice to set on record that Jung's personal views on evil, which inevitably affect much in his interpretation of psychological material besides his conception of the doctrine of the Trinity, are still a very serious stumbling block in the encounter between theologians and Jungian psychologists.[1] Touching as they do on fundamental

---

1. Since Jung's essay on the Trinity was written the discussion on the nature of good and evil has been elaborated with some warmth by both parties, *e.g.*, by the present writer in *Dominican Studies*, Vol. II, 1949, p. 399, and at length by Jung in *Aion* (1951), pp. 69 ff. So far, the discussion appears to have generated more heat than light—an indication that the issues at stake may prove to be of vital importance, and that some strong resistances are yet to be overcome before understanding is to be reached. Of the position of traditional Catholic thought as formulated by Aquinas, the following may be briefly noted: (1) There is no formal dogma of the Church on the subject. (2) But inasmuch as the meaning of basic human words, and those indicative of fundamental human values, is at stake, the matter cannot be lightly dismissed as an academic logomachy. (3) As Jung himself

points of human language, values and *Weltanschauung*—even apart from Catholic faith and practice—the difficulty is not to be belittled. But while this divergence of views must profoundly influence *interpretation*, a Catholic thinker will maintain that the *facts* are at least no less amenable to interpretation in the light of his own conceptions and values, and that these could contribute much to a wholesome development of the invaluable work which Jung has initiated.

But it is less in the Christian doctrine of God than in the Christian doctrine of man that we may reasonably hope for points of contact between theology and analytical psychology. We shall not be disappointed. Emil Brunner, in his essay on 'Biblical Psychology'[1] has written well of the confirmation which contemporary psychology has brought,

---

shows in *Aion*, the conception of evil as a privation of good is asserted by the Fathers of both East and West. (4) They do not deny, as might a 'Christian Scientist', the *reality* of evil (on the contrary, they vigorously affirm it); their concern is with the further question: In what does that reality consist? Or, What is it that constitutes *x* to be 'evil' and not 'good'? (5) Their answer is that it is always the *absence* (the *privatio*, not the negation) of a *real* good from a *real* subject— evil has no positive existence of itself—as blindness is real (but consists in the *absence* of sight from a real man) or darkness is real (but consists in the absence of light). (6) This *absence* may indeed *result from* a presence (as the presence of a cataract causes the absence of sight—and the 'better' the cataract the 'worse' the sight) but does not consist in it. (7) This conception is no *a priori* 'metaphysic', but is empirically verifiable by an *analysis of meaning* whenever the words 'good', 'evil', or their equivalents are used. Jung has our keenest support and sympathy in deploring the minimizing of evil which leads to its repression, with its devastating results for the individual psyche and for society; but we are unable to find evidence that the conception of the *privatio boni* has contributed to this. On the other hand, we are unable to find any intelligible, let alone desirable, meaning in such fundamental Jungian conceptions as the 'assimilation of the shadow' if they are not to be understood as the supplying of some absent good (*e.g.*, consciousness) to what is essentially valuable and of itself 'good'.

1. In *God and Man*, *cf.* his *Man in Revolt*.

in its own restricted sphere, to the revelation of man's radical sinfulness, and of how the disclosure of divine forgiveness in Christ alone meets the 'human contradiction', much of which is acutely brought home to us in depth-psychology. From a theology based on the Protestant tenets of the total depravity of human nature, and of justification by extrinsic imputation, it would be vain to seek for more; and we are not surprised to find that Brunner, having rejected the ancient Catholic belief that human nature is healed by grace, dismisses Jung's psychology of integration as 'romantic' and false.

From the traditional Catholic theology, according to which 'grace perfects nature', and sin, while it disintegrates, does not destroy the inherent goodness of human nature, we may reasonably look for some more positive and constructive contacts with empirical psychology. For such a theology, divine forgiveness is no mere 'imputation', but really healing and integrating on the natural level which comes under psychological scrutiny.

The Christian doctrines of man's nature and destiny, of its fall and disintegration, of its restoration and at-one-ment through the incarnate Word of God, his sacrifice, sacraments and church; all these will be found especially relevant. Only a brief and bald outline can here be offered.

The fundamental Christian doctrine of man, on which all else centres, is that man is made in the image and likeness of God. He fulfils his purpose, his destiny, in the measure in which he conforms to this divine image, and realizes it within himself and in his environment. But the realization of this image is something which exceeds his natural capacities; for it means the attainment of conscious, affective and factual relationship to God, which is possible only if God in his graciousness meets man. It must therefore come from God-given grace; man will need guidance and power which must come, not from his own conscious efforts (though these must accept and co-operate), but from beyond the boundaries of his ego-consciousness—that is to say (from the empirical-psychological standpoint), from the unconscious. Originally (in Paradise), and ideally, man was created with this needful grace; and as a consequence of this positive imaging of his Creator as the source and centre of his life, his constituent parts and functions are balanced and co-ordinated within themselves and with his environment. Grace was thus the co-ordinating and governing principle both of the human individual and of human society. This original and ideal condition is known to theology as the 'state of integrity', of 'original rightness', or of 'innocence'.[1] Analytical psychology shows the persistent power of this 'Eden-archetype'.

The 'Fall', according to this teaching, is brought about by *superbia*, the autonomous self-assertion of the conscious ego over and against God, involving the refusal and rupture of the bond of grace. This 'fall upwards', the revolt of the human spirit from its subordination to the Creator, brings about the disintegration of human personality, and hence of human society, and man's conflict with his natural environment. Thus a 'fall downwards' ensues, in which man's various parts and functions become in varying ways and degrees autonomous and impervious to control and order, and even to consciousness. The rebellion against God— the substitution of the individual or collective ego for God as the centre and hub of the personality—necessarily means a dislocation of the integrity and harmony of the 'natural man', whose constituent elements thus fall asunder, each tending to follow its own bent, insubordinate to the requirements of the whole (the 'self' of Jung). This condition is known to theologians as the 'state of disintegrated or fallen nature'.

Adequately to sketch the 'state of repaired nature', the progressive process of at-one-ment, the whole economy of *salus*, as understood by Catholic Christianity, is impossible in a few paragraphs. But a few salient points of the general pattern may be briefly indicated. At-one-ment, the attain-

---

1. For a fuller development of this doctrine, as expounded by Aquinas, see the present writer's essay in *What the Cross Means to Me* (James Clarke, 1943).

ment of *salus* (salvation and health), is beyond man's unaided powers; it, too, must be an act of God and his grace,
and not of purely human works. It is God in Christ who
reconciles the world to himself (II. Cor. v, 19). Yet it is not
only *by* Christ, but *in* Christ that the atoning work is efficacious; for Christ is not only the external cause but the model
to whom man must be conformed. Not only does the Son of
God himself become human, and show us the way to the
unknown God (for 'no man has seen God at any time, the
only-begotten Son has shown him', John i, 18), he accepts
to the full the consequences of human sin; and it is only by
'putting on Christ' as 'members of his body', and by taking
up our own cross,[1] that we can, with the grace and power
conveyed in his word and sacraments, make real in ourselves
the effects of his atoning work.

Catholic Christianity understands this as a progressive
process, begun in baptism, continued and developed in the
Christian life, but never brought to completion in the
dimensions of this world. The lost innocence of paradise
cannot be regained; although the baptismal rebirth re-
establishes the bond with God, its full effects on the 'natural'
and empirical level do not at once and automatically ensue.
Man's fallen and disintegrated condition, the disorder of
desires (*concupiscentia inordinata*) and the lust of spirit against
flesh and of flesh against spirit, must be humbly accepted
if they are to be transmuted. There is no way back to the
innocence, harmony and irresponsibility of Eden, and any
attempt to find one's way thither through escapist phantasy
and idealism is to reject the way of Christ, as Jung has rightly
seen. There is no escape from world, flesh and devil; they
are to be renounced only by being faced and overcome. Jung
only echoes the teaching of Christian writers like Walter
Hilton when he insists that the first step in the way to
re-integration—which the Christian understands as con-
formation to the pattern of Christ—is the recognition and

---

1. Each his own, and not by a slavish imitation as Jung seems
   to fear in *Modern Man in Search of a Soul*, pp. 273 ff.

acceptance of the 'Shadow'.[1] When Jung writes that 'The
Personality as a full realization of the wholeness of our being
is an unattainable ideal',[2] he confirms, though necessarily
only negatively, the Christian belief that the fulfilment of this
atoning process awaits an eschatological realization, and so
lies beyond the field of present psychological observation.

But nor can a Catholic think of it as a task for the individual alone. The Gospels relate only what Jesus *began* to
do and teach (Acts, i, 1), and it is the task of his whole body,
with its many and different members, to expand and develop
it, to await and prepare his second coming, to grow 'unto a
perfect man, unto the measure of the age of the fullness of
Christ' (Eph. iv, 13).

Jung himself, from his psychological experience, has
written with startling insight on details concerning the
Christian sacrifice, sacraments and scriptures, in a way
which must often astonish and stimulate, and sometimes
shame, the theologian. Enormous possibilities for mutual
aid and enrichment open up. The essays which follow in this
volume, some philosophical, others more theological, are
small offerings on some subjects which would seem to be of
particular interest and importance to psychologist and theologian alike. Our next essay would suggest that the ancient
psychological and ethical investigations of Aristotle and
Aquinas have much to offer which deserve the modern
psychologist's attention, and we shall then pass on to a
consideration of the Thomist conception of revelation, with
its many points of contact with the findings of depth-
psychology, and the light it throws on the character of
'saving' or 'healing' truth as distinct from other kinds of truth.

---

1. Hilton stresses that grace does not rid us of the shadow,
   but prevents our being dominated by it. In the man in
   whom the Christ-likeness is being realized, 'the soul is not
   borne *in* the shadow, though he feel it; but *he* beareth *it.*
   For through grace he is made mighty, and strong for to
   bear his body and all the stirrings of it, without hurting or
   defiling of himself'. *cf.* Victor White, *Walter Hilton, An English
   Spiritual Guide* (Guild of Pastoral Psychology, Lecture 31).
2. *Integration of the Personality*, p. 287.

VI

ARISTOTLE, AQUINAS AND MAN

THE conception of man which we find in Aristotle and Aquinas could hardly concern us at all had they themselves not been men, and big men, who had struggled boldly and realistically with the same problems of human life, death and destiny which confront us all. Legend and misuse, accumulating through the course of centuries, have done much to obscure and prejudice our vision of both of them, and we owe an incalculable debt to those patient research workers, who, in comparatively recent years, have enabled us to view them in historical human proportions. 'With Aristotle man ceases to be problematic', pronounces Professor Buber, quoting Bernhard Groethuysen and echoing a widespread opinion.[1] Every page of the *De Anima* and the *Ethics* seems to belie so facile a judgment, but it is a common one, and it is understandable. There have been times when uncritical adulation, vested interests and sheer intellectual inertia, have made of Aristotle, no less than of Aquinas, a superhuman oracle whose *ipse dixit* solved every question, whose observations and reasonings could be neither bettered nor questioned, whose divine intellect provided a convenient refuge from the necessity of observing and thinking for ourselves. Aristotle and St Thomas themselves would be the first to rejoice that many of the finest minds of subsequent ages have revolted indignantly against this stultifying despotism, at times threatening to paralyse every expansion of human consciousness. But now the reconstructions of a Werner Jaeger,[2] for instance, however open to criticism in important points of detail,[3] enable us to see in the stark,

---

1. M. Buber, *Between Man and Man*, p. 126.
2. Werner Jaeger, *Aristotle* (tr. R. Robinson).
3. *cf.* A. Mansion, 'La genèse de l'oeuvre d' Aristote d'après les travaux récents' (*Revue Néoscholastique*, 1927, pp. 307 ff, 423 ff)

crabbed, ill-edited lecture notes of the later Aristotle (which
form the bulk of what remains to us of his work) the fruit of
a profound experience of the tragedy of human existence, of a
veritably existential *pensée engagée*, of an almost Faustian
ἀγὼν περὶ τῆς ψυχῆς (struggle for the soul). 'The young
Aristotle had really felt the pain of man's dualistic existence.'[1]
A keen biological research-worker, a tutor and adviser of
practical politicians, an inexorable logician, and withal a
devoted disciple of the Academy, he had experienced for
himself the conflicting claims of plain fact, logical necessity
and sublime idea. He had known, too, of the catharsis
of dramatic imagery, and had sensed at least something
of the bliss of passionless, godlike contemplation. Knowing
more of his earlier worshipping devotion to his master
Plato, we can sense the poignancy of his *Plato amicus, magis
amica veritas*[2] ('Plato is my friend but truth is my greater
friend') and read something of that bitter experience
of uprooted loves and loyalties in the detached, shrewd,
worldly-wise pages of his *De Amicitia.* Jaeger has shown
us, too, how there were still deeper sources of functional
conflict and integration, marked for us by the transition
from the 'pious' pages of the *Eudemean* to the more matter-
of-fact, sceptical pages of the *Nicomachean Ethics*; not to
speak of that never forgotten whisper of the Mysteries
that 'the whole of human life is a penance for some heavy
guilt that the soul has incurred in an earlier existence'[3]:
their promises of liberation and immortality. What Jaeger
and others have done to display and rehabilitate Aristotle
as a man among men, Gilson, Grabmann, Mandonnet,
Chenu and many another have done for St Thomas Aquinas.

Neither Aristotle nor Aquinas, nor any of their most
ambitious disciples, has ever been so foolish as to write a
treatise *De Homine.* Had they done so, we might hope to
condense it. As it is, we are faced with an *embarras de choix*,

---

1. W. Jaeger, *op. cit.*, p. 100.
2. A condensation of *Nicomachean Ethics*, 1096a, 16.
3. W. Jaeger, *op. loc. cit.*, *cf.* Chapter IX *passim*.

and a painful decision of selection. For there is nothing whatever in the pages of Aristotle and Aquinas which they did not deem relevant to the theoretic understanding or to the practical guidance of man, and a résumé of all their works is as unpractical as it would be tiresome. Much must be neglected which might be found of exceptional interest to the practising psychologist. We have seen how Jung's forerunner, C. G. Carus, singled out the psychology of Aristotle and Aquinas as especially praiseworthy. Professor Walter Wili[1] has drawn attention to many of the affinities which will be found in Aristotle's *Ethics* to fundamental conceptions in the psychology of Jung himself. This theme could be augmented and developed considerably. And when he turns from Aristotle to Aquinas, the modern psychologist will find much more that may well astonish him, even in his own field of empirical psychological observation. The emotions, their classification and their mutual interplay, the causes and remedies of depression, aggression and fear, and certainly their concomitant enervation processes, have been studied with much greater thoroughness and detail since St Thomas's day. But it may be doubted whether a more comprehensive and systematic picture of the subject has been painted since the treatise 'On the Emotions' (*De Passionibus*) in the second part of his *Summa Theologica*. It alone should dispose of the legend that medieval psychology was purely *a priori*, concerned only with the 'higher', purely intellectual process of the psyche, and abysmally unmindful of empirical observation and practical therapy. In Question 38, for instance, that on the remedies for depression (*De Remediis Tristitiæ*), we find a surprisingly up-to-date application of the principle of functional opposition and compensation, recognition of both the organic and the psychological function of weeping, an exact description and explanation of the releasing effect of the positive transference through 'a certain imagination that others bear the sufferer's burden' ('*quaedam imaginatio quod onus alii cum*

---

1. *Eranos Jahrbuch*, Vol. XII, 1946.

ipso ferant'), and more than a hint of such 'modern' methods as hydrotherapy and prolonged narcosis.

But I would suggest that it is less in *its* own empirical sphere that Aristotle and St. Thomas have anything to offer analytical psychology, rather than in *their* own spheres of trans-empirical philosophy and theology. Their contribution, as I see it, is to supplement and to complement, rather than to supplant, modern psychological findings and methods. Modern psychology owes to C. G. Jung the candid and oft-repeated recognition of the inherent limitations of its own empirical method of phenomenal observation, description and functional correlation. On the one hand he has insisted repeatedly on the inescapable necessity for the empirical psychologist to make postulates—*e.g.*, the unconscious, *libido*, the psyche itself—which transcend empirical observation,[1] and on the inability of empirical psychology to affirm or deny the transcendental validity of the psyche's own images and judgments.   On the other hand he has boldly, and with growing emphasis, proclaimed the impossibility for the honest analyst or analysant to evade problems of *Weltanschauung*, especially such as are concerned with the purpose or purposelessness of human existence.[2] Practical necessity no less than scientific integrity will, I believe, increasingly compel analytical psychology to a more conscious and critical scrutiny, not only of the psyche's own inherent aims, and consequently those of psychotherapy, but also of the manner in which it is to understand and define its own postulates. A purely empirical science can, undoubtedly, proceed for some time on the basis of rough

---

1. See especially 'The Basic Postulates of Analytical Psychology' (*Modern Man in Search of a Soul*, pp. 200 ff.).
2. 'Der eine wie der andere wird zu einer weltanschaulichen Auseinandersetzung mit sich selber sowohl mit dem Partner gezwungen. . . . Die Psychotherapie ist aus dermassen praktischen und behelfsmässigen Methode hervorgegangen, da sie lange Zeit Mühe hatte, sich auf ihre eigenen denkerischen Grundlagen zu besinnen'. (C. G. Jung, 'Psychotherapie und Weltanschauung', *Aufsätze zur Zeitgesch.*, pp. 59, 62).

and ready, and even unconsciously assumed, working hypotheses; but sooner or later it will be compelled to attempt to examine and define those postulates with greater precision. Especially is this the case with psychotherapy, for whatever the human psyche may be found to be, it certainly refuses to be 'nothing but' empiricist, and satisfied with factual descriptions of functional and quantitative relations or statistical frequency. It is, among other things, incurably rationalist, and persists in asking such empirically unanswerable questions as 'What?' and 'Why?' and 'Whence?' and 'Whither?' Our rigid *scientisme* may deplore this propensity as an infantile regression to pre-Kantian naïveté, but in fact it is impossible to interpret the simplest psychological phenomena without at least tacit trans-empirical assumptions.

Let me suggest one example. I may, for instance, call a particular psychological phenomenon a *projection*, and I may accurately describe a projection as an unconscious 'process of dissimilation wherein a subjective content is estranged from the subject and, in a sense, incorporated in the object'.[1] Provided I understand by 'subject' and 'object' no more than descriptions of conscious phenomena, *i.e.*, what is *perceived* as 'I' or 'not-I' respectively, I do not seriously transgress the strict limits of purely empirical observation. But then my definition precisely does *not* describe the phenomena as the projector perceives them; the content which, on other grounds, the psychologist calls subjective, he, in virtue of the projection itself, experiences as objective. Once he has assimilated the content to his empirical ego-consciousness, it is no longer a projection. I am driven therefore, wittingly or unwittingly, to assertions which overstep my empirical datum: to affirmations not merely of what 'appears' but of what 'really is'—even in spite of appearances. Thus, with Professor Jung, I shall go on to describe a projection in much more absolute terms: '*Im Dunkel eines Aeusserlichen finde ich, ohne es als solches zu erkennen, mein eigenes Innerliches oder Seelisches*'. ('In the obscurity of something outside of me I discover, without recognizing it to be such, something

---

1. C. G. Jung, *Psychological Types*, p. 582.

which belongs inside me and to my own psyche'.)[1] But in so speaking I at once raise a hornet's nest of questions and assumptions which take us very far beyond the bare phenomena, or the scientist's cautious 'provisional view of the psyche as a relatively closed energic system'.[2] If I am to be entitled to dismiss the old alchemists' *Lehre der Entsprechung* (correspondence theory) as a rationalization,[3] and to establish my own projection-theory of the same phenomenon as genuinely rational and scientific, I must be able to give a rational and critical account of my own terms. A purely pragmatic 'suitability' for attaining practical results,[4] to σώζειν τὰ φαινόμενα (preserve the phenomena) will no longer suffice; for by that criterion the alchemists' theory was at least as successful as my own. If I am to claim validity and even meaningfulness for my statement that the phenomenon is a projection, I must claim also the reality of a subject other than that of the phenomenal empirical ego, an objectivity other than that of the phenomenal objectivity experienced by the empirical ego (for this the alchemist or the patient also experiences and affirms). I claim, albeit tacitly, that I can define the psyche at least sufficiently to enable me to attribute to it an 'outside' and an 'inside'—again other than the purely phenomenal (for it is 'without recognizing it to be such')—and this in its turn implies that I have found justification for applying these or any other spatial concepts to the psyche. In further asserting that the projected content is really not 'outside' but 'belongs to my own psyche', I am claiming in effect that I can discriminate what belongs

---

1. C. G. Jung, *Psycholgie und Alchemie*, p. 336.
2. C. G. Jung 'On Psychical Energy' in *Contributions to Analytical Psychology*, p. 6.
3. cf. *Psychologie und Alchemie*, loc. cit.
4. cf. 'On Psychical Energy', op. cit. p. 7. The immense value, as measured by results, of conceiving the psyche as a relatively closed energic system, is not of course questioned. But among these results cannot be included the justification of qualitative, let alone ontological, interpretations of phenomena, as Professor Jung in this important essay expressly recognizes (cf. p. 15, etc.).

essentially to the psyche from what merely *happens in* it and *to* it, perhaps from 'external' agency or energy: that in this particular phenomenal event, at any rate, the psyche functions, not as a merely relatively, but as an absolutely, closed system. I am furthermore assuming that I can talk of it as 'it' at all, and that I have some intelligent meaning when I refer to 'it' by nouns and pronouns indicative of 'things' rather than by adjectives indicative of attributes of (for instance) the organism, or verbs indicative of operations.

I adduce the projection-theory as only one example (but perhaps a particularly acute one) of the fashion in which the practical necessities of analysis, and indeed of any interpretation of psychological phenomena which goes beyond the merely descriptive or quantitative, drive us willy-nilly into a maze of philosophical, you may call them 'metaphysical', problems. I am driven, in fact, to pose the very questions which the Aristotelian-Thomist *psychologia rationalis* sets out, and attempts to resolve.

Most of these questions are already set out in the first chapter of Aristotle's *De Anima*. What is *psyche*, what is meant by the word, what its nature and essence (φύσις καὶ οὐσία)? What attributes and events are peculiarly psychological (τὰ ἴδια πάθη τῆς ψυχῆς), and what are also organic? Is any general definition of psyche, which will cover all cases, in any way possible, and if so by what method is it to be attained? Is it an 'it' or 'something' (τί ἐστι καὶ τόδε τι) at all, and if so, in what sense: as an independent existent subject (as Plato had implied), or only as a component of such an existent, and if so what sort of component and what sort of existent? Or is psyche only a qualitative, quantitative or otherwise secondary (*i.e.*, accidental) predicate of some other existent? Is it legitimate to attribute psyche only to man, or is there an animal and even a plant psyche? Wherein precisely do the human and non-human psyches converge and diverge? Can we admit a multiplicity of psyches in one individual? In what way, if any, can psyche be analysed into a number of component parts? Is psyche

quantitative, divisible, localized? How is psyche related to
space and time, that I can attribute to it an 'inner' and an
'outer', a 'before' and 'after'? If intrinsically indivisible, in
what sense can it be analysed into parts? If only in terms of
potentialities to phenomenal operations (ἔργα), how are
these to be characterized and classified? Are we to argue
a priori from the psyche and its potentialities to the ἔργα, or
inductively from the ἔργα to the potentialities and to the
psyche itself? Are all the ἔργα and πάθη (happenings) attributed to psyche dependent on organic processes, and do all
(as some evidently do) involve affect? How is to be distinguished the psychological and the physiological treatment of
the same phenomenon? Are there also operations of psyche
which can be *only* of the psyche and which, even though pre-
supposing organic activities, can in no way be their product,
but must be inherently independent or 'separated' (χωριστή)?
Must not a psyche, capable of activity independent of the
corruptible body, be itself incorruptible and capable of
independent existence? How are the various phenomenal
activities of the psyche, whether cognitional or orectic or
wholly non-conscious, to be rationally stated or classified?
What is to be thought of attempts to conceive the psyche
solely in terms of physical kinetic force, as by many of the
earlier Greek thinkers? Can psyche be identified with, and
limited to, consciousness, as already by Democritus? Can
consciousness itself be accounted for in terms of micro-
macrocosmic correspondence, whether in the crude, materialistic form of Empedocles, or the more refined mathematical
fashion of Plato's *Timæus*? If neither dynamic nor quantitative
concepts cover all the facts, can they be combined as in the
'self-moving number' of the later Plato?[1] Or can we conceive
psyche solely in terms of functional pairs of opposites
(ἐναντιώσεις) as perhaps by Heraclitus? Or as a *Gestalt*, a
harmony (ἁρμονία) of opposites? Or as a wholly independent

---

1. Aristotle's argument in *De Anima* 404 b, 28 ff. on the inherent
    incompatibility of quantitative and dynamic concepts of
    the psyche may be compared with that of Professor Jung in
    'On Psychical Energy'.

entity, mysteriously indwelling the body, but with no essential relation to the organism, as by Plato and the Pythagoreans?[1]

Such are the questions which Aristotle poses as the subject-matter of his *De Anima*. He has no illusions as to the immense difficulty which they present to the human mind.[2] Whatever we may think of his attempts to resolve them, and of the attempts of his commentators and successors, we cannot say that the questions have lost any of their urgency. And if there be temperaments which are inclined to dismiss all such questionings as 'intellectualism', we may do well to reflect that, at the lowest estimate, thinking is a function also for the modern psychologist, and an unavoidable one. If conscious, methodical, directed thinking is a labour and a bore, and doubtless, if over-valued, a menace to health and harmony, unconscious, inferior, 'animus' thinking is no less deleterious both to the psyche and to psychology.

It should not be supposed that Aristotle's interests in the psyche were confined to these questions of principle and general theory, and that the actual empirical phenomena were for him nothing but data for the construction of theory. The *Parva Naturalia*, especially the *De Sensu et Sensato* and the *De Memoria et Reminiscentia* (still recognized as having laid the foundations of the laws of the association of ideas), show him to have been keenly interested in actual psychological events, and their mutual interrelation, for their own sake. But the *De Anima* remains Aristotle's most important and distinctive contribution to psychology; and his value to us to-day lies less in the field of pure observation and experiment, in which he was often mistaken, and always limited in his equipment, than in his genius for inferring from his observations general principles and potentialities as a comprehensive psychological framework.

---

1. Nearly all these questions, and many others, will be found set out in the first four chapters of Aristotle's *De Anima*. A few are not explicitly raised until Books II and III, and some received little attention before the Moslem and medieval commentators.

2. *De Anima*, 402a 11.

It cannot be pretended that, notwithstanding the occasional relief of some sublime passages and some entertaining *obiter dicta*, the *De Anima* of Aristotle is easy or attractive reading. Its emotional appeal is *nil*, its demands on hard methodical thinking are considerable. We shall be disappointed if we look to Aristotle or Aquinas for psychological 'material' or for a 'mythology of the soul'; what they offer to us is unrelieved intellectual thinking *about* the psyche, or it is nothing.

There is little to inspire us in the formula which Aristotle finally reaches to define the psyche: 'The first entelechy [act or completion] of a natural body in potency to possess life, *i.e.*, of an organic body'.[1] Contrasted with the psychological insights of Plato, the *De Anima* of Aristotle is cold and arid. But it is important to understand what Aristotle is about. Professor Wili charges him with overthrowing the whole Orphic-Platonic experience of the psyche as a subsistent entity, temporarily imprisoned in the body, '*Um den Preis, eine nicht gewöhnliche forscherliche Arbeitshypothese fur die Bewegung und das Werden gefunden zu haben*' ('In order to have found an unusual and academic working hypothesis to account for change and process').[2] For Aristotle himself his definition of the psyche was certainly no mere working-hypothesis.[3] He describes it as logically necessary (ἀναγκαῖον) and, as Père Festugière has shown,[4] he reached it, not by way of hypothesis, but as the ineluctable conclusion of a carefully considered and exact method of empirical observation, induction and deduction—a method which he himself describes and works out in detail in his *Analytics*. Certainly it is '*die Bewegung und das Werden*' that must be taken as the factual starting point; for change or process

1. *De Anima*, 412a, 20.
2. 'Probleme der aristotelischen Seelenlehre', *Eranos Jahrbuch*, Vol. XII, p. 63.
3. *De Anima*, 412a, 20.
4. A. Festugière, O.P.: 'Les méthodes de la définition de l'âme' (*Revue des sciences théologiques et philosophiques*, 1931, pp. 83 ff.). *Cf.* A. D. Hicks, *Aristotle: De Anima*, Introduction, pp. xl ff.

is by common consent the distinguishing characteristic of that to which we attribute 'psyche'. Aristotle insists, as Professor Jung has insisted, that the scientific definition of words must be based on common experience and common speech,[1] and common speech ascribes 'psyche' to the living as distinct from the dead. The most elemental of human experiences—life and death—this is what gives rise to the everyday ascription of 'psyche' to what is alive, and the denial of psyche to what is dead. And what distinguishes the 'live' body from the 'dead' body is movement, change, process. Not *any* movement, but spontaneous, immanent, self-produced movement. The living being is distinguished from the non-living being by the fact that it moves or changes itself; it changes not only when acted upon by other agents or forces, but by its own forces it at least nourishes, conserves, repairs and reproduces itself, as already in the vegetable kingdom. In the higher forms of life, the animals (ζῷα), properly so called, come higher forms of self-transmutation —locomotion, sensation, memory, phantasy and corresponding forms of desire or appetite (ὄρεξις).[2] In man there is also mind (νοῦς)—the power of transcending his own mechanically conditioned organism altogether, of forming conceptions which likewise transcend material spatio-temporal limitations, and the conceiving of, and arguing to, affirmations about reality which lies beyond sense-perception entirely.[3] Aristotle knew nothing of cells, but nothing in modern biology has invalidated his common-sense observations of the elementary manifestations of life.

But why, it will be objected, this concern to formulate psyche in terms of pure reason? Why, more precisely, in the narrow terms of Act and Potency? What theoretic or practical value is to be found in this insistence, as against Plato, that psyche is not a complete 'it', but that *by* which we live (ᾧ ζῶμεν):[4] not 'something that is' (*quod est*) but 'that *by* which it is' (*quo est*); not that *which* lives but that *by which* we

---

1. *e.g.*, throughout Book IV of the *Metaphysics*.
2. Desire, inclination, drive; *De Anima* II, *passim*.
3. *De Anima* III. 3, *passim.*   4. *De Anima*, 414a, 5.

live; not an independent entity but the formal, determining, constituent principle of a living compositum?[1]

The answer to the first question is simple. To present the psyche in rational, conceptual terms was the task he set himself: or more exactly the task which he believed was set him by his place in history and the evolution of human culture. In the first two chapters of his *Metaphysics* (which Jaeger has shown to be an epitome of a much more detailed history of human thought)[2] he tells us, by implication, what he believes that task to be. Greek man has at last attained the ability and the leisure to investigate the ultimate problems of reality and of life, to ask not merely what *seems*, but what *is*: to aspire to the godlike prerogative of disinterested reflection on his own thinking. No longer could human curiosity be satisfied by the imaginative constructions of myth: the men who are wise in myths (μυθικῶς σοφιζόμενοι) must now be neglected for those who speak by demonstration (ἀποδείξεως) and offer proof for their assertions,[3] although the lover of myths or 'philomyth' (φιλόμυθος) is already an incipient lover of wisdom or 'philosopher' (φιλόσοφος).[4] Aristotle's aim in all his later and more mature writing is not an esoteric, imaginative insight or gnosis (γνῶσις), nor a subjectively conditioned view, or opinion (δόξᾰ), but a universal and certain knowledge (ἐπιστήμη), painstakingly established on undeniable axioms applied (so far as possible) to equally undeniable fact by indisputably cogent argument. We may decry this ambition to rational certitude as a deplorable *hubris* of the puny human intellect, and we are entitled so to do if our own boasted modesty is the fruit of equal pains and no mere cloak for mental sloth, or a preference

1. It is difficult to understand how Jung can assert that, 'It was universally believed in the Middle Ages as well as in the Greco-Roman world that the soul is a substance', if by 'substance' is to be understood, as we are assured by his translator, 'that which has independent existence'. (*Modern Man in Search of a Soul*, p. 200).

2. W. Jaeger, *op. cit.*, p. 128.

3. *cf. Metaph*, 1000a, 18.

4. *ibid.* 982b, 19.

for uncriticized, undifferentiated intellectual assumptions. We may say that there are regions of investigation which do not admit of such clear-cut accuracy, and Aristotle himself will take the words out of our mouths.[1] We may assert the remoteness from concrete fact of universal concepts divorced from observation and experience, and Aristotle will agree with us again.[2] We cannot so easily deny him the right to pay the heavy price which fidelity to logic applied to observation demanded of him, or complain that he failed to fulfil a task wholly different from that which he set out to accomplish.

So, for Aristotle in his *De Anima*, the question was not how the psyche can be imaginatively or mythologically perceived, but how it is to be rationally conceived. And we must not read into him the very error which he repudiates in Plato— the reification of concepts. Because the psyche can be formulated in rational terms, this does not mean—he asserts the contrary over and over again—that the psyche is nothing but a rational entity. A concept for the Aristotelian is not that which is thought (*quod intelligitur*) but that in which (*in quo*) the data of sense-experience are considered.[3]

This leads us at once to the answer to our second question: Why is it in terms of Act and Potency, Matter and Form, that Aristotle defines psyche? This question brings us to the heart of Aristotle's solution of the perennial problem of cultivated man: a problem which had, in his time, reached acute dimensions and still threatens a deep psychological split in every man who has started to reflect on his own thinking. It was not for nothing that Aristotle had brushed aside (perhaps a little too easily)—with the assurance that 'poets tell many a lie'—the threat of the jealous vengeance

---

1. *cf. Nic. Ethics* 1094b, 13. In fact, as Jaeger shows, the claims of the later Plato to certainty were very much more extensive than those of Aristotle. The more differentiated the intellect, the more it is aware of its own capacities and limitations.
2. *cf. Metaph.* 981a, 13, 983a, 10.
3. *cf.* Thomas Aquinas, *Summa Theol.* I 85, 2.

of the gods for the *hubris* of the philosopher, the perils of the soul that await the Promethean robber of godlike theoretic wisdom[1]—*la grandeur et la misère de la métaphysique.*

For such a man finds himself claimed and challenged by two opposing worlds: the changeless world of νοῦς, of Pure Thought, of Being, of Changeless Certainty, of 'It *Is*': and the world of sense-perception, of αἴσθησις, of Becoming, Instability, Change and Enantiodromia, of 'It *Seems*'. The demands of each appear as totalitarian, exclusive: as of two jealous masters who will brook no allegiance to, nor compromise with, the other. As in India the Vedanta had affirmed the unique and sole reality of the Atman, the 'one without a Second', and had dissolved the rest into the play of Maya, so in Hellas, at the very beginning of all we mean by Europe, Parmenides and the Eleatics had proclaimed the uniqueness and indivisibility of Being and dimissed the rest as illusory appearance. Parmenides' argument was powerful enough: what is not is nothing, but nothing cannot differentiate what is, therefore there can be only one Reality, and the seeming multiplicity of this world of change and decay and its conflict of opposites is unthinkable and therefore No-Thing. Zeno had supported this monism with his celebrated 'demonstrations' of the impossibility of motion. On the other hand, Heraclitus had opted for the sole reality of change: 'All is flux and nothing is stable' (πάντα ῥεῖ · οὐδὲν μένει); one cannot plunge the same stick into the same river twice. If all is flux, came the Eleatic reply, then one cannot plunge the same stick into the same river once, for not only is there no same river, there is no same stick, and no same one. A world which is nothing but change is unthinkable and indescribable—for change itself is undefinable except there be some stable terms of reference, as we ourselves have discovered in trying to define a projection. So the strife went on; and it was no mere academic discussion: it was the initial struggle for the whole-

---

1. *Metaph.* 983a, 4.

ness of European man. Was man *nothing but* an automatic process of enantiodromia, a battlefield of opposing forces, and was his aspiration to affirm reality, to transcend spatio-temporal processes and formulate timeless truths (as in mathematics) an illusion? Or was he, contrariwise, *nothing but* a divine, spiritual, immortal being, strangely incarcerated in a material body and involved in the unreal, weary wheel of purposeless Becoming—liberation from which could be his sole aspiration?

Plato and the early Academy had inclined heavily towards the latter alternative. Somehow, unaccountably, the world of sense-perception did 'participate' in the realm of eternal Ideas and 'remind' us of them. But only among these Ideas, in that transcendent realm of pure thought, was man's true home: thence he came, and thither it should be his business to return. Man, in short, was not Soul *and* Body. Man *was* Soul, and Soul was the godlike mind (Νοῦς). The body was not even a servant of the soul; it was its unfitting prison-house. At best, man's steed.

Act and Potency, ἐντελέχεια or ἐνέργεια and δύναμις—the passive correlative of ἐνέργεια—was Aristotle's closely reasoned answer to the dilemma of νοῦς and αἴσθησις, of Understanding and Experience, of Being and Becoming, of the One and the Many. '*Actus et Potentia dividunt ens, et quodlibet genus entis*' ('Act and Potency differentiate being, and every category of being'). The corollary of Act and Potency, the analogical (non-synonymous, but related) predication of Being, will make possible the affirmation of the unique reality of the Absolute One, and the relative reality of the Many. Act and Potency alone, it is claimed, make change strictly intelligible, and supply a basis for the rational discussion of process. This is not the place to discuss the argument: for that I must refer you to the sources and the text-books. But if that is so, then psyche also must be defined in terms of act and potency; in terms likewise of act and potency must its 'parts' and operations be classified. Definition in these terms—or their equivalents —could alone meet the claims of rigorous metaphysic and dialectic on the one hand, and the empirical data of vital processes on the other.

Aristotle's struggle with Plato was a costly one indeed. But whatever we may think of the validity of Aristotle's definition of psyche as the ineluctable conclusion of a cogent argument, we cannot lightly dismiss its implications as, at least, a possible working hypothesis. Instead of the 'Either-Or' of the Upanishads, of early Greek and much subsequent thought, it enables us to work on the hypothesis of 'Both-And'. It enables us, as it enabled Aristotle himself,[1] to see psychology on the one hand, and biology and physiology on the other, as concerned, neither with two separate and disparate fields of inquiry, nor yet with two purely subjective aspects of the same reality, but as concerned with the potential and the determining constituents respectively of the integral *humanum*. Whatever its own difficulties, it enables us to avoid the difficulties of such hypotheses as psycho-physical parallelism, as psychological epiphenomenalism, as those of a psychology which restricts psychology to conscious mentation, and of all *a priori* limitations which would banish the irrational and the unconscious from psychological consideration.[2] Aristotle's general conceptions of the relationship of form to matter, and of both to quantity and extension, enable us to give some precise meaning to the application of spatial concepts to the psyche—it is only incidentally (*per accidens*, κατὰ συμβεβηκὸς), by reason of its being the form of a body which alone is *secundum se* localized, that we can speak, for instance, of an 'inside' and an 'outside' of the psyche. They enable us to view human psychology, neither as simply a branch of pure metaphysics, nor as only a branch of natural

---

1. *De Anima*, 403a, 25 ff.
2. 'The products of my labours', wrote Wundt in his *Grundzüge der physiologischen Psychologie* (4th edn., p. 633) 'do not square with the materialistic hypothesis nor with the dualistic theories of Plato or Descartes. It is only the animism of Aristotle, in which psychology is combined with biology, that issues in a plausible metaphysical conclusion for experimental psychology'. The λόγοι ἔνυλοι of *De Anima*, 403a 25 is a remarkable adumbration of Jung's 'archetypes'.

science, but as necessarily combining the conclusions of *both*.[1] Also, of supreme importance, they enable us to see psychology as concerned with the whole man—as soul and body. For although the body and its processes are as such the concern of 'physical' physiology, the psyche, given the Aristotelian definition, being the animating principle of the body, the whole of man, and no mere part of him, comes within its field.

It was this vigorous affirmation of the flesh as being of the very essence of man which finally recommended the Aristotelian formula to Catholic Christianity. Notwithstanding Aristotle's hesitations concerning immortality, the denial—at least by most of his school—of the individuality of νοῦς (mind), and the absence from his later work of the 'numinous', 'religious', 'other-worldly' qualities which we find in Plato, and which had attracted the preferences of many Christian Fathers in East and West, Aristotle's definition gradually gained acceptance in the Catholic Church, and at the Council of Vienne its denial was even accounted heresy.[2] Nor is this so surprising as might at first sight appear. Already Tertullian[3] and others had in early times seen the incompatibility of Platonic 'spiritualism', and the relative compatibility of Aristotle's hylomorphism, with the Gospel whose central message was that of man's psychophysical integrity—the message of health (*salus*) wrought in and through the flesh and the hope of glory through the resurrection of the body. Platonist psychology leads directly to gnostic and Manichaean contempt for the flesh and the search for liberation from its shackles. Aristotle's psychology, it must be admitted, dashes all such aspirations: though man has a divine and immortal principle dwelling in him he is *essentially* body as well as soul, and nothing he can do can make him otherwise. Only the revelation that Divine Power enters history and assumes the flesh, and through the

---

1. *Metaph.* 1026a 6.
2. A.D. 1311 (Denzinger-Bannwart, *Enchiridion Symbolorum* No. 481).
3. Tertullian, *De Anima*, esp. chapters 4, 12.

death of the flesh gives eternal life to the risen flesh, could make sense of human destiny, given the rigorous rational psychology of Aristotle. But Aristotle himself could not discover that. It was St Thomas, with the Bible in one hand and Aristotle in the other, who could give both their due and show how the Gospel could meet the inherent insufficiencies and contrarieties which Aristotle had analysed and exposed.

But the very same principles of Act and Potency which compelled Aristotle to define psyche-in-general as the first entelechy of an organic body, compelled him also to the conclusion 'summing up all that has been said about the psyche', that the human psyche is in a sense the whole existing universe—the soul is in some manner all existing things (ἡ ψυχὴ τὰ ὄντα πώς ἐστι πάντα)[1]. This is so, he explains, because the whole universe—the only universe we can talk about—consists of things thought and *sensa* sensed. At first this assertion may sound like an astonishing concession to extreme idealism, coming as it does from one whom historians (even Jaeger)[2] agree in labelling as a naïve realist, innocent of the Enlightenment, and living centuries before the Copernican revolution of Kant's *Kritik*. It is true that Aristotle can have little validity for us if we suppose the *Kritik* to be beyond criticism, or if we try to fit him into our own divisions of Idealist or Realist. It is true that to understand Aristotle, and especially his equation of the human psyche with everything, we have to think ourselves out of the whole body of post-Cartesian preconceptions. We must get behind that fateful day (was it cause or symptom of the split in the post-Renaissance European psyche?) when René Descartes was left alone with his stove, and, forgetful of the stove, and conscious only of René Descartes, attempted to rebuild Western thought on the *Cogito*.[3] Only now,

1. *De Anima* 431b 20.
2. *op. cit.*, p. 379.
3. 'If I were asked what was the most disastrous moment in the history of Europe I should be strongly tempted to answer that it was that period of leisure when René Descartes,

thanks to phenomenology and existentialism, perhaps also to Einstein, are we beginning to free ourselves from the effects of that venture to build thought on a thought which was never a fact. For the pure *Cogito* never was nor will be in human experience: it is an arbitrary abstraction from a fact, and one which *a priori* mutilates it, and irreparably divorces the ego from the non-ego without which it is no conscious ego at all. I cannot be conscious of my thought, still less of an 'I' as the subject of that thought, unless I am thinking the 'Not-I'—things, objects. Aristotle (and still more clearly St Thomas) knew that subject and object were unknowable except in function one of the other. '*Intellectus, in actu est intellectum in actu*', and Aristotle's parallel analysis of the processes of sensation should leave us in no doubt of his meaning. When I think, I think things, and in that thinking both 'I' and the 'things' emerge, on reflection, as potencies to one unique and identical act of knowing and being known. Subject and object are not ultimate *a prioris*: they are conscious data which presuppose a pre-conscious identity, a *participation mystique* in the deepest sense. Thought is precisely that act in which, in experiencing the 'not-I', I experience my ego, and from which I infer the human psyche itself.[1] But an act of psyche it is, by definition, and it is in that vitally important sense that Aristotle knows that, while the first function of the psyche is to animate the body, its wider functions are indeed all embracing (τὰ ὄντα πάντα). The human psyche, by its powers of νοῦς and αἴσθησις both, makes and becomes the whole world.[2]

---

having no claims to meet, remained for a whole day "shut up with a stove". . . . That many of our worst troubles not only in philosophy, but also in politics and economics, with all this means for human happiness and misery, are closely associated with the habit of thought then established, I cannot doubt.'—William Temple, 'The Cartesian Faux-Pas', *Nature, Man and God*, p. 57.

1. This is not explicitly stated by Aristotle, but drawn from his premisses by Aquinas in *Summa* I, 87 and in *De Veritate* VIII. *passim*.
2. *De Anima* 430a 14.

It should be clear enough what Aristotle held νοῦς to do. It has been much more controverted what he held νοῦς to be. Did he indeed hold νοῦς to be 'separate' only from material organs and quantitative extension, or to be a single separate entity, distinct from each individual psyche, as has been maintained by most of his commentators? From the standpoint of pure textual exegesis, strong arguments can be brought on both sides. I confess that I find the arguments for the first adduced by St Thomas Aquinas in his *De Unitate Intellectus* completely convincing, even as exegesis of Aristotle's text. But difficulties remain. We must remember that Aristotle is first and foremost a rigorous logician, and the force of logic could only drive him to antinomies which pure reason—without revelation—is impotent to resolve, for they are inherent in human nature as we know it. On the one hand, there can be no doubt that for Aristotle νοῦς was a potency (δύναμις) and a part of the psyche,[1] and the psyche was the actuality of a living body and as such inseparable from it. The evident fact of death and bodily corruption seemed to preclude survival of the psyche, and if the psyche could not survive, neither could its potency (δύναμις). On the other hand, the activity of νοῦς was undoubtedly immaterial, and independent of space-time conditions, and since the activity of a thing corresponds to its being (*actio sequitur esse*), the conclusion should be that it was incorruptible and immortal, and the psyche with it. It seems likely that, to the end, Aristotle was unable to decide whether νοῦς was literally divine (and hence a substance) or only relatively divine or godlike,[2] and we know how that same problem has haunted Indian thought in its discussions of the significance of the formula 'thou art that', (*Tat twam asi*). Without the faith of the 'People of the Book',[3] that man is made in the image of God and not vice-versa, the problem is indeed a difficult one to resolve. The revelation of creation will enable St Thomas to distin-

---

1. *De Anima* 429a 10.
2. *cf. Nic. Eth.*, 117a 16.
3. *i.e.*, Jews, Christians and Moslems.

guish clearly between the indwelling, uncreated God, the source of all truth and knowledge, and the godlike, but finite, created intellect which is essentially and only a potentiality of the psyche, the latter in its turn being individuated by the body of which it is the form. In so doing he can reconcile the implications of both of Aristotle's sets of observations without inconsistency.

I cannot find that Aristotle came ever explicitly to deny the immortality of the human psyche: the passages adduced by Festugière and others do not seem conclusive.[1] But it must be admitted that the convinced affirmation of immortality which we find in the early *Eudemus* finds no place in the *De Anima*, and the whole discussion of the end of man and of the motivation of human character and conduct in the *Nicomachean Ethics* is wholly this-worldly and takes no account whatever of the prospect of an after-life. It is difficult to see how it could do so. The dilemma presented to human reason when unaided by faith, and reflecting on the seeming antinomies in the human psyche itself, was complete.

The *Nicomachean Ethics* translates ruthlessly the theoretic antinomies of the *De Anima* into profound tensions of practical life. They offer no facile Either-Or, but a stern insistence on Both-And. Aristotle himself insists that the *Ethics* presuppose the *De Anima*,[2] notably in its divisions of the potentialities of the psyche into two classes, the ἄλογον or irrational and the λόγον ἔχον,[3] or rational,[1] and the sub-

---

1. *L'idéal religieux des Grecs et l'Evangile* (Paris, 1932), pp. 55 ff.
2. *Nic. Ethics.* 1102a, 24. It is true that Aristotle says in 1102a, 27 that his summary of psychology in the 'exoteric' writings is sufficient for the purposes of the student of Ethics, but it seems that there is no reason to *oppose* this to the *De Anima* as Professor Wili suggests. *De Anima*, 432a, 15 sqq. is clearly a preliminary statement of problems, not of definitive solutions. Aristotle nowhere repudiates the threefold division of the parts of the psyche, which he regards as 'sufficient' for his ethics, but neither is it adequate to specify all the phenomenal functions of the psyche in a manner that may be expected of psychology.
3. *Nic. Eth.* 1102a 29.

division of the first, the irrational class, into the purely
instinctive and those which can participate in directed
reason (λόγος).[1] The latter in their turn may be governed
by the conflicting motivations of desire and aggression.
Aristotle's psychology in effect sets the stage for the notorious
stresses and strains of his ethics. On the one hand, he shows
that the aim of good living must be the humanly possible.
He sets aside the Absolute Good of Plato as the governing
norm of human character and conduct, together with the
attempts of the later Academy to construct an ethic of
mathematical precision, just because 'it is not practicable and
obtainable by man'.[2] Man is body as well as soul; hungry,
sexual, emotional. The aim of ethics must include the integration of all these physical or partly physical factors into 'the
foursquare man without shame'—(τετράγωνος ἄνευ ψόγου).[3]
In this task, man's emotional life, balanced by Temperance
and Fortitude, has its indispensable part to play. The ideal
of impassivity or apathy (ἀπαθέια) proclaimed by Speusippus,
and later fundamental for the Stoic and the Yogi, is set aside
for the harder task of the directed *use* of the emotions.[4] The conflict of the rational and the irrational elements in man is not to
be by-passed.[5] The insufficiency of the human individual
and the necessity of society, even the priority of the social
as against the individual good, is emphasized.[6] Since the
Good *tout court* is irrelevant to and unobtainable by man, the
purpose of ethics, as applied psychology, will be the formation
of the good citizen, who is the truly human being, standing,
as it were, between the bestial masses and the sublime gods.[7]

---

1. *op. cit.*, 1102b 16.
2. *op. cit.*, 1096b 34.
3. *op. cit.*, 1100b 22, from Simonides of Cos, quoted in Plato's
   Protagoras 339b; *cf.* A. Ehrhardt, 'Vir bonus quadrato
   lapidi comparatur', *Harvard Theological Review*, July 1945,
   pp. 177 ff.
4. *op. cit.*, 1104b 24.
5. *op. cit.*, 1102b 20.
6. *e.g.*, *ibid*, 1097b 12.
7. *cf.*, 1095b 9 ff.

The purpose of ethics must be *eudaimonia*, the good life, but only such as is human and humanly possible.[1] It must be acquired by human effort. Aristotle does indeed allow the possibility that, after all, human bliss or fulfilment may be no human acquisition but a Divine gift, but he dismisses it as a question which lies outside the scope of ethics.[2]

But, on the other hand, and alongside all this, Aristotle's own psychology leads him to another set of conclusions which are not easily reconcilable with the foregoing. The good of man's highest part, his νοῦς, is shown to be something very different. Presently there emerges the figure of Aristotle's 'magnanimous' prig: free, self-sufficient, unsocial, even anti-social. And later still, the acme of humanity, the 'theoretician', the godlike contemplator of the divine, who is indeed a parasite on a society based on slavery; he is passion-free, and seeking a godlike life among men in self-sufficient isolation. Perhaps, Aristotle ventures, this 'divine part of man' is even 'the true self of each';[3] but this ideal is super-human and divine.[4] It is by unexceptionable logic that Aristotle, starting from observation of the human psyche, has reached this conclusion that man's bliss must consist in the highest activity of his highest part exercised on the highest objects and with the maximum of perfection and permanence 'so far as this is possible'.[5] But it is hard to square with his equally logical insistence on man's psycho-physical wholeness and on the subordination of the individual to the common good of the city. Of course this godlike bliss is, in this vale of tears, as Aristotle recognizes, seldom possible, and then only for a few, and in some limited degree, and for a moment or two. And that in itself rules out the generality of men, and nearly all the conditions of good citizenship which he had himself laid down as the business of human morals and well-being.

His ruthless logic was not afraid of antinomies; but it was not within the power of logic to resolve them.

---

1. *op. cit.*, 1094b 23.   2. *op. cit.*, 1099b 13.
3. *op. cit.*, 1178a 3, *cf.* 1166a 16.   4. *op. cit.*, 1177b 30.
5. *op. cit.*, Book X, cap. 8 *passim*.

St Thomas Aquinas, assisted certainly by previous commentators, develops, synthesizes, dots the i's and crosses the t's of Aristotle's *De Anima*. But not in this lay his chief contribution to the solution of the problem of man as Aristotle had left it. It was no part of St Thomas's programme to bring Christ to Aristotle; on the contrary, as a Christian theologian, his purpose was to bring Aristotle's reasoning to the service of Christ—'For the more complete showing forth of these things that are contained in divine teaching' *'ad maiorem manifestationem eorum quae in hac sacra doctrina continentur'*.[1] But in so doing he shows, incidentally but inevitably, how the Revelation of God in and through Jesus Christ brings the answer to the human contradiction which Aristotle had so fearlessly investigated and exposed. St Paul had found in the intense experience of that death-bringing conflict between the law of the members and the law of the mind the prerequisite to the 'gift of God' that is 'eternal life in Jesus Christ our Lord', (χάρισμα τοῦ θεοῦ ζωὴ αἰώνιος ἐν Χριστῷ Ἰησοῦ) (Rom. vi, 23). There had been nothing essentially faulty in Aristotle's observation or reasoning. The Absolute Good of Plato was indeed humanly impracticable and unattainable. But now the Christian Revelation showed that in a sense Plato had been fundamentally right, even if for the wrong reasons. For the Absolute Good is no impersonal Idea, no mere principle of intelligibility or ultimate aim of movement and desire (as for Greek speculation generally), but the living God of Abraham, Isaac and Jacob, the Father of the Lord Jesus Christ.[2]

So the *Summa* of St Thomas begins by affirming what at the beginning of his *Ethics* Aristotle had been compelled to deny: the attainability of man's true and last end and bliss and completion.[3] It was true that man could not reach the Absolute Good, but God in Christ showed that the Absolute

---

1. *Summa Theol.* I. i, 5 ad 2.
2. *cf.* E. Gilson, *God and Philosophy.*
3. *Summa Theol.* I. i. 1.

Good not only could, but did, reach out to man and communicate to man its own eternal life. The *Summa*, on its very first page, affirms as a fact that it is a Divine gift. We have seen that the *Ethics* had methodologically dismissed, as a hypothesis which lay outside its own field of inquiry, the suggestion that the good life might be a gift of the gods. The *Summa* begins by affirming, therefore, man's need for a knowledge which transcends rational discovery: a knowledge which is essentially not a human but a divine knowledge (for God only knows what things God has prepared for those that love him), but one which men, nevertheless, may accept in humble faith in God's communication of that knowledge. Faith, St Thomas will explain later, is the humble receptivity of the human mind to the Unseen and the Unknown:[1] in and through faith in the Divine revelation, not through his unaided reasoning processes, man dimly but surely partakes of 'a sort of imprint of God's own knowledge' (*'quaedam impressio divinae scientiae'*).[2] Reason can argue that there is indeed 'what men call God', and can make certain analogically correct statements about him.[3] But the end, the fulfilment, which God has destined for man—the eternal divine life dwelling in him as a free gift of Divine love—can be known only by God and communicated by his revelation, and can be attained only by the power and grace of the indwelling Spirit given by God through Christ: the Christ who attains the immortal life of soul *and* body by first accepting the death which is their separation.

There was a truth in those whispers of the Mysteries of a primeval catastrophe and guilt which Aristotle had heard in his youth. God had made man in his own image and likeness; but that image had become, not annihilated, but disintegrated into autonomous component parts. Therein lies the primitive and fundamental revelation of the meaning

---

1. *Summa Theol.* II-II. i. 2 and 3.
2. *Summa* I. i, 3 ad 2.
3. *Summa*, I. ii ff.

of man, known only to the People of the Book. Man had
fashioned gods in the likeness of his own psychic contents
and aspirations: to Israel is made known that contrariwise
the psyche is made like God, and for God, and to partake in
the eternal life of God. St Thomas will take up and develop
all Aristotle's arguments for the stable character of human
fulfilment in contemplation of the Divine by man's highest
endowment of mind (νοῦς).[1] This νοῦς is itself godlike, not only in its immateriality; but also, in its threefold
co-ordinate function of Memory, Understanding and Love,
it is a 'made Trinity', the created likeness of the One God
who is revealed as Father, Son and Spirit.[2] Radically man
has a capacity for God (*capax Dei*), though that capacity
can be actualized into likeness to God (*conformitas Deo*)
only by divine power and grace. But the way to fulfil that
imaging of, and conformity to, the Divine Threefold in
Eternity is through the Human Fourfold of psycho-physical
man in time: the *Imago Trinitatis* is attained only through
the *Imago Christi*, and conformity through grace to the Life,
Death and Resurrection of the Man who is the Word of
God to men in human flesh, with human body and human
psyche.

All this, human reason, exercised on the purely human
data, cannot discover. A revelation, which transcends
reason, must come to supplement, and perhaps correct, even
the highest flights of mere reason. What, in St Thomas's
mind, is this revelation, and what processes does it involve
in the human psyche? Do they afford any parallels to
processes observed and studied in depth-psychology to-day?

---

1. *Summa* I-II. i-iv.
2. *Summa* I. xciii. *cf.* A. Gardeil, O.P., *La structure de l'âme
et l'expérience mystique.*

VII

REVELATION AND THE UNCONSCIOUS

IT would be a mistake to suppose that Aristotle never had any inkling of the possibility of a revelation which would convey knowledge over and above what man could discover by the directed employment of his own senses and his own intelligence. In his early work *On Prayer* (of which only fragments remain) he had said that 'God is either νοῦς or beyond νοῦς'. If a certain dim but conclusive knowledge that God exists could be attained by strict reasoning (as he argues at length in Book XI of the *Metaphysics*), this could not exhaust all that could be known about him. As Jaeger says:[1] 'Neither Schleiermacher nor Kant distinguished more sharply between faith and knowledge ... than did the originator of speculative argument for God's existence in his classic pronouncement: "Those who are being initiated [into the Mysteries] are not required to engage in active study (μαθεῖν), but to be passive to inner experience (παθεῖν)".'[2] In his *De Divinatione per Somnia* he had raised the question whether dreams might be divine in origin, and a means of communication of divine knowledge; and while he rejects the hypothesis, for reasons which may strike us as extraneous and not wholly convincing, he does not dismiss it as intrinsically impossible.

But when we turn from Aristotle to Aquinas we turn from a purely philosophical thinker to one who was primarily a theologian and only secondarily a philosopher. For the theologian, rational philosophy (whatever its own intrinsic dignity and merit) is primarily of interest as the handmaid of theology (*ancilla theologiae*): a handmaid who may help in

---

1. *op. cit.*, p. 160; *cf.* p. 240.
2. Fragment (Rose) 15.

elucidating the mysteries conveyed in revelation and accepted by faith. Revelation itself now takes pride of place; and we turn to examine St Thomas's treatment of the processes which revelation involves: this *cognitio* which, though subject within limits to rational investigation, is itself no grasping (μαθεῖν) but an experiencing (παθεῖν), and contrasts sharply with the processes of directed thinking.

St Thomas describes the typical apprehension of revelation as 'a kind of clouded awareness mixed up with darkness' ('*quaedam cognitio obumbrata et obscuritati admixta*') (*De Veritate* xii. 12). In the same place he argues that its quality as prophetic insight into the Divine is in inverse ratio to its quality as clear and distinct knowledge. In its most typical forms, it is everything of which the controlled, orderly, logical and scientific reason is most suspicious. It is governed by no laws of logic or method, it is not even subject to the recipient's volition; it may well be—St Thomas here recalls the pathetic protest of Jeremiah—clean contrary to it. It is no permanent disposition (*habitus*) to be used at will, but something momentarily undergone (*passio*); something, not that the recipient does, but that is done to him, which seizes him and overpowers him compulsively (*De Veritate* xii. 1; *Summa Theol.* I-II. 171. 2, etc.).[1] It proceeds by no measured steps, which can be checked by laws of logic and detached scientific observation; it is an *intuitus*, an intuition —a vision—more especially an inward vision or audition— an *instinctus*, an *inspiratio* (*ibid*). Its normal and typical vehicle is not the rational concept, but the concrete image, the phantasy, the dream, the hypnogogic (sleepy) uncontrolled imagination (*De Ver.* xii. 7, 81; I-II. 173, 2, etc.). It thrives under conditions of intense introversion, of alienation from external sense-perceptions, in states of ecstasy, of trance, of frenzy, which, St Thomas recalls, may be induced by solitude

---

1. All subsequent references in the text of this essay, unless otherwise stated, are to the *Summa Theologica* of St Thomas Aquinas. I=Prima Pars; I-II=Prima Secundae; II-II= Secunda Secundae; III=Tertia Pars.

or—as by Saul and Elisha—by the sense-lulling, hypnotizing effects of music (*De Ver.* xii. 9; I-II. 173, 3, etc.). The prophet does not always know what he sees nor even what he says (I-II. 173, 4); nor of these does he invariably discern between what is of divine or superhuman origin, and what is 'from his own spirit' ('*per spiritum proprium*'), a product, as St Thomas himself puts it, of his own instinct (I-II. 171, 5). He may be moved not only to see and say the strangest things, but to do them too, as Hosea was moved to take a succession of harlots to wife. More shocking still perhaps to sweet reasonableness is St Thomas's emphasis that prophetic revelation is as such independent of good morals—let alone of personal sanctity (*De Ver.* xii. 5; I-II. 172, 4). For prophecy is required, he says tersely, not 'goodness of morals' (*bonitas morum*) but 'goodness of imagination' (*bonitas imaginationis*). If sexual excess and worldly pre-occupation, he adds, are inimical to prophetic insight, that is not for any ethical reason, but for the purely psychological one that they withdraw attention and interest (i.e., *libido*) from the interior image to the external world. Aristotle, St Thomas reminds us, had already remarked on the fact that it is not the best people who have the best dreams;[1] he had also remarked that it is 'the melancholic man'— we might render this as the 'introverted intuitive'—who is usually the best dreamer quite irrespective of his morals.[2] St Thomas finds Scriptural warrant for parallel phenomena even in regard to supernatural revelation. Nor does he hesitate to draw the parallel—even while he most carefully marks the differences—between the typical condition of the inspired prophet in the act of perceiving Divine revelation, with that of the psychotic, the 'raging maniac' (*furiosus*), the man whose 'mind is possessed' (*mente captus*). Nay, the prophets are to be likened to the brute beasts inasmuch as 'they are rather acted upon than act' ('*magis aguntur quam agunt*'). (*De Ver.* xii. 3 ad 19).

---

1. *De Div. per Somn.* 463b 15, cf. *De Ver.* xii. 5. obj. 4.
2. *ibid*, 464b 33ff.

Truly enough, as we shall see, that is not the whole picture; but enough doubtless to be something of a scandal to the cultivator of the clear-and-distinct, the cut-and-dried, the methodical and the controlled. It is the scandal which had led Plato[1] to identify prophecy and mania—μαντική and μανική—and to expel the 'enthusiast' and the inspired from the Republic. Aristotle was too open-minded an empiricist and too integral a rationalist so easily to dismiss the manifestations of unreason, embarrassing though he found them to be. For him facts were facts, and to that extent subject to the investigation of reason. However little he may seem to us to be at home with the uncanny subject in his Περὶ τῆς καθ' ὕπνον μαντικῆς (treatise On Divination by Dreams), he did not ignore it. St Thomas had read that perplexed work on dream-interpretation, and his own De Prophetia utilizes some of its ideas.

A narrower rationalism is less patient with irrationality, with anything less than the comprehensive, clear-cut concept, the water-tight argument, the established conclusion. 'Some', said Aristotle in the Second Book of his Metaphysics, 'desire to have all things clear-and-distinct (ἀκριβῶς), while others are annoyed at it'; and both there and early in his Nicomachean Ethics he warns his hearers of the danger of that desire when the object of our study does not permit of such sharpness of outline. St Thomas at the beginning of his Summa quotes from the same book of the Metaphysics the warning that there are objects before which our minds are as the eyes of bats in respect of daylight; but he adapts and stresses it to the point of saying that, in respect of divine things, our minds are as bats' eyes before the naked light of the sun (I. 1, 5 ad 1). Such a situation is a painful one for the adept of the idée claire, of Latin precision, law and order. St Thomas also was a Latin, by culture if not by birth, and never was there one more vigorous in vindicating the function of reason in theology, more thoroughgoing in drawing its logical implications, more dexterous in mani-

---

1. In the Ion.

pulating the concept, the proposition, the syllogism; but
never as ends in themselves, never with the idea that scientific
rational theology was a substitute for, let alone an improvement upon, the original revelations on which it is based
and which it is its purpose to clarify. As we progressively
appreciate how much analogies play in St Thomas's thinking
in the *Summa* itself, its first impression of clarity, of the
clear-and-distinct, of the comprehensible and the cut-and-
dried, rapidly vanishes. It is more to our present point to note
that St Thomas did not neglect to direct his powerful reason
upon the largely non-rational phenomena which underlie it
all and to attempt to account for them in rational fashion and
by rational means. No Christian theologian worthy of the
name can afford to do otherwise. Plato could expel the
inspired and the possessed from the Republic; they can
never be expelled from the Church which is built on the
foundations of the prophets and apostles.

In this essay it will be impossible to present an adequate
didactic account of St Thomas's conception of revelation,
let alone to expound it and to draw out all its implications.
I can do little more than try to indicate that it deserves
more consideration than it commonly receives, and that
it is, once the difficulties of understanding his medieval
terminology have been mastered and related to our modern
language and knowledge, surprisingly up to date in regard
both to the problems which it faces and the postulates it
invokes. But it is idle to pretend that his treatment of the
subject does not present many serious difficulties, especially
for the modern reader.

One difficulty lies in the enormous variety and multiplicity
of the actual phenomena which demand to be considered, a
fact which renders the subject peculiarly impervious to any
facile schematization and generalization. 'God who at
sundry times and in divers manners spoke in times past unto
the fathers by the prophets', (*'Multifarie, multisque modis, olim
Deus loquens patribus in prophetis'*). Commenting on this
first verse of the Epistle to the Hebrews, St Thomas stresses
the extraordinary richness and variety to be found in the

methods which God has devised to make his saving ways known to men—even in the Old Testament alone.

Clearly, then, we must not look to St Thomas for anything so naive as any one single, all-embracing, *a priori* theory of the 'mode' of revelation, such as some modern writers have attempted. There is no one mode. The Spirit of God bloweth where it listeth, and it is unscientific to attempt to contain the infinitely rich and diverse operations of the self-revealing God into any one preconceived human category. At the human end, the receiving end (and, as we shall see, for St Thomas we cannot really speak of revelation until or unless the revelation is received), there is no one thing, no one single event, called Revelation: there are countless revelations of very varying kinds and very varying degrees. The task of theology is not to lay down some *a priori* pattern of how God should reveal and what he should reveal; its task is to bow down in deep humility before the manifold and bewildering variety of what God actually does; to accept it, in the first place, as naked, unchangeable fact, however offensive or otherwise it may be to particular human tastes and preconceptions. If inquiry is to be truly scientific, not to say reverent, it will not attempt to mould and transmute the elementary data in the interests of some preconceived theory. But neither will it be satisfied merely to record and describe; it must analyse the bare phenomena into their constituents, assign causes and purposes in the light of the revelations themselves and with the aid also of knowledge derived from other sources; attempt classification of kinds and degrees of revelation on the basis of the knowledge thus obtained: in short, attempt to reduce the vast body of highly variegated raw material to some intelligible unity without prejudice to its richness and variety, and without loss to the unique individuality of the particular specimens which fall under its consideration. Its method will be primarily inductive; but it will not hesitate to employ the findings of deductive as well as inductive sciences in the accomplishment of its task. The purpose of such an investigation will be that which is, for St Thomas, the purpose of all theological inquiry; the greater clarification to our own minds of what is contained in divine teaching (*'ad maiorem manifestationem eorum quae in hac sacra doctrina continentur'*)— the more intelligent understanding of God's ways with man for his *salus*—his ultimate health and well-being and salvation (*cf.* I. i. 1).

This precisely is the not inconsiderable task which St Thomas has set himself in his two principal treatises *De Prophetia*: in the *De Veritate*, Question XII, and the *Secunda Secundae* of the *Summa*, Questions 171-174. Manifold indeed are the factors which he finds in different ways and at different times to be operative in revelation. Here is no simple picture of a transcendent God periodically 'invading' the natural order according to one single, established scheme, and regardless of natural causes, needs and factors. As often as not, St Thomas finds revelation to be brought about through the most natural and lowly causes and to be reflected in the most commonplace processes, as well as by causes and processes of the most transcendent character.

We shall, I suggest, have gone a long way towards overcoming the difficulties of understanding St Thomas's conception of prophecy and revelation if we are at some pains to understand his terminology as he himself understood it, and not subconsciously to read into it our own meanings derived from current speech, or even from current theology. This warning is especially necessary in the case of the terms *prophetia* and *propheta* themselves. It need hardly be said that for St Thomas a *propheta* is not necessarily one who foretells the future (II-II. 171, 3; *De Ver.* xii. 2). A *propheta*, as he understands the word, does not necessarily *tell* anything at all; when he does so—whether by speech, by writing, by gesture or by dramatic action—that is all secondary and consequential to the essential 'gift of prophecy'; it belongs to the employment (*usus*) or the proclamation (*denuntiatio*) of prophecy. Primarily and essentially prophecy is not a certain kind of speech, but a certain kind of consciousness or knowledge: a cognitive psychological event which the prophetic utterance presupposes and expresses outwardly (II-II. 171, 1; *De Ver.* xii. 1 et 13). At the outset of both treatises St Thomas recalls the passage in 1 Samuel ix. 9, 'He that is now called a Prophet, in times past was called a Seer', a *Videns*. Not, evidently, that anyone whosoever who 'sees' anything whatsoever, in any way whatsoever, is to be called a Seer or Prophet. The distinguishing mark of prophetic sight lies in the remoteness, the distance of what is seen from normal vision and cognition: 'Prophets know those things which are far removed from the knowledge of men' (*'prophetae cognoscunt ea quae sunt procul remota ab hominum cognitione'*): 'they saw things which the rest did not see' (*'videbant ea quae caeteri non videbant'*). We might render this by saying that the prophet is conscious of that of which other men are unconscious: he sees 'as it were, from afar' (*'quasi ex longinquo'*) what is remote or opaque to average consciousness. If foreknowledge of the future is peculiarly characteristic of prophetic insight, that is only because the future is peculiarly remote and opaque to ordinary conscious apprehension, in contrast to the present or the past (II-II. 171, 3; *De Ver.* xii. 2). This does not mean, as we shall presently see more clearly, that the *field* of prophetic vision is necessarily totally different and remote from the field of ordinary vision and apprehension; St Thomas is most emphatic that it is not, and that the field of natural perception and reason may fall within the scope of the prophet's vision. The prophet may see what anybody can see with his own eyes, or reason out in his own brain (*De Ver.* xii. 2); but *within* that field the prophet will see something which our connatural faculties cannot see, and he sees it by means other than those of the consciously directed employment of those faculties. His knowledge is essentially a vision—by which we understand, of course, not merely ocular vision, but any sort of direct perception: it may, and often will, take not only visual but also aural forms, and even forms which altogether transcend the processes of exterior and even interior sensation.

But not only, for St Thomas, is there a distinction between

REVELATION AND THE UNCONSCIOUS 115

the essential prophetic knowledge (*cognitio prophetica*) and its employment (*usus*) or proclamation (*denuntiatio*); the two involve diametrically opposite psychological processes. In regard to the former the *propheta* is purely passive, as 'the atmosphere to the radiation of the sun' (*De Ver.* xii. 1). Here he is in no way a responsible agent, he sees what he sees and cannot help himself; it *happens to* him; he *does* nothing consciously and willingly. Willingly or unwillingly, with or without regard to his own character and predispositions, he is seized by a power, or rather a light, an 'inbreathing' (*inspiratio*), a 'touch' (*tactus*), beyond his control, whether or not he simultaneously retains the normal use of his own faculties. Truly enough there are conditions and psychological predispositions favourable to such experience, and conditions and predispositions which are unfavourable—so Amos protested he was no professional prophet, while the 'sons of the prophets' cultivated solitude and introversion, 'turning away from carnal and earthly things' ('*a carnalibus et terrenis vacantes*')—but divine power can and does overrule the indispositions, or rather (since divine power always acts according to nature and never against it), supplies the dispositions simultaneously with the vision (*De Ver.* xii. 5). But in the 'employment' or 'proclamation' matters are normally very different. Not indeed always, because, as St Thomas recognizes, there are cases when the prophet is precisely overwhelmed by superior power to speak or act in a fashion beyond his cognizance or control (II-II. 173, 4). But normally it is true that in the employment or proclamation, and in the employment or proclamation only, the 'spirits of the prophets are subject to the prophets' (I Cor. xiii. 32; *cf. De Ver.* xii. 4); it is within their power to speak or not to speak, to choose their own words, their own images and language. These they will normally choose in accordance with their own character and experience; thus Amos the shepherd naturally uses language and imagery with pastoral associations. In the *use* of prophetic experience the prophet may receive divine assistance; but, to use the technical language, the prophet is in this a true principal, though secondary, cause, and the divine assistance will be in the nature of co-operative (*gratia co-operans*) rather than of operative grace (*gratia operans*) as in the prophetic knowledge (*cognitio prophetica*) itself.

We are now perhaps in a position to understand why St Thomas can say repeatedly, not just that prophecy receives revelation, but that it *is* revelation: though it is true, as he also says, that not all revelation is prophecy. We are used enough to the idea that to reveal means to uncover, to disclose, to remove a veil; and perhaps we go on to suppose that when we speak of divine revelation we mean that God somehow removes covers and veils from himself. But a moment's reflection will show that such a supposition is an anthropomorphism, which, though picturesque and helpful up to a point, will not bear very much rational scrutiny. We must remember that for St Thomas every action or relation which we attribute to God but which has its effects in time or space, 'adds nothing to God but only to the creature' (*'nihil ponit in Deo, sed solum in creatura'*): it involves no new entity or reality on the side of God who is unchanging *Actus Purus*, but only a new reality or entity in the created universe (*cf.* I. 13. 7., 43. 3. ad 2, etc.). When we say that God reveals—as also when we say that God creates, moves this or that, or even becomes man (*cf.* III. 1. 1, ad 1., 16. 6 ad 2)—we are not saying that something happens in eternity but that something happens in space and time. And what happens when we say that God reveals, is precisely the psychological occurrence in the prophet's mind—the 'prophetic vision' (*visio prophetica*), his awareness of what is commonly hidden from human perception. So, for St Thomas, 'Revelation is the very perception itself of divine things, by which prophecy is brought about; and by this very perception the veil of darkness and ignorance is taken away' (*'Revelatio est ipsa perceptio divinorum in quo perficitur prophetia: et per ipsam removetur obscuritatis et ignorantiae velamen'*. II-II. 171. 1 ad 4). It is not God who is wrapped in veils; the veils are the ignorance and darkness, the unconsciousness, which normally envelops our own minds; and it is these precisely which the very fact of the prophetic vision removes. Similarly, the 'distance' which the prophetic vision traverses is not, and cannot be, a distance of God from the creature, for, St Thomas assures us, God is more intimately present to all his creatures than they are to themselves (I. 8. 1); it is a distance of *cognition*, an absence from human awareness of divine things. God is not absent from us; but our minds are in greater or less degree absent from him, and indeed must remain so until they possess the final consummation of revelation which is the beatific vision itself. 'Prophecy is something imperfect in the category of divine revelation . . . its perfection awaits us in our heavenly home' (*'Prophetia est quiddam imperfectum in genere divinae revelationis . . . perfectio autem divinae revelationis erit in patria'*). (II-II. 171. 4). But already, in varying ways and degrees, prophetic vision removes the veils which cloud our minds and, so to speak, reduces the distance which separates them from God.

But how can we speak of a *Divine* revelation, a supernatural *prophetia*? What is it that the seer sees, and how, and why?

Before settling down to answer these questions, St Thomas drags across our path what at first sight looks like a red herring. St Thomas was in no doubt at all that there is, as well as divine or supernatural prophecy or revelation, such a thing which he calls natural prophecy (*prophetia naturalis*): a *prophetia* or vision, that is to say, which while attributable to no special innate faculty or 'spirit of divination' in human nature, or even in certain favoured human individuals, is yet explicable by purely natural or created finite causes. Until the nineteenth century it had not become respectable to doubt such phenomena as precognition, telepathy and clairvoyance; and since, at the turn of the century, it again became respectable to pay attention to dreams, their existence has been forced on our notice again. It is said that Freud withheld for ten years the considerable body of so-called paranormal material he had accidentally collected in the course of his psycho-analytic work, 'for fear', as he put it, 'of our scientific world-view being menaced by it'.[1] In various parts of his works, St Thomas had gone to considerable pains to study the origin of these phenomena; and since he himself does not attempt to expound supernatural revelation and prophecy without reference to them, we can hardly hope to understand his exposition without at least paying them a passing glance. While he sharply differentiates supernatural from natural *prophetia*, he invokes the latter not only to illustrate what the former is and is not, but also because he insists that, here as always, the supernatural acts not against but in accord with nature, and often employs natural resources and agencies in the pursuit of its own supernatural ends. Any embarrassment we may feel in alluding to such a subject may to some extent be mollified by the reflection that science has recently removed this traditional preserve of the charlatan into the laboratory for the cold inspection of the statistician, and under the name of Parapsychology has rendered such highly emotive words as prognostication, clairvoyance, second-sight, apparitions, mediumship, telepathy and the rest by such innocuous ciphers as 'psi', 'P.C.', and 'E.S.P.'.

Adequately to present St Thomas's treatment of these phenomena would take us very far afield indeed, and into intricacies of medieval psychology, physiology, biology, physics, Ptolemaic astronomy, and cosmography, and finally angelology and demonology. The modern reader whose interest in the matter is more than antiquarian is likely to have little patience with such recondite research, and even were he to undertake it he would then find himself under the necessity of radically revising it and translating it all back again into the appropriate terms of modern science. St Thomas's speculations on the subject were indeed often based on observations which we now know to be thoroughly faulty, but we are in no position to dismiss them all as so much balderdash: in fact they may be read not without profit

---

1. Quoted from Ehrenwald by L. J. Bendit, *Paranormal Cognition*, p. 26.

alongside kindred theorizings of to-day. Any attempt, ancient or modern, to explain such phenomena must in the last resort be driven to postulate factors which in some way transcend the spatial and temporal limitations of the world of ordinary sense-perception, if not also its condition of successive change and decay. This is equally the case whether we postulate the 'Serial Universe' of Mr Dunne, the 'Eternity' of Mr Shepherd, the 'Psychon' systems of Mr Whately Carington, or whether, with Professor Jung, we suppose, in certain states of consciousness, 'a reflex of subatomic conditions which must needs be explained by a four-dimensional continuum'; or whether, finally, with St Thomas, we hold heavenly bodies and angels to be possessed of the required attributes, and also capable, albeit indirectly, of producing images in human consciousness. The requisite factors which Professor Jung seeks in the nuclear physics of our day, St Thomas sought in the astronomy of his own. St Thomas's conception of *prophetia naturalis*, so far as it concerns us at present, may be summarized fairly briefly.

The perceptions of man's external senses are limited to what is 'present' in space and time—indeed, the words present, past and future have meaning only in relation to such perceptions. Not so, however, the human imagination or *phantasia*. This can and does produce images, visual or other, of what is 'absent' or 'distant' from the external senses, of what to *them* is past, future, remote or wholly non-existent. Though fed, so to speak, by sense-impressions, the imagination 'forms' them in its own way, selecting, combining, separating shapes, colours, sounds, rhythms, even tastes, smells and tactile sensations, and makes them into patterns in a space and time which is itself imaginary, and not that of the 'outer world' in the 'here and now' of sensation. It is therefore of the nature of the imagination that it may be a receptacle for forms of what is 'remote' in space or time. But we still have to ask how they can be actually produced. Imagination may be directed by volition—as in the conscious production of art forms—and in the waking state it is more or less influenced by the sense-impressions which the subject is receiving. Not always so, however; it is especially characteristic of the imagination to act '*subito*' (I-II. 74. 7 ad 4) and apparently spontaneously to produce images of whose origin the subject is unconscious. Still more so in sleep, in the dream, in which conscious attention and control are relaxed and in which the external senses are inactive. St Thomas may well astonish us by his 'modernity' when he goes on to attribute these phantasy-formations to biological and even to what we should call biochemical factors: he is well aware of the influence of bodily health and disease on the imagination, as well as of the influence of the imagination in functional disorder (*cf.* III 13. 3 ad 3), and of the diagnostic value of dreams in medicine (II-II. 95. 6); he could hardly be averse to the hypothesis presupposed to much current psycho-therapeutic technique (*i.e.* 'active imagination'), that these are, at least in part, a translation into psychological images of biological instincts, affects and reflexes. Though he speaks here of the activities of such entities as spirits and humours, where modern neurology indicates rather such agencies as endocrine gland secretions and hormones, the case is not thereby materially altered.

But as soul (*Psyche*—the subject of psychology) is subject to the action of the living organism (*Bios*—the subject of biology) so the living organism (*Bios*) in its turn is subject to the action of nature (*Physis*—the subject of physics and chemistry). Most obviously is this so in the transmutation of food and drink into the substance of the organism; but the organism is also subject to many other agents in this sublunary world. But these also in their turn, St Thomas supposed, were subject to the agency of those purer elements and qualitatively unchanging entities, the *meteora*, which Ptolemean cosmography situated in layers beyond the orbit of the moon. Beyond change and decay, they were also beyond time. They were nevertheless conceived to be the source of all movement and change in this changing world, and so to be ultimate finite predeterminants in the production of physical events (of physical as distinct from intellectual and volitional acts, which as such, of course, are extra-temporal). They were therefore the ultimate determinants of occurrences which might be widely separated in space and time. From this it followed that an intelligence which was capable of comprehending their natures, the laws of their movements, and their causal efficacy, would be capable also of knowing the occurrences which result from them; not, it is important to note, that the occurrence itself would be directly perceived as present (which would be a contradiction in terms) but by the presence to the intelligence of the causes which determine its eventual or 'distant' existence. To the extent that such an intelligence (*i.e.*, spirit, angel or demon) could communicate that knowledge to a human mind, that mind would know the future or distant occurrence; that is to say, it would be capable of precognition or telepathy. Not only this, however: the heavenly bodies themselves could act directly or indirectly on the human organism, especially its gaseous and fluid components, which in its turn would produce appropriate images of greater or less clarity and accuracy, and especially in sleep or trance, of the occurrences which fell within the same sphere of celestial influence (see esp. II-II. 95. 6). Though prediction attained in this way would be concerned, *per se*, only with predetermined *physical* occurrences, it could also render a fair measure of probability in predicting human behaviour, and especially in predicting the general direction of human history, the behaviour of man in the mass. For although 'the wise man overcomes even the stars' ('*sapiens homo dominatur et astris*'), the wise are few, and most men most of the time follow their biologically determined and star-ruled imaginations and passions rather than their intelligence (*cf.* I. 115. 5. 4 with I-II. 77. 1).

But whatever might happen in the human imagination through these 'impressions of heavenly bodies', the ability of the sense-locked human intellect to understand the natures, laws and movements of the heavenly bodies was very limited indeed. By sense observation and rational calculation little could be predicted beyond their own positions and such occurrences as eclipses, and perhaps, more optimistically, the weather.

No such limitations, however, would bind the pure separated intelligences, the wholly bodiless minds, the purely spiritual *Daimones* such as had been conceived and refined by Greek and Arabian philosophers, and which Aquinas identifies with angels. These could and would understand the heavenly bodies, and with them their determining activity in mundane events. What was more, it could be shown that they, too, and no less than our own human minds, could and did act upon matter, and so upon the human organism, and through the human organism upon the human imagination. Unfortunately, since these beings had intelligence, they also had will, and their benevolence towards the physical, mental and spiritual health of man could by no means be relied upon. When St Thomas had patiently examined in turn, both as theorist and moralist, the numerous forms of prognostication practised in his time—they still flourish in ours—he had found this fact to be one of the chief deterrents to the deliberate employment of most of them (*cf.* II-II. 96; *De Sortibus, passim*). Human reason usually had no means of discovering whether the phenomena were the work of morally neutral heavenly bodies or of personal entities who, however veracious their predictions, were enticing man to his own undoing. One could not voluntarily invite their services without in fact voluntarily complying with their ulterior motives—this is St Thomas's interpretation of the famous 'pact with the devil'. True, it might be benevolent beings who were operative, and such indeed was one of their appointed functions in the order of the universe. But it was hard to be sure.

We may be tempted to dismiss indignantly this whole idea of spiritual as well as mechanical causation in human phantasy-formation as wholly alien from modern experience and scientific knowledge. But it may be sobering to recall that depth-psychology witnesses to traces of personal and purposive as well as impersonal and mechanical agency in the phenomena which it attributes to what its empirical methodology compels it to call 'the unconscious', and the apparent purposes are not, it would seem, uniformly in the direction either of sanity or sanctity.

I must apologize for what is admittedly a disproportionately long, but still all too condensed, account of *prophetia naturalis* in an essay concerned with divine and supernatural revelation. But it is this, with its wealth of obsolete language and its strange pre-Copernican setting, which is likely to prove the greatest stumbling block to the modern reader of St Thomas's own presentation. And it should have served many relevant purposes. It has introduced us to his conception of the imagination, and may help us to understand why, in divine revelation also, the imagination is *par excellence* the vehicle of prophetic vision (*De Ver.* xii. 7). But in the case of divine revelation there is another reason, arising from the very nature of the Godhead itself. The 'remoteness' from consciousness in space and time of the distant or the future event is purely relative; in itself the event is humanly knowable; where and when it is neither distant nor future, but present to the senses, it is in fact directly known. Not so, however, the eternal, transcendent, infinite Godhead; the ultimate Whence and Why of existence. Short of the beatific vision, it can never be directly known, and even then not comprehended, by the finite intelligence. It is knowable only in and through created, finite effects. In this sense God's 'remoteness' from finite human consciousness, or rather the remoteness of human consciousness and even intelligence from him, is not relative but absolute: in fact, infinite. Hence, in his later work, St Thomas will allow the full value of the word 'prophet'—the *procul videns*, or 'far-seeing'—only to the prophet of supernatural, Divine revelation (II-II. 172. 1). The images he sees are not, to use the modern terminology employed by Jung, mere *signs* for what is otherwise knowable, but true *symbols* for what wholly transcends sense-perception or rational comprehension. Not merely for its own delightfulness, as does the poet, does the teacher of the ultimate Mysteries employ imagery, symbol and metaphor, but *'propter necessitatem et utilitatem'* ('from necessity and to serve further ends') (I. i. 9).

The book has yet to be written which will throw into relief the immensely powerful role which, in St Thomas's view, is played by the imagination in human life. Even our most abstract thinking is dependent upon it, and conditioned by it, inasmuch as it originates in abstractions from images (*abstractio a phantasmatibus*). More to our present purpose is its preponderating role in determining human behaviour, and hence in moulding human history. It is the imagination supremely which constellates or dissipates human emotions, and which by reason of its ability to present the absent, the possible and the future supplies goals to be attained, objects to be avoided, and patterns to be followed in human conduct (*cf*. I-II. 77. 1, etc.). What man imagines does not merely mould history, it is itself one of its most powerful ingredients: we should know by now that the phantasies of the Nazi myth are just as much history as the commencement of war at 11 a.m. on 3rd September, 1939, and were it not for the fact of that phantasy that external fact would not be fact. The interior life of the human psyche, and especially its myths and phantasies, their action upon and reaction to the human environment, are no less history than lists of battles, kings and queens. This should be borne in mind when we are perplexed by the presence in Biblical prophecy of much that, however transmuted, belongs to the common stock of human symbolism and mythology (*i.e.*, the historical collective unconscious). Such things are certainly no less the business of a *prophetia* concerned with the guidance of human life through time to eternity than is a precise chronological record of the names of the kings of Israel.

Less overtly, our allusion to *prophetia naturalis* has introduced us to another most important idea in St Thomas's conception of Divine revelation, that of the ministry of angels in its production. St Thomas takes in all seriousness the assertions of Acts vii. 53 and Galatians iii. 19, that the Old Law was mediated by angels (I-II. 98. 3). This idea is also fundamental to the argument of the Epistle to the Hebrews and indeed, as Père Bouyer has shown, to Pauline conceptions generally.[1] St Thomas presses this to the point of denying categorically that Old Testament revelation was ever the effect of immediate Divine agency. If Exodus xxxiii. 11. had said that 'The Lord spoke to Moses face to face, as a friend speaks to a friend', that could only be because 'Scripture speaks conformably to popular opinion' (*'secundum opinionem populi loquitur Scriptura'. ibid.* ad 2): one of St Thomas's many sweeping concessions to the principle that revelation is often more concerned with what people imagine than with precision of statement about the external world.

But he is also at great pains to give this important theological idea of angelic enlightenment a rational and even scientific explanation. We cannot here go into all the intricacies of his angelology; still less draw out its implications for the idea, stressed by P. Bouyer as Pauline and Patristic, that diabolic agency is also, though very differently, operative in revelation. A few points may, however, be noted. St Thomas, in sharp contradiction to St Albert the Great and many medieval Christian and Jewish divines, had asserted the identity of the 'angels' of the Scripture with the immaterial, separated 'intelligences' of metaphysical speculation. (It is, however, well to remember that he recognized that the very name 'angel' indicates a *function* rather than a substance— *'Angelus est nomen officii tantum et non substantiae'* (*In Matt.* xv. 1.); and in treating of the Scriptural names of the various angelic 'choirs' or 'orders' he shows how they severally signify various *functions* of contemplation and service (I. 108. 2 and 5)). The general name 'angel', however, signifies 'message-bearer', a function therefore of mediating the unknown to consciousness. But how was this possible? The answer must depend on what we understand these functions to be. If angels were immaterial substances, they could therefore do all that such beings could do, but they would do it, not as independent agents to fulfil their own private

---

1. 'Le problème du mal dans le christianisme antique'. *Dieu Vivant*, No. 6.

purposes, good or bad, but as ministers of the divine purpose for the universe, and especially for man. Enjoying the divine vision, they could communicate not merely their own connatural knowledge as in 'natural' prophecy. They certainly could not communicate the incommunicable beatific vision itself; they could only communicate some finite *results* of that vision. But being in touch with eternity, so to speak, they could somehow communicate some knowledge of the eternal purposes and designs for creation to the mind of man in time. This indeed is one of their primary functions in the universe: to give enlightenment to the human mind. Only God, indeed, and that without creaturely mediation, could impart faith, the complete receptivity and self-surrender of the intellect to the Unseen and Unknown, *non visum, non scitum* (*cf.* II-II. 1. 2 and 3). But it belongs to angels to set forth the *contents* of faith, *'proponere credenda'* (I. 111. 1 ad 1). But how? It is beyond angelic power to form ideas in the human intellect—only God penetrates the mind (*'solus Deus illabitur menti'*). It is also beyond angelic power—St Thomas is most emphatic on the subject, though we cannot here pause to follow his argument—directly to form images in the human imagination (I. 111. 3; *De Ver.* xii. 10). Even angels could not overrule the ordinary processes of psychology and biology; working in and through matter they must obey the laws and employ the resources of matter. Only by an agitation of bodily spirits and humours (*'commotio corporalium spirituum et humorum'*) by modifications of the human organism,[1] images are produced, though these in their turn are necessarily limited in range to the material provided by the recipient's sense-experience. Angels could, and more rarely did, St Thomas held, produce shapes and forms on the 'external world', and even without their agency could stimulate the external sense-organs (I. 111. 4). But either way they must act through the organs of the human body.

---

1. We might say by the excitation of the neurones of the cerebral cortex—see J. C. Eccles, F.R.S., 'Hypotheses relating to the Brain-Mind Problem', *Nature*, Vol. 168, pp. 53 ff. (July 14th, 1951).

The important conclusion is inescapable that, in St Thomas's mind, the proximate and immediate causes of supernatural, no less than of natural *prophetia*, were invariably biological or physical in character.

We should be quite mistaken to picture this as an abnormal interference of spirit with natural physical or biological processes; in St Thomas's mind the interpenetration of spirit (*Pneuma*) and life (*Bios*) and nature (*Physis*) and soul (*Psyche*) was part and parcel of the normal order of things, even though not all its manifestations in human consciousness were directly concerned with the transcendence of the created order altogether. Whether we go on to say that the instruments of spiritual purposes are radically biological, or that the purposes of biological processes are ultimately spiritual, depends on the point of view which we take as our starting point. Either way, it is through the sub-rational that the super-rational is brought to human consciousness. And either way, our present knowledge of biology and its psychological counterparts, both ontogenetic and phylogenetic, would seem to be able to complete St Thomas's conception of revelation very much more satisfactorily than could that which he had at his own disposal. The struggle for life, the perpetuation and evolution of life and ever more abundant life, suggest a natural longing (*naturale desiderium*) which can be satisfied only in life absolute and infinite: the 'endless, total, simultaneous and perfect possession of life' ('*interminabilis vitae tota simul et perfecta possessio*')[1] which is eternity. And destiny in eternity, and the relevance of events in space and time to eternity, are, as we now go on to see, the distinguishing characteristic of divine revelation, of supernatural, as distinct from natural, prophecy.

For angels 'enlighten' the human mind, not only by thus indirectly fashioning images in the imagination or the senses, but also by a certain 'strengthening' (*confortatio*) of the human understanding (I. 111. 1). This idea is not, it proves on investigation, such a crude anthropomorphism as might at first sight appear, though the language is, as St Thomas admits, metaphorical (*cf.* I. 106. 1). It implies no further

1. Boethius's classical definition of eternity.

influx of new ideas or images; but rather an increase in the intellect's ability to *judge*, to connect or disconnect, the ideas it already possesses or the images presented to it (*cf. De Malo*, xvi. 12; *De Ver.* xi. 3). It is, so to speak, an increase in the light in which the relations between ideas or images are seen. What can be done by angels in this fashion, can *a fortiori* be done by God. Perhaps we may find a clue to this rather difficult theory in the approximations, suggested by the pseudo-Denys, Ruysbroeck and other mystical writers, of levels of mystical contemplation to the functions of the several angelic 'choirs'. St Thomas himself suggests something of the sort when he writes of this intellectual 'strengthening', in both supernatural and natural *prophetia*, that by its means 'the human mind is raised to understand in a certain way conformably to the manner of immaterial substances, so that with utmost certitude it sees, not only principles, but also conclusions, by mere intuition (*simplici intuitu*)' (*De Ver.* xii. 3).

This particular theory that the prophet's enlarged power of judgment comes through angelic mediation is not perhaps indispensable to St Thomas's general theory of revelation. What, however, is essential, and indeed fundamental, is the primary importance of the *judgment* itself. There is no apprehension of truth, indeed no question of truth or falsehood, nor of veracious vision as opposed to hallucination (*cf.* I-II. 77. 2; *De Malo* III. 3 ad 9), without a judgment or its equivalent (I. 16. 2). Moreover, unless an idea or image is related to something else, it has no meaning, no *significatio*. It is not a sign nor symbol nor in any way significant; it tells me nothing, it is just itself. My hearing of a sound, my sight of a cat, my concept of a triangle have no meaning, true or false, unless related to something else; they just *are*. Similarly, I may have the most vivid dream of the exact number on the flanks of a Derby winner, but unless I can judge and interpret, relate it to this year's, next year's, last year's, or a wholly non-existent Derby, it profiteth me nothing. I may have all sorts of paranormal dreams and visions, even God-given dreams and visions, but if I cannot judge of them, I am no prophet. Pharaoh, St Thomas reminds us, had excellent dreams, but not Pharaoh who had the dreams, but Joseph, who could judge their meaning, was the prophet (*De Ver.* xii. 7); he judged of their meaning in the light of some higher knowledge of the eternal designs of God, even though their immediate meaning concerned nothing more transcendental than providing guidance for pagan Egypt's food supply.

So Aristotle likewise distinguishes clearly between the dream and the μαντική, the divination or interpretation, of the dream. We know that at the Delphic Oracle the function of the Pythonic priestess was confined to her ecstatic utterances; there were other functionaries whose business it was to find some significance in them. But in Greece, as in Israel, these two functions of receiving and judging were often combined in the same person. Aeschylus, in his portrayal of the prophetess Cassandra, shows us with consummate art the psychological development of a typical prophetic experience; from deep unaccountable physical pain and emotional horror, through the passing into trance and the gradual shaping and unfolding of hideous images, to the final terrified realization of the relation of those interior forms to events imminent in exterior reality. We may see similar and no less dramatic processes in the Bible itself, for instance in Jeremiah iv:

> My bowels, my bowels! I am in anguish.
> Oh, the walls of my heart!
> My heart is in tumult;
> I cannot keep silence—
> Now I hear the sound of a trumpet,
> The alarm of war.

> Shock upon shock has come,
> The whole land is shattered. . . .

Then the judgment on the reason for it all:—

> For my people is foolish,
> They have not known me,
> They are sottish children. . . . .

And finally the application to the world of fact: it is

> The daughter of *Sion* that bewaileth herself,
> That spreadeth her hands, saying,
> Woe is me now.

That brings us to what is for St Thomas the distinguishing characteristic of divine revelation, of supernatural from merely natural *prophetia*. Primarily it lies in its very *purpose*; though this supernatural *prophetia* may be brought about through purely natural causes, and indeed *must* be realized in natural, psychological media, its end, its purpose or *finis*, transcends finite, created nature altogether (*De Ver*. xii. 3 ad 11).

Divine revelation is needful, St Thomas had said in the very first article of the *Summa*, because the purpose and meaning of human existence is ultimately to be found only in the invisible and incomprehensible Divinity, and yet that purpose must somehow be made known to man if his objectives and activities are to be adjusted to that purpose. In the attainment of that purpose and the fulfilment of that meaning alone lies his *salus*—his ultimate health and weal. And such knowledge can come ultimately only from the one source that possesses that knowledge, God himself. Hence the 'remote' or the 'distant' with which the supernatural *propheta* is ultimately concerned (whether he himself knows it or not) is not the remote or distant in time but in eternity; he is concerned with the things of time only from the standpoint of eternity. While the natural *propheta*, at his best, is concerned with future good or bad 'fortune' as predetermined by the 'Fates'—the mechanical laws of cause and effect immanent in nature (*karma*)—the supernatural prophet is concerned with the ultimate designs of the Author and Finisher of men and stars. Inasmuch as he, too, may foresee the future, his sources of information, so to speak, are not (as with the 'natural' visionary) contemporaneous pre-determinants of things to come, but issue from the Eternal to whom events, which to us are past, present and future, are equally present. Here we may see the striking difference between the characteristic prophet of Israel and of, let us say, Greece. True, even in Greece, we may see strivings towards this sort of prophecy; the transformation of the Fates from Furies into Graces on the emergence of the 'younger gods'; but, only, it might seem, to deliver man from slavery to inexorable Fate to slavery to incalculable Caprice. A harder path awaited the people of Israel than was promised to the citizens of Athens in the closing chants of *The Eumenides*. Through repeated desolation and exile they had to learn to withdraw their *libido* from their national capital in order that they might recognize that their earthly home was less a 'thing in itself' than a symbol and a stepping stone to an incomprehensible, and yet picturable, 'Jerusalem which is above, which is our mother' (Gal. iv. 3).[1] It is not at all, St Thomas insists, that the Biblical prophet sees eternity, any more than the natural prophet, strictly speaking, sees the future. As the 'natural prophet' sees something *present* which is *significant* of the future, so the 'supernatural prophet' sees something *present* which is *significant* of eternity, or, more exactly, whose significance or meaning lies ultimately in eternity. So St Thomas accepts the traditional phrase that the prophet sees *in speculo aeternitatis* (II-II. 173. 1; *De Ver.* xii. 6), but he is most insistent that we understand this quite literally as the 'mirror *of* eternity' and not the 'mirror which *is* eternity', if only because eternity is in no sense a mirror; it is not the reflector but the reflected. And even if it were a mirror, the prophet could not see it. The mirror *of* eternity is precisely events in time.

But the mere perception of an occurrence is not a revelation, still less the occurrence itself; what concerns the prophet is the *outcome* of the occurrence, its *eventus*, what it is leading to from the standpoint of the eternal designs for man and his *salus*. For, St Thomas insists, the supernatural prophet, as well as the 'natural' prophet, is particularly concerned with the future; in so far as his prophetic judg-

---

1. See K. L. Schmidt, 'Jerusalem als Urbild und Abbild', *Eranos Jahrbuch.* XVIII, pp. 207 ff.

ment falls also on the present or the past (or, more exactly, on present memories or records of the past), it is from the standpoint of whither they are leading man in accord with the eternal designs. He is concerned with the past in so far as it throws light on what man is, and is doing, from the standpoint of eternity; with the present in so far as it is pregnant with the future, what will come of it (II-II. 171. 3; *De Pot.* iv. 1: *Quodlibet.* vii. 14 ad 5).

But because the *standpoint* of the supernatural prophet is different from that of the natural prophet, his field of vision is immeasurably widened. The paranormal vision which 'sees' the future as predetermined in finite causes is at most paranormal—a rarity. But there is nothing whatever in space or time, in the length and breadth of creation, which is not a reflection of eternity, and whose ultimate significance and meaning does not lie in eternity. The *cognitio prophetica*, St Thomas writes, being itself a reflection of the divine knowledge, a judgment passed from the standpoint of eternity, may extend to anything whatever that is subject to the divine knowledge itself, 'divine things and human, spiritual things and material' (II-II. 171. 3); to anything, in fact, 'knowledge of which can serve man's *salus*: past things, present things, future things, eternal things'. (*De Ver.* xii 6) from the lowest to the highest. The prophet's judgment—his assertion or denial—may indeed fall on what we would call paranormal occurrences, the very *acceptio* or reception of images may be preternatural or supernatural. But it need not be so; it may be perfectly everyday and normal (II-II. 174. 2; *De Ver.* xii. 2). Thus Jeremiah saw eternal significance in an almond tree, and the position of a pot; Amos in a basket of fruit.

The prophets of Israel did not meddle in politics, they got up to their necks in politics, and they became so because of their eternal relevance in God's designs for his people's welfare. The humdrum records of the Books of Kings, the copybook platitudes of Proverbs, no less than the visions of Ezechiel and Daniel, the sublime utterances of the Divine *Sophia*—all have their place within this comprehensive conception. As for the strange and meticulous ritual prescriptions of the Pentateuch, St Thomas devoted the longest articles in the whole *Summa* to set forth their revelational symbolism (I-II. 102) and two commentaries are attributed to his pen which attempted the same task for the love songs of *Canticles*. Thus, there are grades or degrees of prophecy or revelation, and it would be interesting, did space permit, to study St Thomas's classification of those grades (*De Ver*. xii. II-II. 174. 3).

Much else must be omitted from our account; including St Thomas's interesting distinction between kinds of precognitional prophecy, with its explanation why certain prophetic foretellings, though divine and infallible, do not come to pass—as Jonah found to his chagrin (*De Ver*. xii. 10; II-II. 174. 1). This chapter has omitted very much that would be necessary to complete the picture, and its brevity has unavoidably given a somewhat lopsided picture which has stressed certain features at the expense of others. We cannot, however, leave the subject without a few words about what must seem a far more serious and extraordinary omission, an omission which is not mine but from St Thomas's own treatises *De Prophetia*.

What sort of theory of revelation is this, it may be asked, which takes all its examples from the Old Testament, and has practically nothing to say about the New, about revelation in the Person of Christ, the Word made flesh? This omission from the treatises *De Prophetia* is certainly remarkable; it must, however, be remembered that the whole Third Part of the *Summa* treats of 'our Healer, the Lord Christ Jesus . . . who showed us the true way in his own person' (III *Prologus*). It is, however, true that St Thomas nowhere systematically and *ex professo* links up his treatment of the Incarnation with the general conceptions of revelation which he had given in his *De Prophetia*; neither has he very much to say which would enable us to compare the apostolic witness of the New Testament with the prophetic witness of the Old, nor does he methodically study the respective roles of revelation and prophecy under the two dispensations. If we would know his mind on these matters we shall have to depend largely on scattered remarks incidental to his treatment of other questions. The task demands a whole paper to itself, and I must be content with a few tentative indications.

Already in the *De Prophetia* he offers two thought-provoking suggestions. One is the idea borrowed from St Gregory that there is, as it were, a twofold movement in Old Testament history, a movement *away from* the sublime visions of the Divine Transcendence and Majesty given to the Patriarchs and on Sinai; and a movement *towards* a progressively clearer vision of the Incarnation to come, the revelation of God in human nature (*De Ver.* xii. 14; *cf.* II-II. 174. 6). Progressively in the Old Testament is there prophetic realization of the eternal relevance of the commonplace as distinct from the extraordinary, and with it a progressive realization of human responsibility. It is not too much to say that whereas 'natural prophecy' is mainly concerned with human irresponsibility, man's dependence on mechanical law and spiritual caprice outside his own control, supernatural prophecy in the Old Testament is increasingly a realization of man's independence and answerableness for his own actions. If we like the quaint language of the 'Higher Anthropomorphism' (against the dangers of which St Thomas will nevertheless warn us—I. 1. 9 ad 3) we may call this a 'progressive revelation of the ethical character of God', but it is really a progressive revelation of the ethical character and freedom of man; indeed of the primordial revelation that man is made to the image of God. Biblical revelation progressively *is* redemption, liberation from servitude to finite causality; but simultaneously a revelation of the eternal relevance of everything in space and time, and supremely of human perceptions, imaginations, thoughts and actions. The fulfilment of that process is the recognition of God in and through human flesh. The New Testament is not merely a fulfilment of the content of the Old, it is a fulfilment of its *mode*. No longer does the Word of God merely *use* human flesh and the natural operations of *Bios* and *Psyche*, he *becomes* it.

A second line of thought is suggested at the very end of St Thomas's *De Prophetia* (*De Ver.* xii. 14 ad 5). He writes: 'When Moses is said to be superior to other prophets, this is to be understood of prophets of the Old Testament; for to that epoch, while Christ, to whom all prophecy was orientated, was still awaited, prophecy especially belongs. But John the Baptist belongs to the New Testament; and in the New Testament a clearer revelation was made, on which account the Apostle in II Corinthians 3. 18 expressly sets himself and all other Apostles above Moses.' Already (*De Ver.* xii. 12 ad 3), St Thomas had given his account of how the Baptist was 'a prophet and more than a prophet'; the 'more than prophecy' consisted in the fact that '*digito demonstravit Christum*'—he did what no previous prophet could do, and which was not itself *prophetia* but a *denuntiatio* of *prophetia*: he pointed to Christ with his finger. I suggest we shall not be far from St. Thomas's mind if we see in this the distinguishing characteristic not only of the Baptist's, but of New Testament revelation generally. The apostolic witness is not something which is to be set over against prophetic revelation, but something which presupposes and includes it. Revelation is still no less a psychological event; but now it is an event of recognition of the interior image or idea in the exterior. Whatever the prophets knew the apostles knew, says St Thomas (I. 57. 5 ad 3), and they knew still more inasmuch as they found it 'in the mystery of Christ, which was not known to other generations, as it is revealed to the holy Apostles' (Eph. iii. 4). But it is only in the interior perception of the *mystery* of Christ that there is revelation. No more than were Jeremiah's almond tree, the invasion of Sennacherib or Pharaoh's dream, are the mere occurrences of the New Testament revelation. For there to be revelation there must be perception, not merely of the historic occurrence of the Crucifixion or the Empty Tomb, but also and principally of their *meaning* in the eternal designs of God.

Christ is the One who realizes—makes real—the prophetic symbol in his own person, and who for that reason is no mere contemplator and seer of the symbol—he *is* it. But the revelation of that is still a vision; a vision in the inspired mind of the Apostle and Evangelist, if not also and foremost in the prophetic and human mind of Jesus Christ himself (III. 7. 8). The Evangelist, says St Thomas, tells of the way in which was realized the selfsame reality (*substantia facti*) that had been seen and proclaimed by the Old Testament prophets (*Comm. in Sent.* II. xi. 2. 4). In the New Testament, I suggest, we still have prophecy, but we have something more—the pointing with the finger to the outward embodiment of the mystery.

In the New Dispensation, it is true, precognitional prophecy has lost its supreme importance (*cf.* II-II. 95. 2 ad 3); both the proclamation and the ritual of the Christian Church will be concerned, not only as were those of the Temple and Synagogue, to make present the future, but also to make present the past—the redemptive act done 'once for all' by Jesus. But that also only with a view to eternity; and for St Thomas, as we have seen, the consummation of revelation is not in the Incarnation in time, but '*erit in patria*', it awaits us in heaven. It is expedient for us that Jesus also goes away that the Spirit may come; and his departure is followed by a renewed and unprecedented outpouring of the spirit of prophecy. It is true that, in one supremely important sense, revelation is closed; there can be no further increase of revelation of things to be believed by all. The Catholic faith is the universal and all-embracing faith (*cf. In Boeth., de Trin.* III. 3) which admits of no increase or addition (II-II. 1. 6). There is no more to be revealed than is contained in that Figure to which the Apostles point with their fingers; but the hidden Heart within that external Figure, says St Thomas, is the Holy Scripture of the prophetic vision.[1]

But though, once God's Word is made flesh, there is no

---

1. 'Sacra Scriptura dicitur Cor Christi, quia manifestat illud' (*In. Ps. XX.*; *Quodlib.* XII. 27. cf. Peter of Bergamo's *Tabula Aurea* s.v. Scriptura).

more for God to say, there is still plenty—nay more than ever—for man to see. Prophetic vision and revelation must still continue. It must still continue, in the first place, for the famous *homo in silvis*—the 'man in the woods' who has never heard from human lips the apostolic message of the Gospel, and of whom, St Thomas says, it is most firmly to be held that he will have an interior revelation at least of what is necessary to his ultimate *salus* (*De Ver.* xiv. 11 ad 1). We know of many millions more men in different sorts of woods than St Thomas ever imagined. But within the Christian community also prophecy and revelation continue. Certainly as sporadic *charismata*; but also, I would suggest, though the connection is not made by St Thomas himself, in the operations of the Gifts of the Holy Ghost. The perceptive function of the Gift of Understanding, the judgment functions of Wisdom, Knowledge and Counsel are, on St Thomas's showing, closely akin to those which he has described as pertaining to prophecy, and it is difficult on his principles to see how they can be other than truly revelational. They seem to differ from *prophetia* only in this, that they are no transient *charismata*, but proceed from a permanent disposition or *habitus* whereby the baptized Christian is *bene mobilis a Spiritu sancto* ('readily subject to the movement of the Holy Spirit'). Every baptized Christian, it might be inferred, is a *propheta*, a receiver of revelation, by calling and status and inherent quality, in a way in which no Old Testament prophet could be.

St Thomas had learned from St Paul that prophetic revelation is the greatest and most desirable of *charismata* (I Cor. xiv. 1); that to it are subordinated all other *charismata* (II-II. 171. *Prol.*); that on it depends Faith, and on Faith depend Hope and Charity (II-II. 4. 7). But 'the greatest of these is charity' (I Cor. xiii, 8-13). It was not for nothing that St Thomas had joined the Order of Preachers which had come into being to combat the esoteric, dualistic Albigensian Gnosticism which equated spiritual vision with goodness and holiness, and matter—especially sex and worldly occupation—with badness and sin. 'Not every good man,' he writes, 'is more suited to having prophetic visions than any bad man, for some who are lacking in charity have minds very apt to perceive spiritual things, and this because they are immune from carnal and terrestrial interests and are endowed with natural insight. While on the other hand there are some who are much occupied with earthly affairs and who are busied about fleshly reproduction (*carnal. dantibus operam generationi*), and who have not penetrating minds, but who do have charity. And so sometimes prophetic vision is given to some who are bad and denied to some who are good.' (*De Ver.* xii. 5 ad 6).

Unsublimated sexuality and extravert activity, the two factors which had been alleged to be the main obstacles to spiritual insight, may, if at the service of charity, be of more eternal worth than the spiritual perceptions themselves. With that fine confession of Christian materialism we may fittingly close this investigation of high spiritual things.

There are problems, certainly, concerning revelation which have been forced upon us by modern science, Biblical and secular, of which St Thomas knew nothing. There are perhaps gaps and lacunae in St Thomas's own presentation; there have certainly been many in mine. There are correlations to be made even of his own ideas which he himself did not explicitly make. Perhaps, had he completed the vast symphony of his *Summa*, he would have gathered together these scattered themes in an all-unifying coda. What a gigantic effort it had been! And in nothing so much as in its conception of that very revelation which it had set out to elucidate. It had employed every instrument known to the science of his time; it had played in every register from the highest to the lowest. It had presented everything in creation, from the loftiest angels to the humblest processes of human metabolism, from the wildest dreams of men to their tritest observations and platitudes, as all contributing to the unveiling to the human mind of man's ultimate significance and destiny and his guidance through time to eternity.

But the symphony was to be an unfinished symphony.

In the early morning of 6th December, 1273, at Naples, something mysterious happened to Thomas Aquinas; something which inhibited and paralysed further composition. It was no news to him that, as compared with revelation itself, his *Summa* was like straw; the *Summa* itself had implied as much in its opening pages. But even straw had been useful, if only to show which way the prophetic spirit blows. Now even that was a thing of the past. Revelation had come to him, no longer as a subject for intellectual analysis and explanation, but as overwhelming reality. 'I can write no more,' he told his companion, 'for everything that I have written seems like straw, by comparison with the things which I have now *seen*, and which have been *revealed* to me.'

VIII

PSYCHOTHERAPY AND ETHICS

THE moral aspect of psychotherapy has received little serious and thorough-going consideration from Christian theologians or moral philosophers. This is due in part to the fact that contemporary psychotherapeutic theory and practice is in so variegated, amorphous and contradictory a state that few generalizations about it are possible, let alone any critical examination of it as a whole in the light of any body of ethical principles. It is possible, indeed, to take the written works of a given writer on psychological theory and methods, and to subject them to ethical scrutiny, and a certain amount of work of varying merit has been done in this direction; work which is itself, perhaps, by no means impervious to serious criticism. But even such work as this, within its own inevitable limitations, is not always very practically helpful. The theoretic expositions of psychologists and the accounts which they give of their methods are not infrequently both better and worse than their actual practice; and in any case do not afford very adequate material for judgment and fair discussion on the part of those who themselves lack either active or passive psychotherapeutic experience.

But the practical urgency of the problem is too acute to allow us Catholics to wait indefinitely for some decisive and all-inclusive ethico-psychotherapeutical synthesis. The problem is brought home to most of us in its most challenging and concrete form when the question arises of committing ourselves or others to psychological treatment. Do we not, in doing so, risk the undermining of our moral principles, perhaps of our religion and our faith? Rumours have reached us, perhaps, of alleged psychotherapists who, after long and costly weeks of treatment, prescribe some such homely old palliatives as a dose of fornication, divorce, cutting loose from hearth and home, or some other form of uncleanness, injustice, or impiety. We may have heard vaguely that one whole and important school of psychological analysis regards the elimination of God and conscience, thinly disguised as a super-ego, as the chief desideratum in any successful analysis. Ugly rumours have reached us, too, of dark doings in the treatment itself: of conditioning to certain patterns of behaviour under compulsions induced by hypnosis or drugs; of confessions of dark secrets and immoral abreactions compelled by drugs or shock; of analysts who conceive it to be their first task to induce their patients to fall in love with them and whose whole treatment consists in conducting morbid and pornographic conversations. Even if we do not credit such rumours, there remains a fundamental misgiving not lightly to be set aside. Are we not in any case, in submitting to psychological treatment, subjecting our minds to the direction, perhaps to the domination, of another mind, and one whose moral and religious standards may be fundamentally unsound, and are in any case fallible? Even if we could be assured on that, must not the whole end and aim of any psychologist who knows his business be to fashion the mind of his patient to his own standard of 'normality', and must not the 'normal' inevitably be in accordance with the standard of the majority of men, *i.e.*, in accordance with the standard of conformity to this wicked world? Will he not inevitably filch from us our religion and whatever ethical standards we may have which are not those of the world around us?

To these and suchlike misgivings a number of answers are commonly offered. Perhaps the most common—and in my opinion the most specious and dangerous—is that which will spirit away our misgivings with the magic name of 'science'. Psychotherapy, we shall be told, is a respectable branch of medicine; it is the employment of purely scientific methods for the curing of purely mental disorder. It has nothing whatever to do with religion or with morality; and mental disorder (it is further implied) has nothing to do with spiritual or moral disorder; neither with a man's religious convictions, nor with virtue or vice. Psychoneurosis (it is suggested) is a disease as cancer is a disease; the methods of curing it are parallel, and are neither affected by, nor do they affect, the religion or the morals of either practitioner or patient. Cure can and should be achieved without tampering with the patient's religion or his morality in the slightest. The genuine psychotherapist will be solely concerned, as is the medical man, with correct diagnosis, discovering the neurological or psychological cause of the complaint, and applying the appropriate remedy. The concern of the truly scientific psychotherapist is with an autonomous psychological sphere and with scientific remedies as ethically neutral as a bottle of physic or the surgeon's knife. Indeed, should religious or moral issues arise, he will, in his own interests and that of the cure, respect his patient's convictions and keep carefully off the grass. We are assured that there is really nothing whatever to fear; and the priest and the moralist will kindly mind their own business and not meddle in a scientific world which they cannot expect to understand. While it may be true that, for instance, the philosophy of a Freud may be materialistic and atheistic, and that the tendency among some who call themselves his disciples falls short of traditional ethical standards, the philosophy, the *Weltanschauung*, the moral principles of these men, can and must always be distinguished from their science and from their scientific therapeutic technique.

Some such line as this to allay our misgivings is taken by many who should, in my opinion, know better. It is, roughly speaking, the line taken by quite a few Catholic psychologists and their friends. These will indeed be found to allow that religion may be a useful adjunct in the effecting of the cure, but only, it would seem, as something purely adventitious and extraneous to the therapeutic process. Some will further admit a negative role to the moralist, inasmuch as it belongs to him to decide (in the same way as for any medical practitioner) what is permissible and not permissible in the treatment and the remedy. The idea that the Freudian

technique may be safely applied without subscribing to the
Freudian philosophy has been argued by Roland Dalbiez,
and his position has been supported by Maritain. Among
non-Catholics, Dr William Brown is noteworthy as accepting in the main Freudian 'science' and 'technique', but
repudiating Freudian 'philosophy' and 'irreligion'. This is
not the place to enter into a discussion of this very special
question: we must ask in more general terms whether an
answer on the lines suggested is really adequate to allay
our misgivings.

Now it is perfectly true that psychotherapy is, or should
strive to be, rigorously scientific. By this I mean that, at a
very minimum, it should be based solely upon observation
and experience of psychological fact and phenomena and on
no *a priori* theory; and that it should not, as such, invoke
postulates, hypotheses and theories beyond such as are
demanded and verifiable by the factual evidence. We need
not, at this stage, press our would-be comforters to too
precise a definition of what *they* understand by 'scientific',
or to state what range they would give to the term 'psychological data', or inquire whether they are prepared to take a
comprehensive view of *all* the data or limit them solely to
such facts or aspects of facts as will fit into the categories of
mechanical and historical causation. It may also be allowed
that psychotherapy is a branch of medicine in the historical
sense that all forms of contemporary psychotherapeutic
practice, even depth-analysis, have their origin, directly or
indirectly, in the medical clinic. We need not, at this stage,
inquire whether this fact has been altogether to their advantage. We may, however, inquire whether this idea of
psychotherapy as a specialized branch of medicine does not
sometimes presuppose a purely materialistic conception of
the function of medicine itself which is now very much less
self-evident than it was for our fathers, and which seems to be
being abandoned largely owing to the impetus of psychology
itself: it is with dubious propriety that psychotherapy can
hide behind medicine from the challenge of moral and
spiritual factors when these are being increasingly recognized

by hard-bitten surgeons and neurologists in the etiology of functional and even organic health and disease.

But we need not enter into these somewhat intricate and recondite matters in order to question the equation between the cure of cancer and the cure of a psychoneurosis. The plain fact is that the latter is directly concerned with the patient's mental outlook on life, and with patterns and principles of behaviour, with the whole order of values, motives and duties, in a sense in which the former is not. If psychological treatment does not issue in the change of a man's mentality, his outlook, his manner of conduct, his attitude to the world and his own place in the world, it surely fails entirely in its own set purpose. And, however we may choose to define ethics, or for that matter religion, surely we must agree that they are both concerned with precisely these very things. It is therefore hard to see how we can agree with such a distinction between mental and spiritual or moral disorder as is sometimes suggested, nor how a responsible and conscientious psychotherapist can disclaim any concern with his patient's religion and morals, and treat these as an untouchable sphere which is no concern of his. Must we not at least suspect that if religion is concerned with a man's ultimate values and motives, if its business is to constellate and give unity and direction to his interior attitudes and external behaviour, then if a man is suffering from any form of conflict, or is at the mercy of fears and compulsions which inhibit that unification and orientation, there is something wrong with that man's religion and his religion is itself involved in his disorder? To suppose that such a man can be brought to achieve anything like a change of outlook and behaviour while his religion remains unaffected seems like trying to make him achieve a self-contradiction. And experience would seem to confirm that, in the case of patients who consciously subscribe to, or have been brought up in, some religious belief or practice, their religion or ethical code is not only an element in their problem, but also often appears quite openly as one of its principal factors. Even in the case of patients who profess no religion, fundamental religious issues are found to emerge in depth-analysis as roots of the trouble, and also as the vehicles of its solution. C. G. Jung, as is well known, goes so far as to maintain that there can be no successful 'cure' of adult psychoneurosis which does not involve the attainment of a new religious attitude and the abandonment of previous religious or irreligious attitudes: something, therefore, very like a conversion. We may ask, indeed, whether any word can better sum up what must be sought from psychotherapy than *metanoia*—which is the Biblical word for a change of mind and heart; and we may recall that the very word *religio*, like the Sanscrit *yoga*, probably means to bind back or together: it is that which should bind a man together by binding him to God—or whatever he may call his ultimate value and the aim of his life.

It does therefore seem unscientific to contend that, in the name of science, psychotherapy can and should disregard religious and moral issues. Even from the purely therapeutic standpoint it seems that a patient's religion and moral principles cannot be regarded by the practitioner as a tabu, a constant which can remain unchanged throughout the process. And we would further venture to contend that the psychotherapist who supposes otherwise is of all the most to be regarded with suspicion, for he is of all the most unconscious of his responsibilities, of the principal factors and of the inevitable outcome of any effective treatment he may give. Moreover, an analyst who is so minded will be unaware of, and so incapable of transforming, the religious and moral transferences which the patient will be all the more likely to project upon him.

Before turning to see if we can make some more constructive contribution to the solution of our problem, we must take a respectful glance at those who would go to the opposite extreme. There are many, otherwise of very different schools of thought, who would agree in the main with all we have said, but would deny that our problem of correlating ethics with psychotherapy really exists. This they will do, though in very different and contradictory ways, by asserting more or less openly that they are really one and the same thing. It would take us too far away from our principal subject to discuss what may be called 'pan-psychologism'—I mean the theory, more or less openly avowed, that religion, morality, indeed everything, is 'nothing but' psychology, and which tends in practice to substitute psychological techniques for religion. It may be mentioned, incidentally, that pan-psychologism has been frequently and formally repudiated by C. G. Jung, and that it can easily be shown that it goes far beyond what is warranted by his own data and scientific postulates if they be rightly understood; but a certain tendency in this direction among some of his disciples, which can claim some measure of support from some of his own less careful writing, cannot easily be denied.

But we are, most of us, more familiar with what may be called a crude 'pan-religionism'. This denies our problem by saying in effect that there is no room for psychotherapy because religion supplies all our needs. 'Keep the faith; keep the commandments; go to the sacraments; be resigned to the will of God; say your prayers; consult a priest; read good books—and then you will be quite all right and won't want to get involved with psychologists.' We are probably familiar with the cheery advice, and many a neurotic is perhaps dimly aware that, had he consistently followed it, he would have found therein an effective prophylactic against his present condition. But he has tried all these things, and his condition seems worse rather than better. And naturally so; for the very essence of any psychoneurotic condition lies in the inability of consciousness and conscious will to cope with or relate itself to some autonomous and automatic system, whose power is increased rather than lessened by reinforcement of the habitual conscious attitude and pattern of behaviour. His religion, it must be repeated, is precisely one of the elements or factors in the disorder, and it is precisely failing to fulfil its function of integration and co-ordination. Not only does he experience fears or compulsions which are not wholly at the disposition of

conscious will (for that is the lot of fallen humanity generally); he is at their mercy, their unwilling victim; with them
he is precisely impotent to enter into any satisfactory
relationship. It is not that his religion is objectively and in
itself incapable of forming a bridge; but his personal religion
is itself infected with the disorder. It is not to be denied that
competent and understanding religious or moral instruction
on the conscious level may in some measure remove intellectual misunderstandings which foster the neurotic condition; but in the measure in which it is truly neurotic, it
seems impossible to bring about a revision of purely intellectual judgment which will resolve the automatism of the
complex and place it at the disposal of consciousness.

The priest, then, as such, is no more a satisfactory substitute for the analyst than the analyst is a satisfactory
substitute for the priest. Furthermore, it may be doubted
whether our problem would necessarily be satisfactorily
solved if only we could find an analyst whose own religious
beliefs and ethical principles were unexceptionable. It is
not to the psychologist we should go if what we seek and
need were moral, theological or religious instruction: the
psychologist is not, and ought not to be, any substitute for
the religious or moral teacher. But such a one, it may be
urged, can at least be relied upon not to make us lose our
faith or our morals; if, as Catholics (for instance) we seek
treatment solely from a Catholic psychologist, we can at
least be assured that his treatment will make us 'good' and
not make us 'bad'.

Now it is just here, I would submit, that the real crux of
our problem confronts us. For, it seems to me, the real
question at issue is not merely the risk that the psychologist
will make us bad, but that he will *make* us anything. Have
we any right to be made anything, even to be made good?
Are we not merely delivering ourselves from one compulsive
automatism to another? Is an imposed and compulsive
goodness really goodness at all? Is the scientific employment
of psychological knowledge, even for our alleged good, and
whether on the mass-scale of the State propaganda-machine

or for the individual in the consulting room, a thing which is ethically tolerable—or even, for matter of that, therapeutically successful? Are we really paragons of virtue—or even psychologically healthy—if we are so conditioned by external means that we cannot very well help ourselves? The problem narrows itself down to what seems at first sight to be an insoluble dilemma between freedom and determinism.

، Though of all the various schools of psychology the Behaviourist would alone seem to be explicitly committed to absolute determinism, it seems that any psychology which claims to be scientific in the sense of being bound by the principles of mechanistic causality or sequence must to that extent be deterministic; and any psychotherapy which claims to be rigidly scientific must be likewise committed to determinism. Whatever means it employs, whether physical or not, it is bound by the laws of mechanical causation. This means that, in diagnosis, it must exclude moral choice as a factor in the origin of the complaint and regard any sense of guilt as a morbid delusion. What is more serious and to the point, it must in its curative methods work on the sole assumption that the positing of a certain cause will produce a certain effect, and the whole task of the physician will consist in finding and positing the appropriate stimulus to induce a preconceived and desired response. And if it is indeed true that by 'scientific' we are to understand solely that which can be dealt with in terms and categories of historical and mechanical causation, then it is difficult to see a way out of this dilemma. The psychotherapist, the more he claims to be in this sense a detached and rigid scientist, the more he is in fact a magician who employs an esoteric and superior knowledge whereby he gains power over other people's minds and hearts, and fashions them in accord with his own preconceived idea of 'normality'; and whether he be a black magician or a white magician, may be thought to be of considerably less importance from the religious and ethical standpoint than the fact that he is a magician at all.

We Catholics are not, of course, concerned to deny every sort of psychological determinism, or to suppose that psychological characteristics and events are the outcome of chance. We do not have to repudiate the basic postulate of Freudian psycho-analysis, and most other psychologies, that much of our mental life is causally predetermined in much the same way as are events in the physical universe. We must not confuse freedom with omnipotence, but humbly recognize that our psychological, no less than our physical, life is in very great measure the outcome of necessity and of necessitating factors, many of which are beyond our knowledge and control. But we must maintain that man is not *only* a product of conditioned and conditioning agencies, but also is himself an agent capable of self-determination—of perceiving alternatives and choosing from among them. He is capable of judging and choosing values, of acting for a purpose, of responding consciously and freely to his very predeterminations. In this we see the specific characteristic of a human being, without which he is less than human. Nor can we exclude free choices which we have made in the past from among the very factors which later condition us. We must therefore regard with considerable suspicion any psychology which ignores, makes light of, or repudiates this characteristic; still more any psychotherapy whose open or covert aim is to treat us *as if* we were only reflexes to given stimuli, passive effects to determined and determining causes. On the other hand we shall tend to welcome a psychotherapy whose aim is precisely to enlarge our knowledge of the factors that determine us, which will extend and strengthen our self-mastery, and enable us to increase our sphere of freedom. We Catholics ask of psychotherapy, not to make us good, nor to tell us what to do or not to do in order to be good, nor even to make us 'normal' in accord with any given norm, however estimable; but only to help us to achieve a greater freedom through a better knowledge of our necessity and compulsions. We must decline to be 'made' anything by psychotherapy; we want to be helped to be able to make or mar ourselves.

(In parentheses, and to avoid possible misunderstanding, we may remark that here, and throughout this chapter, we are talking of *psychotherapy* and ethics—and by psychotherapy we understand the treatment of psychoneurosis by psychological methods, mostly conducted by dialogue or conversation between the therapist and the patient. *Psychiatry*, in the stricter sense of the word, the medical and usually physical treatment of psychosis, also raises many moral issues, but they are of another order.)

My own very limited reading and experience of contemporary psychology compels me to record the opinion that by far the greater bulk of it seems to presuppose, more or less openly, these exclusively mechanistic assumptions and to be conditioned by their limitations. The more it claims to be respectably 'scientific' and to eschew all quackery, and the more it aspires to the condition of an exact science in the traditional sense, the more will a psychotherapy based exclusively upon it be closed to the primary claims of human freedom and responsibility. Fortunately, in practice, instinct and common sense admit the surreptitious introduction of factors which cannot, in this narrow sense, be regarded as 'scientific'. But there is, to my knowledge, only one school of psychotherapy which openly, consistently and methodically repudiates the sufficiency and primacy of the principles of mechanistic and historical causality in psychotherapeutic practice.

C. G. Jung, as is well known, broke with Freud on the issue of the all-sufficiency of infantile sexuality, the Oedipus complex, and repression, to provide the etiology of every mental disorder. But, specializing in the treatment of *dementia praecox*, or introversion-neurosis as he prefers to call it, he was led to discover that Freud's preoccupation with historical causation was apt only to confirm the patient in his regression and in his morbid shirking of personal responsibility. Jung was not concerned with formal morals as such, but as an empirical and practical therapist he was very much concerned to help his patients to get better. He was driven to the conclusion that the concepts of historical and mechanical causation, with their exclusive reference to the historical past, were inappropriate and inadequate to handle a practical therapy which was of its nature concerned with the patient's present and future. Furthermore, he found that they failed as adequate vehicles to exhaust the latent content of his patient's dream-material, which he found to have a present and prognostic reference as well as a retrospective one. The practice, of course, preceded the theory, as the theory was later to provide a valuable working hypothesis for the improvement of the practice; but Jung was soon led, by way of his substitution of undifferentiated 'energy' or 'libido' for Freud's 'sexuality', to contend that, however valuable the employment of causal concepts might be, the decisive ones to be employed in psychotherapy were energic rather than causal. Just as a physical event, as is recognized by the physicists, can be regarded both causally and energically, so could a psychic event; and so by the psychotherapist it should be. He thus stated his basic postulates, postulates which involve a break, not only with Freud, but with the assumptions that to this day underlie by far the greater part of psychotherapeutic theory and practice:

> It is a generally recognized truth that physical events can be looked at in two ways, that is from the mechanistic and from the energic standpoint. The mechanistic view is purely causal; from this standpoint an event is conceived as the result of a cause. . . . The energic viewpoint on the other hand is in essence final; the event is traced from effect to cause on the assumption that energy forms the essential basis of changes in phenomena, that it maintains itself as a constant throughout these changes, and finally leads to an entropy, a condition of general equilibrium.
>
> The flow of energy has a definite direction or goal, in that it follows the fall of potential in a way that cannot be reversed.[1]

This is not the place to expound in detail Jung's application of the concepts and laws of quantum-physics and

---

1. *Contributions to Analytical Psychology*, p.1.

thermodynamics to psychological data.[1] It is undoubtedly daring, and perhaps not beyond criticism; but it cannot easily be denied that as a working hypothesis it has proved in practice immensely fruitful. What is important to our present purpose is that the theory issues from and issues in a practice which, at the lowest estimate, offers a way out of our dilemma. The psyche and its phenomenal manifestations are no longer to be conceived purely or primarily in terms of determined cause and effect, but as a relatively closed self-regulating system possessing its own potentialities of recovery and renewal through the interplay of simulstaneous co-efficient functions. Reductive analysis still has its part to play, but only as a subordinate means to the differentiation of functions; these functions are conceived as correlative, mutually exclusive but compensating *quanta*. The concept of a preconceived 'normality' as the goal of psychotherapy gives place to that of 'individuation' or 'integration'; *i.e.*, a conscious balance of equilibrium of differentiated and mutually-compensating functions whose qualitative content emerges in the analysis itself and can in no way be determined in advance.

We need not here discuss the later, and perhaps more familiar, features of Jung's psychology—the irreducible four functions (Sensation and Intuition; Thought and Feeling) and their interrelation; the four irreducible 'directions' of psychic energy (introversion and extroversion; progression and regression); the collective unconscious with its immense implications for the role of religious symbolism in the task of analysis; the concept of the symbol itself as the instrument of psychic transformation. All these elaborations have been rendered possible only by the emancipation of psychotherapy from the exclusive standpoint of predetermining causality. Dr Jacobi expresses the matter admirably when she writes:

---

1. For a detailed exposition of the theory and its elaborations, see Jung's own books, and such authoritative systematisers of his work as Jolan Jacobi, *The Psychology of C. G. Jung* (Kegan Paul) and Toni Wolff, *The Guild of Pastoral Psychology Tutorial Reading Course*, Part VII.

Sigmund Freud looks for the *causae efficientes*, the causes of later psychic disturbances. Alfred Adler considers and treats the initial situation with regard to a *causa finalis*, and both see in the drives the *causae materiales*. Jung, on the contrary, although he, too, naturally takes account of the *causae materiales* and likewise takes the *causae finales* as starting and end-points, adds to them something further in the *causae formales*, those formative forces that are represented above all through the symbol as mediators between the unconscious and consciousness or between all the pairs of psychic opposites. . . . Freud employs a reductive method, Jung a *prospective* one.[1]

The practical consequences for our present discussion are important. Dr Jacobi continues, paraphrasing and quoting Jung himself:

Jung's method is therefore not only to this extent a 'dialectical procedure' in that it is a dialogue between two persons . . . it is also in itself dialectic, as a process which, by confronting the contents of consciousness with those of the unconscious, calls forth a reaction between these two psychic realities that aims towards and results in bridging over both with a *tertium quid*, a synthesis. It is accordingly, too, from the therapeutic standpoint a preliminary condition that the psychologist accept this dialectic principle equally as binding. He does not 'analyse' an object at a theoretic distance, but is quite as much in the analysis as the patient. . . . But the patient alone determines the interpretation to be given to the material he brings. Only his individuality is decisive here; for he must have a vital feeling of assent, not a rational consent but a true experience. 'Whoever would avoid suggestion must therefore look upon a dream interpretation as invalid until the formula is found that wins the patient's agreement.' Otherwise the next dream or the next vision inevitably brings up the same problem and keeps bringing it up until the patient has taken a new objection as a result of his experience. The often heard attitude that the therapist could suggestively influence

1. J. Jacobi, *op. cit.*, p. 66.

the patient with his interpretation could therefore only be made by one who does not know the nature of the unconscious; for 'the possibility and danger of prejudicing the patient is greatly over-estimated. The objective-psychic, the unconscious, is, as experience proves, in the highest degree independent. If this were not so it could not at all exercise its characteristic function, the compensation of consciousness. Consciousness can be trained like a parrot, but not the unconscious.'[1]

This writer's more limited experience strikingly confirms that it is indeed a fact that any attempt on the part of the analyst to interfere with the patient's endopsychic process and independence, whether consciously by trying to indoctrinate the patient with his own ideas, or unconsciously by involving the patient in his own projections, will invariably call forth a vigorous protest from the patient's unconscious— it may be by way of a dream which criticizes the analyst, or by a strong negative transference which, if not speedily resolved, will wreck the whole analysis, or by an acute recurrence of symptoms or a recurrence of dreams which represent the identical unresolved problem. 'The patient is always right'—psychologically right—may be said to be the Golden Rule for a Jungian analyst; and perhaps no quality is more demanded of the analyst than the humility and the capacity for self-effacement and self-criticism which its observance requires. His task is solely that of mediator, translator; the patient's companion in the journey into his own depths. He is always to follow; never to lead. He may interpret, amplify—but interpret and amplify the patient's own material in a fashion that wins the patient's own assent. To do this, the reduction of effects to causes will be necessary; but the artificial positing of causes to produce effects, never. The analyst is in no sense the efficient cause of the patient's 'cure' by the imposition of an agency *ab extra*; his task is solely to assist the *vis medicatrix naturae* within. For Jung's is

1. J. Jacobi, *op. cit.*, p. 68. Quotations from Jung: *Modern Man in Search of a Soul*, p. 12, and *Integration of the Personality*, p. 101.

a therapy in which the practitioner makes no arrogant claim to 'suggest', still less to force, the patient into any preconceived mould of alleged 'normality', but, on the contrary, one in which his task is solely to assist in uncovering the sources which hinder the patient from fulfilling his individual destiny, enabling the patient himself to reconstruct his own life and to transform the unconscious sources of life, power and integrity. A therapy, therefore, whose aim and effect is in no way to restrict the patient's freedom and responsibility, but on the contrary one which makes the fullest demands upon them as the decisive factors both in the process and the result. Its effect is precisely to *liberate* from the inevitability of the historical-causal sequence. Or, as Dr Jacobi has expressed it, it is, as a 'way to self-knowledge and self-control', precisely 'an activation of the ethical function'.

The point could, did space permit, be elaborated with a wealth of concrete example; the proof of the pudding must always be in the eating and not in the cookery books. But we must draw to such a conclusion as the situation allows. It is not suggested that no conceivable theoretical hypotheses other than those of C. G. Jung can be ethically acceptable. Nor would we imply that no psychotherapist who does not claim discipleship of Jung is reliable, or that therapists of other schools may not attain equally admirable results because of (or in spite of) other theories; nor that every psychotherapist who wears a 'Jungian' label on that account deserves our unqualified confidence. But we venture to submit that Jungian theory and practice at least offer possibilities of a way out from the dilemma with which we have been occupied.

It would, however, be idle to suppose that even fidelity to Jungian theory and practice will immediately solve all the difficulties which in practice may arise. The special case of the Catholic patient, and the collaboration of priest and therapist in his treatment, is by itself a vast, complex and practically untouched subject. It is difficult to see any existing, ready-made solution to our problem; the solution does not exist, it is a job yet to be done.

The task before us is gigantic indeed; I can do no more than allude to what appear to be the most pressing needs. In the field of psychology itself there is, it seems, the urgent business of the delimitation and co-ordination of neurological, psychiatrical and analytical methods. There is the crying need for more, and still more, reliable analysts; analysts who are not only technically experienced and equipped, but who are possessed of the moral and spiritual integrity, the intellectual and emotional discipline, the humility, patience, and fearlessness—above all, the capacity for self-sacrificing and disinterested *love*—which fruitful analysis demands. Closely associated with this is the need for some method whereby both the training and the consulting of analysts can be made very much less financially prohibitive than they usually are at present.

Then, from the point of view of our special preoccupations as Catholics, there is the need for the theoretic co-ordination of psychology with theology; for consideration of the very special practical problems of the spiritual direction of analysants and their after-care: the peculiar needs of Catholic patients and of those many who, as an outcome of analysis, are brought to the threshold of the Church, but who, all too often, are sent empty away to find some spurious substitute in gnostic cults. Due consideration of each of these subjects would require a paper to itself.

Also, we would suggest that we cannot complacently suppose that all the work to be done lies only with the psychologists, and that religious and moral education among us Catholics is in so happy a state that we need do nothing about it. Aristotle said that ethical inquiry and teaching cannot be undertaken without a knowledge of the human *psyche*; and rightly so, for what is ethics but the pattern of habit and conduct with a view to the *telos*, the end and fulfilment, the balance and health, of the whole human soul and all its parts? This standpoint, which is that of St Thomas Aquinas, not to speak of the Fathers of the Church, seems to be virtually ignored in the kind of teaching which presents morality solely as an extrinsically imposed code of arbitrary regulations rather than as a *life* of *virtue*, of a 'second nature' which responds to and integrates the innate needs and tendencies of the whole man. The morality of the intricate 'moral systems', which filters from some of our 'moral theology' textbooks into our schools and homes in effect substitutes an external and casuistic jurisprudence for the cultivation of an immanent Prudence;[1] resistance to, and suppression of, instinctive desire for its heightening and transformation by the disposition of Temperance *within* the *appetitus concupiscibilis* (the pleasure principle) itself; cold, dutiful, anti-instinctual effort for the virtue of Fortitude *within* the *appetitus irascibilis* (the instinctive 'will to power'). This loss of the traditional pre-Reformation Catholic moral theology is a veritable breeding ground of psychological conflict, frustration, psychoneurosis—and 'leakage'.[2] Can we say either that Christian *doctrine* is commonly presented among us in all its psychological relevance as the *Verbum salutis*, the Divine message and pattern of integral human health and wholeness? Each of these questions, in their turn, raises vast issues which require whole books to themselves.

While the above pages were being written appeared Professor J. C. Flugel's *Man, Morals and Society*.[3] Perhaps it still remains among the most important contributions to the subject of psychotherapy and ethics written from the psychologist's point of view. The views it expresses are, in any case, not outmoded, and a few reflections upon it may not be out of place.

Dr. Flugel's approach is, naturally enough, very different from our own. He writes as a psychologist pure and simple, and with a minimum (at least in intention) of extra-psychological presuppositions. He is moreover a convinced and

---

1. See T. Deman, O.P., *Dictionnaire de théologie catholique*, s.v. 'Prudence'.
2. The colloquialism used by Catholics to denote the abandonment of Catholic practice, especially by adolescents.
3. *Man, Morals and Society: A Psycho-analytical Study* (Duckworth, London, 1945).

orthodox—though also a 'progressive' and by no means uncritical—Freudian; but he is unusually open to interests and considerations outside his own professional province and writes with an ease, an urbanity and a humour uncommon to his kind.

In certain important matters, Flugel's conclusions strikingly anticipate and confirm our own. In particular we would draw attention to the frankness with which he dismisses the contention that psychotherapy as a 'pure science', can confine its attention to the *means* of human conduct and disregard consideration of the ends and values which are the province of ethics (pp. 12 ff., 30 ff.). Indeed, it is precisely because he believes that the analytical exploration of psychological means modifies our apprehension of these ends and values that he has written and published the book at all; in the belief, that is to say, that from psychoanalysis (notwithstanding its many candidly recognized insufficiencies) many lessons may be learned 'concerning the general nature of human morality and the general lines of moral progress' (p. 240, *cf*. Preface). A student of Aristotle and St Thomas cannot fail to recognize in the 'Cognitive (Psychological)' judgment which Dr Flugel opposes to 'Orectic (Moral)' judgment, something very much like what he himself understands by the rational ethics of traditional philosophy; and indeed the 'guiding notions concerning the main lines of moral progress and development' (p. 241) which Dr Flugel believes to be indicated by psychoanalysis conform strikingly with many of the main principles of Aristotelian-Thomist ethics. His contrast between the ethics of 'facing and expressing' and the ethics of 'avoidance' (p. 29) seems almost identical with that of Aristotle between ἀρετή (virtue) and ἐγκράτεια (control), and his emphasis on the 'spontaneous goodness' of *habit* recalls the basic conception in traditional ethics of the 'good life' as a life of virtue. His plea for 'the epicritic discriminatory power of consciousness' as against 'the protopathic methods of the unconscious' is scarcely intelligible except as a modern restatement of Aristotle's conception of the participation by the ἄλογον (irrational) in λόγος (reasonableness), and his conception of 'autonomy' (pp. 252 ff.) is in principle indistinguishable from Aristotle's aim of 'magnanimity'. However much we must dissent from many of Dr Flugel's concrete applications of these 'guiding notions', it is difficult to avoid the conclusion that, in their main direction, they represent a return to those of the 'intellectualist' ethics of the *philosophia perennis* rather than (as he himself seems to suppose) an advance to some new and hitherto unknown peak of human evolution discovered by psycho-analysis. Indeed it may well be asked whether the 'stupidity', 'infantilism' and 'archaism' of modern man's 'super-ego', which Dr Flugel so ruthlessly exposes, and which he shows to be at the root of much of the conflict and neurosis of our time, is not due in considerable measure to the vacuum left by the abandonment of this precious heritage.

But the average reader will naturally look to Dr Flugel's book to learn what practical recommendations psycho-analysis has to offer us in order to recover it, and here the book is profoundly disappointing. Indeed after two hundred and forty pages, most of which are employed in exposing the intricate complexities and bewildering depth of the factors in human perversity, the author, in a passage of profound pessimism, 'passes the buck' back to the biologists. Psycho-analysis, it appears, can show man to how great an extent 'even his mental and moral characteristics are far from being completely amenable to conscious will and deliberation', but 'our ultimate mental and moral capacities, like our ultimate physical characteristics, can probably be changed only by biological methods' (p. 241).[1]

Without cynicism, and without disparaging the real

---

1. The biologists, physiologists and neurologists on their side, seem to be increasingly anxious to pass the ball back to the psychologists: the physician Alexis Carrel's *Man the Unknown*, the surgeon Kenneth Walker's *Diagnosis of Man* and the remarkable last chapter of the neurologist V. H. Mottram's 'Pelican' book on *The Physical Basis of Personality* bear witness to the game of shuttle-cock which the specialists play with poor Modern Man!

positive contribution which Dr Flugel has made to the study of the etiology of modern man's moral and psychological problems, it may be said that perhaps the chief value of his book lies in its implicit exposure of the impotence of the exclusively 'reductive' and 'historical causal' method of treatment, an exposure which is all the more impressive because the method is here followed with unprecedented thoroughness and brilliance. From the very first page Dr Flugel envisages his task solely in terms of 'diagnosis and prescription' with a view to discovering the 'origin and nature' of man's moral impulses (p. 9). The bulk of the book is in fact occupied with the complexities of the conflicting factors which bring about man's moral problems and achievements, and in particular with the causal factors which contribute to the construction of the 'super-ego' and its conflict with the 'id'.[1] It shows indeed how very far Freudian psychoanalysis has advanced from what Dr Flugel himself calls the 'crude hedonism' of its early formulations, yet its basic postulates are nowhere abandoned. If the categories of purpose and finality be excluded from the study of psychological phenomena, it is inevitable that the axiological is still confused with the etiological; what is prior in time is regarded as prior in importance and value, and the most psychology can do is to suggest some knowledge of what we ought to do; the psyche is incapable of showing how to obtain the power to do it. Religion, art, culture, politics, morality are logically viewed as 'displacements' of infantile sexuality and parental relationships—much as if a grown man were regarded as a 'displacement' of an embryo.

Invaluable as the book will be to the professional analyst, of whatever school, as a guide to the countless and complex factors to be looked for in the origin of his patient's troubles, the average reader, and still more the neurotic reader, will find little in the book which will not confirm him in the belief that he is the victim of a tangle of intricate mechanisms from which psychology is powerless to extricate him. Never

---

1. The uninitiated will find no more lucid explanation of these uncouth terms than in Dr Flugel's own book.

before, perhaps, has the baffling complexity at the origin of the conflict between the 'law of my members' and the 'law of my mind' been so ruthlessly revealed; but Dr Flugel can offer no glimpse of hope of such reconciliation of the conflict as St Paul found in the grace of our Lord Jesus Christ.[1] The emergence of a 'transcendent' or 'reconciling' function, a *tertium quid*, such as has been observed by Jung as the vehicle of solution, integration and healing (or its recognition should it emerge) is precluded *a priori* by a psychology whose whole preoccupation is with historical causation, which belittles 'intuition' as unscientific (*cf.* p.9) and which disregards the functional and teleological aspects of psychological phenomena. Notwithstanding the immense advances which Freudian psychoanalysis is shown to have made in its recognition of the importance of 'super-ego' factors in psychological health and disease, it is still apt to conceive the way of health and happiness to lie in the murder (however 'symbolic') of the Father rather than in reconciliation with the Father through the self-sacrifice of the co-equal Son. It is only consistent with these pre-suppositions that Dr Flugel misses the inner psychological relevance of sacrifice and asceticism, and indeed of Christianity generally, and that he can seriously advocate so sophisticated a product of ego-consciousness as Cattell's 'Theopsyche' as a substitute for God.

---

1. Epistle to the Romans, vii. 7 ff.

IX

THE ANALYST AND THE CONFESSOR

W E are often assured by those who should know best that sacramental confession and psychological analysis[1] are very much the same thing. On this point at least there would seem to be a considerable measure of agreement between many Catholic spokesmen and many psychologists: if they differ, it is only in the assertion of the superiority of their own respective wares. While the psychologists will tell us that sacramental confession is a sort of naïve and undeveloped, pre-scientific forerunner of psychological analysis, it has become almost a commonplace among many Catholic apologists that analysis is a secularized and truncated form of sacramental confession.

The equation deserves somewhat more critical examination than it customarily receives. Doubtless there are certain superficial resemblances which might incline us to put them both into the same category, and it is probable that a more careful comparison of the two procedures may reveal still deeper affinities and connections between them than at first sight appear. But there are still more obvious and essential differences between them which cannot be overlooked without risk of great confusion both in theory and in practice. We have only to take a look at what actually takes place in the confessional and what actually takes place in the analyst's consulting room to see that the differences, even on the surface, are very marked indeed; and a closer acquaintance

---

1. I use this somewhat clumsy term rather than 'psychoanalysis' lest I be thought to have in mind only Freudian analysis, of which alone the term 'psychoanalysis' can strictly be used. By 'psychological analysis' I understand any psychotherapy which employs depth-analysis, whether Freudian, Jungian, or any other.

with their respective aims and presuppositions will reveal still further the chasm that divides them. We shall soon learn that the analyst who plays the confessor will be as bad an analyst as the confessor who plays the analyst will be a bad confessor, and we shall be put on our guard against the dangerous type of apologetic which might be understood as offering the confessional as a substitute for psychotherapy: dangerous because of the disappointment it must arouse in those who know no better than to suppose it to be a cure for psychoneurosis, and the contempt it must arouse in those who do. Nothing but good, we believe, can come from a closer acquaintance by the analyst of the practice of the sacrament of penance, or by the confessor of the practice of analysis. But before we can hope to see how the one can illuminate, and perhaps subserve, the other, it is of the greatest importance to avoid all initial blurring of their basic differences. Here, as always, *distinguer pour unir* is the indispensable precondition for accurate thinking.

And the distinctions are indeed basic, as becomes evident so soon as we attempt to sort out and compare the constituent ingredients of sacramental confession with those of psychological analysis.

Few analysts, and those hardly the most trustworthy, would be prepared to present us with a formula which would cover all the component elements which go to make up an analysis. Just how an analysis will proceed, of what it will consist, what part in it will be taken by the analyst and what by the patient, what it will and will not achieve and what paths it will follow: none of these can be determined in advance. Its starting-point, its development, its procedure and its term will alike be determined by the material which emerges in the analysis itself, by the patient's response and the analyst's skill. It is an adventure of exploration into uncharted territory: there may be compasses, but there are no ready-made maps. It is a medicine, but one for which there is no uniform prescription. The ingredients of which it is to be made will differ widely in every case, and will be dictated by the material itself and no *a priori* preconceptions.

Indeed its therapeutic success will depend on nothing so much as on the ability of both analyst and analysant to rid themselves of predetermined plans and prejudices.

In striking contrast, thanks to centuries of actual practice and theological reflection, the ingredients of the sacrament of penance are neatly and definitely sorted out, formulated and tabulated. These ingredients, with their technical names, are familiar to most Catholics from their very catechisms. The instructed Catholic 'going to confession' knows fairly exactly what will happen; what he has to do and what the confessor has to do. He is probably familiar with the traditional dissection of the sacrament of penance into its component parts: he knows that, like all the sacraments, it consists of certain definite 'matter' and certain definite 'form'. He may not appreciate the logical and metaphysical considerations which have established this matter-form analogy as a technical device whereby theologians analyse the sacraments into their components; but at least he knows the authoritative character of its results. And he knows that the constituent elements of the sacrament of penance are thus authoritatively classified under three heads: (1) remote matter; (2) proximate matter; and (3) form. These may well serve us here as terms of comparison.

The 'remote matter' of the sacrament of penance—that is to say, 'what it is all about', the subject with which it is concerned, the material of which it is made and to which the 'form' gives a specific 'shape' or significance—is stated to be *the sins of the penitent committed since baptism.*

At once a striking contrast jumps to the eye when we turn to the counterpart of this 'remote matter' in psychological analysis. Sin, truly, is an evil; and psychotherapy is also concerned, as is every therapy, with an evil. Moreover, both the sacrament and the analysis are concerned to remedy the evil. But the evils with which each is concerned are essentially different, even mutually opposed. Sin is defined as an evil human act; that is, a human activity which lacks the goodness and rightness it should have in conformity with the divine mind. In theological language it is *malum culpae*—

'the evil men *do*'. It is, of its very nature as a human act, in some measure voluntary: and a sin is sinful in the precise measure in which it is willed. A psychoneurosis, on the contrary, is a certain *malum poenae*—an 'evil men *suffer*' or '*undergo*'. It is a sickness, and as such something essentially involuntary and usually contrary to the sufferer's will both in itself and in its symptoms and manifestations. It is something that *happens to* us, not something we *do*; though it may condition actions, these actions are neurotic symptoms in the precise measure in which they are involuntary. We may say that while the sacrament of penance deals with certain evil results of human *freedom*, psychotherapy deals with certain results of human *compulsions*: with thoughts, feelings, emotions, conflicts, patterns of behaviour which the patient 'cannot help', which are uncontrollable by his will and usually clean contrary to it. Confession presupposes the power to sin and to turn from sin and seek forgiveness; analysis usually presupposes necessity and impotence and seeks liberation and freedom. In short, the primary and direct concern of the sacrament is with wilful *misdeeds*: the primary and direct concern of analysis is with a certain kind of involuntary *misfortune*.

This difference is quite fundamental. Whatever resemblances may be found, we cannot overlook the essential difference in the material with which the sacrament of penance and any kind of psychotherapy are respectively concerned.

From this basic difference spring others which are hardly less striking. Sin, being essentially voluntary, is also essentially conscious, while it is of the very definition of any analytical psychotherapy that it is concerned, at least no less, with the unconscious. Sacramental confession, as we have already remarked, is concerned solely with actual sins committed after baptism: it is not concerned with inherited sin, whose remedy lies within the province of baptism itself. In contrast, psychotherapy cannot confine itself to factors acquired in the patient's own lifetime, still less limit itself to any definite date in the patient's history. It can on no account neglect inherited factors and dispositions: least of all can any depth-analysis which, under whatever name, recognizes a 'collective unconscious' as an important factor in mental health and sickness.

The 'proximate matter' of the sacrament of penance is said to be the three acts on the part of the penitent: confession, contrition and satisfaction. Here we have three definite and deliberate acts, interiorly performed and exteriorly expressed, required of the penitent as a *sine qua non* constituent of the sacrament. Each represents a predetermined attitude or operation of mind or will in regard to the 'remote matter'. Confession implies conscious acknowledgment of that 'remote matter', and its expression in words. Contrition implies the turning of the will *from* the same, and its turning *to* God and the divine will. Satisfaction implies the willing acceptance and performance of some task imposed as compensation and as a token of good faith and willingness to accept the penal consequences of sin.

It is presumably in the first of these—the act of confessing —that the resemblances between sacramental confession and psychological analysis are more particularly supposed to lie.

But the 'confession' required of the penitent and the 'confession' required of the analysant are two very different things; and the difference lies in the difference of 'remote matter' which we have already noted. What a penitent is expected to confess is very clearly defined and restricted to the sins committed since his baptism or his previous confession. No such limitation can bind the analysant. Though no analyst who knows his business will want to exclude such material, he will still less seek to limit his patient's 'confessions' to his real or alleged misdeeds. And he will be concerned with them, not precisely as moral offences, but at causes or symptoms of neurosis, and as providing—together with the patient's conscious or unconscious attitudes so them—important elements in the total picture of the personality with which he has to do. The patient's 'good deeds' will interest him no less than his 'bad' ones (confessors are notoriously, and rightly, impatient with rehearsals of the penitent's virtues!) while dreams, free associations, spontaneous reactions and other manifestations of the unconscious will interest him still more. His business is less with what the patient does than why he does it. Only from this totally different standpoint may there be some overlapping, but never complete identity, between sacramental and analytical 'confession'. The psychological processes demanded by each differ correspondingly: the former requires a certain concentration of conscious memory and the orderly recital of a selection of its contents; the second, contrariwise, a mental and physical relaxation which permits the free flow of uncontrolled phantasy and the suspension of regular 'directed' mental activity. The uncomfortable confessional box with its hard kneeler, and the couch or armchair of the analyst's room, admirably express and promote the two very different kinds of 'confession' for which each is appointed.

Psychological analysis knows nothing of contrition or satisfaction as predetermined acts to be required of the patient: it would fail entirely of its purpose were it to lay down in advance the conscious attitude which the analysant was to adopt to his material. This can no more be predetermined than can the material itself.

Still less is there any equivalent in psychological analysis to the *form* of the sacrament of penance. This 'form' is the words of forgiveness pronounced by the priest: it is the specifying and determining element which makes the sacrament of penance to be what it is; it is the efficacious sign of reconciliation with God, and so the very remedy for the evil which is the sacrament's 'remote matter'. Nothing of the sort is to be found in psychological analysis. Some very superficial resemblance might be suspected in certain cases in which reconciliation is effected with some *imago* projected upon the analyst; but there will be no 'remedy' except in so far as the transference is resolved, the projection withdrawn and assimilated to the patient's own conscious ego. There is still considerable disagreement among analysts as to what their own precise role in analysis should be. But few, even of those who most strongly advocate his 'active' intervention in the process, would maintain that the ultimate remedy comes from the analyst rather than the analysant and his own response to his own material. None certainly would claim Divine power and authority to forgive sin.

Moreover, a confessor is required to act as *judge* of the objective moral rightness or wrongness of what is told him, and to give such authorized guidance on moral issues as is asked of him, or as circumstances seem to demand. An analyst has no like authority to pronounce moral judgments, and for therapeutic reasons will usually refuse resolutely to do so.

So the differences between sacramental confession as understood and practised in the Catholic Church and psychological analysis as known and practised to-day are considerable and profound. Are we then to conclude that there are no connections between them, and that they are so wholly diverse that they can hardly be spoken of in the same breath?

To say this would, we think, be a grave mistake. We may not overlook either the psychological value of sacramental confession or the 'religious' features of many an analysis and the close connections which may be found between them. Here is a subject which deserves much more careful exploration and consideration than has yet been given it, or is possible in this brief essay. But once the essential differences between the two have been understood, we may offer a few suggestions as to where such exploration might profitably be directed.

It should be remembered that although *malum culpae* and *malum poenae*, sin and misfortune, are essentially different, and even opposite in their voluntariness and involuntariness respectively, there is a close causal link between them. It is elementary Christian (and not only Christian) teaching that the first is the ultimate cause of the second. Sin results in temporal (as well as eternal) punishments and consequences, and St Thomas Aquinas explains how the disorder and disharmony of man's psychological powers and activities are, more especially, the automatic outcome of sin (*cf. Summa Theol.* I-II. 82. 3 and 85. 3). This must not be misunderstood in the sense of the cruel and unchristian assumption that all suffering, especially mental suffering, must always be attributed to the sufferer's own personal and actual sins (such as constitute the 'matter' of the sacrament of penance): we are forbidden straightway to ascribe it to the sins of 'this man or his parents' (John ix.2). But it is true that original sin is the ultimate, though indirect, cause (by removing the original grace which was the source of man's psychological integrity and harmony) of all such disorder, and that this perversity *can* be enhanced by personal, actual sin. It should further be remembered that not all such disorder (being quite 'normal' in fallen human nature) can be characterized as pathological or neurotic. But psychology itself finds it increasingly difficult to eliminate moral disorder from the etiology of mental disorder. The materialistic and mechanistic belief that a neurosis could be diagnosed without consideration of the patient's ethical valuations or behaviour, and that it could be 'cured' without any moral response or alteration, dies hard, but becomes increasingly difficult to maintain.

So while sacramental confession (including contrition and amendment) does not deal directly with psychoneurosis, we need not be surprised to find cases in which it is indirectly therapeutic: indirectly in so far as it may remove one of its causes. But it is perhaps as prevention rather than cure that sacramental confession, especially if practised with regularity and with frank and unflinching self-examination, may serve the ends, if not of psychotherapy, then at least of mental hygiene and prophylaxis. Analytic experience witnesses to the very great extent to which unconsciousness of the 'shadow' side of life contributes to the formation and persistence of neurotic complexes. A patient's failure to meet consciously and deliberately the challenges ('temptations' or 'tests' in Catholic parlance) which life brings him, whether they arise from his own character or from his environment or from their mutual impact; his shady compromises, never fully faced, with life's conflicting demands; his narcissistic idealization of ego and corresponding neglect of the less acceptable traits of his character: all these, notoriously, are a common breeding ground of neurosis. Frequent and honest self-examination, and the necessity of formulating its findings in the confessional, may alone do much to promote a more complete self-awareness, and so prevent these less pleasing features of a personality from sinking into unconsciousness, where alone they can generate neurotic symptoms. Hence, while sacramental confession is not ordained to cure, it may do much to prevent, the disorders with which psychotherapy is concerned. We say, 'it may'; indeed it should. But other factors, inherited or environmental, may enter in to prevent its exercising this particular efficacy; and indeed in certain cases (notably those known to Catholics by the tragic symptoms of 'scruples') it may occasion an increase of the virulence of the disease.

On the other hand, while psychological analysis is not ordained to forgive sin, it may do much to free the patient from those compulsions which make both sin and repentance from sin—and even any clear-eyed self-examination—difficult or impossible.

It should also be remarked that, although psychological analysis cannot demand contrition of the patient, it is seldom successful unless it brings about something which, at very least, is not unlike it: a radical change of the patient's conscious outlook, a *metanoia* or change of mind, and with it of his moral valuations and behaviour. It is a truism that if an analysis does not change the patient's outlook on life, his whole mentality in greater or less degree, it achieves nothing. The very enlargement of his consciousness automatically involves a shifting of his whole centre of awareness, and with it of his standard of values. This change, however, is not something that he brings to analysis, but something which emerges from the process and its material themselves. Numerous case histories show striking resemblances, not only between the results of analysis and those of religious and moral conversions, but also in the very symbols which eventually emerge from unconscious sources to induce the transformation. We may again recall C. G. Jung's celebrated declaration made in 1932: 'During the past thirty years, people from all the civilized countries of the earth have consulted me. I have treated many hundreds of patients, the larger number being Protestants, a small number of Jews, and not more than five or six believing Catholics. Among all my patients in the second half of life . . . there has not been one whose problem in the last resort was not that of finding a religious outlook on life. It is safe to say that every one of them fell ill because he had lost that which the living religions of every age had given to their followers, and none of them has been really healed who did not regain his religious outlook.' He added that 'This, of course, has nothing to do with a particular creed or membership of a church'; but he has also called constant attention to the parallels between dream processes and their healing symbolism, and those of recorded religious initiations, conversions and illuminations. He has also remarked on the similarities, both in their mode and in their results, of the healing factors and experiences in analysis with what religious belief holds to be the effects of the operations of divine grace. That they are such in fact we can never have sufficient grounds to affirm with certitude; but neither can we *a priori* deny the possibility. While man is limited to the appointed channels of grace and forgiveness, God is not so limited; and there seems to be no reason why the theologian should deny to dream-symbolism the *ex opere operantis* efficacy he must allow to the sacraments of the Old Law, the baptism of John, the sacramentals of the Church or—it may be added—the dream-symbols of the Scriptures. Though little can be affirmed or denied with certainty, the resemblances are sometimes too impressive to be totally ignored.

The most that can be said in summary is that although sacramental confession and psychological analysis are two wholly different things, pursuing two different but inter-related purposes, the purposes of the one may sometimes happen (*per accidens*) to be attained through the other. But when the prevention, or more rarely the cure, of psycho-neurosis sometimes results from sacramental confession, this arises from the conscious human activities which it involves. If, however, divine grace and forgiveness are sometimes attained through the processes of psychological analysis, this can only be from the patient's response to God's uncove-nanted mercies through the inner life of his soul.

X

DEVILS AND COMPLEXES

THE Devil and his works is a subject which we might approach from very many different points of view. We could confine ourselves to a purely positive, factual, phenomenal approach: to anecdotes of events that might claim to indicate diabolic possession or some other kind of devilry. Anthropologists, missionaries, folklorists and psychical researchers may be found ready to give us plenty of such material at first-hand. Or we might search the records of the past—the autobiographies of those who were or thought they were possessed by a devil, the innumerable reports of processes for witchcraft and sorcery which became an epidemic in Europe from the end of the fifteenth century—inspect the *Malleus Maleficarum* and the whole mass of strange and seamy literature which that epidemic of witch-hunting produced. Or we might examine modern, clinical, psychopathological case-material, and see what parallels it affords with alleged diabolical possession, and inquire whether psychological science has in fact disposed of the allegations, and improved on the therapy of past ages to any notable extent. We could spend a great deal of time in verifying and correlating these records and also in theorizing about them. Again, we could cover all the countries and cultures of the globe, and go back to the beginnings of recorded history, to study human beliefs and myths concerning evil spirits and their influence on the human mind and on human behaviour, the very varying valuations put on such supposed influences in different societies, the different rituals, techniques and practices adopted—now to overcome, now to be rid of, now to evade, now to use and harness to human ends, such alleged influences. We might attempt to trace the development of such beliefs and practices—the metamorphoses they undergo, their changing variety of symbolic representation, the varying conceptions of the interrelation of demons and diseases. Epilepsy, the *morbus sacer*, the holy disease which is widely believed to be a seizure by a divine or demonic spirit, could alone absorb our attention. On all these things there is already a considerable literature, and much work still remains to be done. In this essay we can hardly even touch upon them.

We must, however, touch—however superficially and lightly—on the Biblical data concerning demons and evil spirits, and more especially on Satan. For here we have the primitive raw material which the Christian theology of the devil and all his works seeks to illuminate, and which such Christian practices as exorcism etc., presuppose. There can be little doubt that, in the Hebrew Scriptures, the emergence of evil spirits as somehow distinct entities, distinct both from God and from his emissaries or theophanies, the good angels or spirits, was a gradual process. When we compare the Old Testament as a whole with cognate records in neighbouring lands—Babylonia or Egypt, for example—we must agree that malevolent preternatural powers, call them gods, spirits, devils or what you will, are relatively conspicuous by their absence. They have no part to play in the cosmogony of Genesis (in sharp contrast to Babylonian and most other cosmogonies). And although later reflexion will identify the serpent in the Garden of Eden with the devil, there is no hint of this in the original story. It is noteworthy that the name *Satan*, as a proper name, without the article, occurs only once in the Hebrew Old Testament—in I Chron. (Vulgate, I Paralip.) 21. 1. 'And Satan rose up against Israel, and moved David to number [*i.e.*, take a census of] Israel.' This passage is particularly significant, for it is clearly a later re-editing of II Samuel (Vulgate, II Kings) 24. 1, where we have 'The *wrath of Jahweh* was kindled against Israel, and stirred up David among them saying: Go number Israel and Juda'. This appears to be not the only, but perhaps the clearest, example of the gradual differentiation in the Old Testament of Satan from God, in which, with the gradual emergence of a more moral and merciful conception of God, his more wrathful and disagreeable activites can no longer be attributed directly to him, and Satan—the 'adversary'— emerges as the agent of such activities. These activities, however disagreeable and evil they may appear to man, are always in the Old Testament believed to be beneficial to him in the long run, and Satan is and remains the *Mal'ak Jahweh*—the emissary, representative or 'angel' of God. Thus in Numbers 22. 22 it is a *Mal'ak Jahweh* who stands in the way of (in Hebrew 'satans') Balaam and his ass. In the opening chapters of Job, the Adversary or the Satan is one of the *Bene Elohim*—the sons of God who stand in the Divine Presence (1. 6)—whose business it is to put man to the test, humiliate him and expose his unrighteousness, and indeed to serve the Divine purpose by manifesting God's less amiable characteristics. This Divine benevolence, underlying Satanic malevolence, is implicit in the New Testament also, and quite explicit in such a passage as St Paul's 'Lest the greatness of the revelations should exalt me there was given me . . . an angel of Satan to buffet me'. (I Cor. 12. 7).

Satan is not, of course, the only malevolent power or spirit in the Old Testament. Apart from the serpent in the garden, there are the mysterious sons of God who went into the daughters of men (in Genesis 6), there is Azazel in Leviticus 16, Lilith in Isaiah 34, Leviathan and Behemoth in Job, the unnamed evil melancholic spirit that fell on Saul, the ones that inspired the witch of Endor, the lying spirits that seize the false prophets, Baal and the other pagan gods of the neighbourhood—*Omnes dii gentium daemonia*. All of these might be claimed to be in some way diabolic, and in varying degrees to possess the minds and hearts of man. All of them are presented as having some functions, however obscure, in the mysterious designs of God for the salvation of his people. Although they are all pictorially represented as somehow personal, anthropomorphic or theriomorphic, the Bible is less interested in what they are than in what they do, in their functions rather than their essence. *We* might say that they are purely personifications of divine functions or projections of unconscious contents of the human mind, but it would be an anachronism to attribute such sophisticated interpretations to the minds of the Old Testament writers—for them it would be entirely to miss the point of their narrations, which is less with what devils are than what they do, and how they affect human behaviour.

Only among the later Rabbis does the question arise—*What* is Satan anyway? And it is interesting to note that sometimes they favour an 'objective' interpretation which would identify Satan with the 'dark side' of God himself (dark and fearsome, that is to say, to human apprehension) or as a distinct but rebellious manifestation of God who is nevertheless an agent of the divine purposes for man, a fallen angel; but sometimes they favour a more 'subjective' —we might say 'psychological'—interpretation and identify Satan with the *'yetzer ha-ra'*—the 'evil inclination' or imagination inherent in man of which we read first in Genesis—and then frequently in the Old Testament.[1] So also St Paul, in Romans 7, will almost personify what he calls 'the sin that dwells within me'. The functions of this 'indwelling sin' are precisely those elsewhere ascribed to Satan. It is the adversary which is contrary to the 'mind', the conscious ego, which delights in the law of God. It is the accuser which shows us up for what we really are despite our claims to righteousness. It is, in the jejune language of analytical psychology, an autonomous complex, a shadow, which acts in and through us in spite of ourselves: 'If I do what I do not want, it is no longer I that do it, but sin that dwells within me' (Rom. 7. 20).

Comparatively rare and secondary as are allusions to devils in the Old Testament, they—together with the 'good' angels—play an increasingly important role in later Jewish thought and apocalyptic—perhaps a preponderant role in popular, rural Jewish religion. The priestly and prophetic emphasis on the transcendence of Jahweh, whose very name might not be uttered, the concentration of his official litur-

---

1. See Rivkah Schärf 'Die Gestalt des Satans im Alten Testament', in *Symbolik des Geistes* (Zürich, 1948).

gical worship in the Temple at Jerusalem, perhaps made it inevitable that popular interest would be more occupied with powers and spirits who were deemed to have more immediate concern with helping or hindering the daily lives of ordinary people.

In the pages of the New Testament, Satan and the devils may be said to be fairly ubiquitous from the beginning to the end. The polite efforts of nineteenth-century Liberal criticism to exorcize the demons from the New Testament, to explain away its more 'devilish' passages as a later and superstitious adulteration of the pure ethical milk of the Gospel, or at least to apologize for them as an unimportant concession to contemporary illusions, have proved a dismal failure. Even the most radical criticism of *Formgeschichte* holds that these passages belong to the most primitive strata, the essential core, of the evangelical tradition. Especially since Schweitzer and Otto, it has become difficult to read the Gospels at all otherwise than as an account of the struggle between the *de jure* Reign of God and the *de facto* Reign of Satan—the actual 'prince' or 'god' of this world over human hearts, minds and affairs. 'The devil', Tertullian will say, with customary exaggeration and insight, 'is fully known only to Christians.'[1] The coming of Christ itself evokes the spirit of anti-Christ; only when the full light shines in the darkness is the intensity of the darkness made manifest.[2] Not only the words and actions of Christ as related in the Gospels, but also the Epistles, and still more obviously the Apocalypse, are largely unintelligible except on the supposition of the reality and activity of Satan and other malevolent spirits.

We cannot here attempt even a summary of New Testament manifestations of diabolic power, still less of the implications of New Testament teaching about the Devil, his characteristics and functions. Something, however, must be said, more immediately relevant to our subject, about New Testament and early Christian belief concerning the devil and disease—physical and mental. Satan is believed

1. *De Testimonio Animae*, iii.
2. *cf.* C. G. Jung, *Aion*, pp. 72 ff.

to be somehow at the origin of all human sin and way-
wardness, and therefore of its consequences—suffering,
disease and death. Christ, however, firmly rejects the belief
that disease is necessarily the 'fault' of the individual sufferer,
or an inherited result of that of his immediate forebears.
'Neither this man hath sinned, nor his parents' (John 9. 3).

Although it is nowhere categorically stated, disease is
commonly presented as a work of the devil, and the healing
work of Jesus, not as a mere ridding of symptoms, but as a
release from diabolic domination. This is so because sickness,
from the religious standpoint, is itself a testing or temptation
which (as with Job) may lead a man from—or to—God. But
this diabolic domination differs widely in degree, in imme-
diacy, and even in kind, in different cases. In Luke 13. 11, for
instance, we read of 'a woman who had a spirit of infirmity'
for eighteen years; she was bent over and could not straighten
herself. And Jesus said to her, 'Woman, you are freed from
your infirmity'. So far there is mention only of 'infirmity'
(ἀσθένεια—literally, absence of strength or health). But
in verse 16, Christ refers to her as 'this woman whom *Satan*
bound for eighteen years'. Only by a wild stretch of language
could this be called diabolic *possession*, but somehow it is
Satan who is operative in the spinal curvature. In the
language of a later day we may say that, though Satan is
not the proximate, secondary cause, he is a remote cause,
or at least is using the infirmity to withhold the sufferer
from the praise and love of God into which she bursts so
soon as she is healed.

Quite different is the case of the 'man with an unclean
spirit'—of whom we read for instance in Mark 5. 1-20
(*cf.* Mt. 8. 25 ff.; Lk. 8. 26 ff.). A psychiatrist will recognize
in this account the dissociation and the prodigious strength
of the maniac; and the 'legion' of devils who take possession
of the man, controlling him, and speaking and acting in and
through him, can hardly fail to remind the alienist of the
phenomena of dissociation. Here, as also in the case of the
mediumistic slave girl of Acts 16. 16 ff., we find the 'possessed'
displaying paranormal knowledge—an apparently not

unknown concomitant of insanity, which can only with difficulty be accounted for *purely* in terms of brain-lesion, glandular irregularities, or repression.

Time will not permit us to linger further on New Testament ideas of diabolic influences in man's mental and physical health, nor on the beliefs and practices of the early Church in this matter.[1] Systematic curiosity about the natures—the what, whence and why—of good or evil spirits hardly troubled the Biblical writers, nor, in any very serious degree, the early Fathers of the Church. Only with the rise of scholasticism, Jewish, Moslem and Christian, do such questions become acute. Only then is the serious effort made to construct a methodical angelology and demonology, abstracted from mere picture-thinking, in purely rational and conceptual terms, which will be free from uncritical anthropomorphism and would satisfy the demands of logic and hermeneutics. This became (as is well known) one of the principal occupations of the scholastic theologians. Of these efforts, probably the most successful and coherent, as well as the most influential, was that of St Thomas Aquinas, who earned the title of the 'Angelic Doctor' largely in consequence of his treatises on the angels. These treatises are notoriously among the most difficult in all his writings. We cannot here examine in detail their methodology, the validity of the premises and arguments which they employ, nor even list all the conclusions which they reach. But it may be worth while to note a few of the conclusions which may be more relevant to our general theme.

To our question—'Do angels and devils exist at all anyway?'—St Thomas will not give us what we might consider an entirely unambiguous answer. He will want to know what we mean by 'exist'. If we limit existence to what is immediately perceptible to our minds or senses, then certainly they do not. Neither do they exist as material reality

---

1. Those interested in the latter might be referred to the valuable collection from early Christian literature on the subject in Dr Evelyn Frost's *Christian Healing*, Appendix to Part I.

is said to exist, nor as contained in the categories of space and time, even though he holds them to be *operative* in space and time. Only by some *analogy* with the material reality of our experience can we apply the verb 'to be' (*esse*) of them, but they are in their own way real enough. For St Thomas the theologian, this is of course guaranteed by the Scriptures, but he finds the reality of incorporeal intelligences asserted also in writings of the philosophers—notably in the Neo-Platonists, and above all in Avicenna. He himself argues to the same conclusion, both *a priori* from the hierarchy of creation, and *a posteriori* from observable phenomena in the universe, and notably in the mind of man himself, which require the positing of intelligent and purposive agency, which transcends purely physical causation, as well as human intelligence, volition or ability. What is active must be actual —if it acts it must somehow *be*.

To the question, *what* are angels?—he replies with a *docta ignorantia*. Strictly, he says, we do not and cannot know *what* they are, but rather what they are not. All that we, or the objects of our experience, strictly have in common with them is creatureliness, finiteness—they *have* being, only God *is* being. But we are nevertheless able to make certain predications about them *per viam remotionis*, i.e., by stripping our concepts of their material time-and-space conditioned content, and then applying them analogically (*i.e.*, in a non-identical but related sense). Notably, we are able to reflect upon our own intellectual and volitional operations, abstract from them every notion and condition of succession, change and sense-limitation, and then affirm them analogically of the subject 'Angel'. In Aristotelian terminology, angelology must be conducted entirely in the third degree of abstraction. Perhaps we can attempt to paraphrase the result by saying that angels are a purely mental and not a physical reality: they are *intelligibilia intelligentia*—thinking thoughts. But like our own conscious thinking and thoughts, they are nevertheless effective in bringing about changes and events in the corporeal world of space and time, including apparition in visual or imaginary form to human perceptions. Angelic or diabolic apparitions are not them-selves angels or devils, they are at best corporeal forms assumed for man's benefit.

This catalogue of bald conclusions from Thomist angelo-logy may lack even plausibility: their verification pre-supposes a complex and taxing type of methodology to which few of us nowadays are accustomed. But we must hasten from this rapid glance at St Thomas's general angelology to his demonology.

It stands to reason for Aquinas that there can be no such thing as an essentially and naturally evil spirit. Evil cannot exist of itself, evil (as an abstract noun, *i.e.*, badness) is the absence of some appropriate good in something which of itself is good. 'God saw that all he had made was very good' declares Genesis: '*bonum et ens convertuntur*'—'the "real" and the "good" are interchangeable'—affirmed the ancient philosophers. So far as their natures and being are concerned, the demons are very good indeed, and St Thomas favours the view that Lucifer or Satan is by nature the very noblest and highest and most Godlike of all God's creatures. But—*corruptio optimi pessima*—the badness of the best is the worst sort of badness.

How did Lucifer go bad? How, in metaphorical language, did some angels fall? In their essence, their being, St Thomas insists, they did not, and (being immaterial, and therefore essentially changeless and incorruptible) could not. But they sinned—their evil was and is a moral, not a physical, evil. But how? St Thomas argues, by a process of elimination, that a bodiless, timeless, passionless 'thinking thought', such as angels are conceived to be, could be capable of only one sin, *superbia* (which is perhaps better translated as uppish-ness or ambition or even self-complacency, than as pride) with its concomitant, *invidia* or envy. The essentially Satanic sin is thus autonomy over against God, satisfaction with natural endowments and happiness, and consequent refusal to accept the offer of a share in Divine life, grace, bliss and glory. It is to this that Satan first instigates man ('You shall be as God'), and to the extent that man succumbs to this temptation, he imitates Satan. Satan is the spirit of self-centredness, as against God-centredness.

But Satan cannot *make* man sin. Human sin cannot come about except from man's own willing consent. Satan can tempt, try, test—he can never compel, and if he did compel the result would not be the sin of the one compelled. He can only offer us objects which will lure us from God-centredness, by way of attraction or repulsion. He can entice the human mind and will by presenting to it beliefs, hopes, fears, loves, which, whether illusory or real as far as they go, are not belief, hope, fear and love of the true God and of his designs for man. Or he can oppress the human mind by the presentation of evils which, again, may be real enough as well as illusory, and yet are not the supreme evil of turning from God. Misfortune, sickness, physical or mental, anxiety, melancholy, and the rest, are not sin, but they may induce us to rebellion and despair. Satan may elate us with wishful thinking, or depress us with affliction; either way he is the master of illusion, the father of lies. Either way the intended end-result is the same—to solicit our assent to the half-truth or to illusion as the ultimate truth, and to entice our consent to autonomy over against God and the Divine ordinance.

But how could it be supposed that these *intelligentia intelligibilia*, be they benevolent angels or malevolent demons, would be able to affect the human mind? This is a question to which St Thomas gave a good deal of attention, and again we must confine ourselves to some of his more noteworthy conclusions without recording the arguments that led him to them. The nature and power of angels and demons being, *ex hypothesi*, finite, they cannot directly implant new conceptions into the human intellect any more than they can compel the human will. Neither can they directly form new phantasies in the human imagination. But just as our minds have a certain power to modify and transmute matter for their own ends, so have angels and demons. St Thomas has no doubt at all about what we should now call the physical basis of the human mind, and in particular of the spontaneous products of what we would now call undirected mentation or free phantasy. Still less has he any doubt about the physical basis of feelings, attitudes, moods and emotions. His language about these things is not ours; he takes for granted the whole paraphernalia of medieval physiology, and talks about spirits and humours, spleen and bile, where we might talk about glandular secretions, blood-pressure, and the activity of neurones in the cerebral cortex. But the principle remains very much the same. Agencies which are able to modify the physical preconditions of phantasy, feeling and emotion, will be able indirectly, but none the less effectively, to modify a man's psychology—especially his emotion-toned attitudes, dreams and day-dreams—as well. This ability will not, however, be unlimited. Just as our ability to modify matter is limited by the potentialities and recourses of the matter at our disposal, so will be that of angels and demons. Satan (we may suppose) will exploit the psycho-physical make-up of those he favours with his attentions: the sanguine man will tend to mania, the melancholic to depression—the former will be more amenable to temptations to presumption, the latter to temptations to despair. But only when there is the surrender of the will to these predetermined conditions can there by any question of sin: only then can Satan be said to have triumphed. All the rest, even what might be called diabolic possession, are only means, and in themselves can be equally well an occasion for the triumph of grace as for the triumph of evil. St Thomas knows nothing of the facile distinction, which we find, for instance, in the *Catholic Encyclopedia* and most latter-day Catholic literature, between mental disorder which comes from 'natural causes' and mental disorder which comes from diabolic agency. For him, the devils can *only* act upon the human mind through natural, physical and psychological causes; and conversely all natural physical causes can be instruments of diabolic purposes. Truly enough, there are cases in which paranormal phenomena are more in evidence, but we seem to have no warrant at all for limiting diabolic agency and purpose to these, as some Catholic theologians and psychiatrists to-day seem inclined to do.

Nothing has yet been said about diabolic *possession* as distinct from any other diabolic activity in human affairs. There would indeed seem to be no very hard and fast distinction or any generally accepted definition: it would seem to differ only in degree, and the term is generally used only in those cases in which the subject appears to be under the more or less chronic control of an 'alter ego' which manifests paranormal knowledge or powers. For very good practical reasons the *Roman Ritual* lays down strict conditions for the diagnosis of the possessed if the spectacular rite of solemn, public, exorcism is to be held. It enjoins that this rite is to be performed only very exceptionally and with the greatest caution: the candidate must be able to talk fluently, or at least to understand, languages which he has never learned, or to be telesthaesic or clairvoyant (*ignota lingua loqui pluribus verbis vel loquentem intelligere: distantia et occulta patefacere; vires supra aetatis seu conditionis naturam ostendere, et id genus alia*). But it must not be supposed that possession must be limited to these cases in which the extreme and spectacular measure of solemn public exorcism may be thought to be warranted; neither does the Church limit exorcism (by which is to be understood the invocation of superior, divine and angelic power, to defeat the diabolic) to these solemn occasions. There are regular liturgical exorcisms for all at the times of entry and departure in the life of grace (*i.e.*, for candidates for baptism and in danger of death). Although, for weal or woe, exorcism is less commonly practised than heretofore, its frequent use is encouraged even by the most respectable and conservative authors. We may quote, for instance, Fr Prümmer's *Manual of Moral Theology*: 'For solemn and public exorcism . . . is required the express and specific permission of the Bishop, to whom it belongs to decide if the case in question is truly one of diabolic possession, and whether or not a public exorcism is expedient. . . . But privately and without public solemnity, not only clerics . . . but also laypeople may pronounce exorcisms; for nowhere is this forbidden to the laity . . . and we read in history of such holy laypeople as St Catherine of Siena and St Anthony the Hermit casting out devils. . . .'[1] Prümmer quotes the moral theologian Noldin: 'It is much to be desired that the ministers of the Church should perform simple exorcism more frequently, remembering the words of the Lord, "In my name they shall cast out devils"'—with or without the knowledge of the subject. He warns us, however, that of course exorcism is not automatic: it does not necessarily always produce any immediate or visible effect, or perhaps any effect at all. The exorcist does not act in his own name; he invokes Divine power, a power, that is to say, which is beyond his own control. It is essentially a religious and not a magical act, that is to say, a commission of the affair to higher power, not the utilization of higher power for predetermined ends. The casting out of devils by Beelzebub is recognized by Christ as perfectly possible (Luke 11. 15 ff.), but though the perceptible result may be the same, it is to be sharply distinguished, both in purpose and in method, from casting them out 'by the finger of God'.

Finally, the question must be asked, has not modern psychopathology disposed of the whole conception of diabolic possession? Has not science made it plain that what more credulous ages considered to be the signs of an indwelling devil are now all tabbed and docketed as manic-depression, schizophrenia, epilepsy, hysteria, paranoia and the rest? Do we now not know that what were then thought to be devils are 'really' unassimilated unconscious complexes? It is dangerous to be dogmatic, or to attempt a definitive answer to these questions without a more thorough understanding of all the terms than this writer possesses. We need to beware of assuming too readily that a new name necessarily involves a new explanation which refutes the old. This writer's limited acquaintance with psychiatric literature,

---

1. D. M. Prümmer, O. P., *Manuale Theologie Moralis* (1923), Vol. ii, pp. 463 ff.

confirmed by discussions with psychiatrist friends, strongly
suggests that the names whereby mental diseases are classified
are purely descriptive, and in no sense at all cover etiological
explanations: that is to say they are no more than labels
for certain syndromes or symptoms which are commonly
associated together. To the extent that their respective
psychosomatic 'causes' are understood (which would not
seem, in most cases, to be to any great extent), this would
seem in no way to invalidate such conceptions of their
diabolic origin as we find, for instance, in St Thomas, for
whom, as we have seen, the devil must always employ
psychophysical dispositions and agency. The word 'complex',
although indispensable in psychotherapy, will, it seems, be
found on examination to take us little further. So long as it
could be supposed, as it was by Freud in his earlier and
more sanguine days, that the unconscious consisted of
nothing but the rejected or repressed material that had once
been in the individual's consciousness, the mind's automatically produced waste by-product, there could be some hope
that the devil could be scientifically vapourized. But (as we
have seen elsewhere in this volume) this watertight conception of the unconscious was later abandoned even by Freud
himself, and there can be little doubt that it fails entirely to
'save the phenomena', more especially such paranormal
phenomena as have historically been associated with diabolic
possession. Probably few serious depth-psychologists to-day
would presume to offer any positive definition or complete
causal explanation of the unconscious at all, let alone offer
it as an adequate causal explanation of anything else. For
Jung, as we have seen, the term 'unconscious' is purely a
hypothetical *Grenzbegriff*, a boundary concept which (to
quote from his glossary in *Psychological Types*) 'covers all
those psychic contents or processes which are not conscious,
i.e., not related to the ego in a perceptible way'. His definition of unconscious complexes in the same glossary is particularly interesting and relevant: he calls them 'groups of
psychic contents, isolated from consciousness, functioning
arbitrarily and autonomously, leading thus a life of their

own in the unconscious, whence they can at any moment hinder or further conscious acts'. The definition might be a very good description of Thomist devils — or angels. Nor does the therapeutic success of psychiatry or analysis dispose of diabolic agency. Medieval man rightly saw no inconsistency between subjecting the insane to shock-treatment (a ducking in a cold pond or a vigorous thrashing), or to something like narcotherapy (incubation in a cave, a church or a tomb), and the belief that the devil was behind it all— on the contrary the victim could thus be released from the devil by depriving him of the instruments of his dominion. Whether by exorcism, *i.e.*, the invoking of superior power against the devil himself, or by some psychological or physical performance on or by the sufferer, the hoped-for result was the same—the casting *out* of the devil. We can describe this 'casting out' in the language of depth-psychology as the objectification of the complex, and its dissociation from the conscious ego, but the net result on the symptomatic level does not seem to be anything very different. Deep analysis itself will commonly mean a confrontation with the Adversary, a progressive assimilation of the Shadow, which (as Dom Oswald Sumner has shown in a study on St John Climacus)[1] has much in common with the recorded conflicts of the Desert Fathers with devils.

Finally, it must be made clear that we do not of course contend that 'devils' and 'complexes' are altogether synonymous and interchangeable terms. When the theologian says that somebody is afflicted by the devil, he is describing his situation in relationship to God. When the psychologist says he is suffering from an unassimilated autonomous complex, he is describing an inherent functional disorder. Each speaks a different language; each describes an observed occurrence from a different viewpoint, or, as the scholastics would say, in a different *ratio formalis qua.* Our contention is that the meanings of the two sets of terms (the

1. Oswald Sumner, O.S.B., *St John Climacus; The Psychology of the Desert Fathers* (Guild of Pastoral Psychology, Lecture 63).

theological and the psychopathological) are, however, not mutually exclusive; and we would offer for expert consideration the suggestion that, while the meanings are different, each term may be, and commonly is, referable to the selfsame phenomenon or occurrence.

XI

GNOSIS, GNOSTICISM AND FAITH

IT was the numerous references to gnosis and gnostics
in the writings of C. G. Jung that first gave me any idea
that there might be more to it than a bygone form of non-
sensical, fanatical superstition—of no interest to myself or
to any modern man. One passage in particular aroused
my interest:

[Modern Man] is somehow fascinated by the almost
pathological manifestations of the unconscious mind. We
must admit the fact, however difficult it is for us to understand that something which previous ages have discarded
should suddenly command our attention. That there is a
general interest in these matters is a truth which cannot
be denied, their offence to good taste notwithstanding. I
am not thinking merely of the interest in the psycho-
analysis of Freud, but of the widespread interest in all
sorts of psychic phenomena as manifested in the growth
of spiritualism, astrology, theosophy, and so forth. . . .
We can compare it only to the flowering of Gnostic thought
in the first and second centuries after Christ. The spiritual
currents of the present have, in fact, a deep affinity with
Gnosticism. There is even a Gnostic church in France
to-day, and I know of two schools in Germany which
openly declare themselves Gnostic. The modern movement
which is numerically most impressive is undoubtedly
Theosophy, together with its continental sister, Anthro-
posophy; these are pure Gnosticism in a Hindu dress.
Compared with these movements the interest in scientific
psychology is negligible. What is striking about Gnostic
systems is that they are based exclusively upon the manifestations of the unconscious, and that their moral
teachings do not baulk at the shadow-side of life. Even in
the form of its European revival, the Hindu *Kundalini-
Yoga* shows this clearly. And as every person informed on

191

the subject of occultism will testify, the statement holds true in this field as well.

The passionate interest in these movements arises undoubtedly from psychic energy which can no longer be invested in obsolete forms of religion. . . . .

I do not believe that I am going too far when I say that modern man, in contrast to his nineteenth-century brother, turns his attention to the psyche with very great expectations; and that he does so without reference to any traditional creed, but rather in the Gnostic sense of religious experience. We should be wrong in seeing mere caricature or masquerade when the movements already mentioned try to give themselves scientific airs; their doing so is rather an indication that they are actually pursuing 'science' or knowledge instead of the *faith* which is the essence of Western religions. The modern man abhors dogmatic postulates taken on faith and the religions based upon them. He holds them valid only in so far as their knowledge-content seems to accord with his own experience of the deeps of psychic life.[1]

Readers of Jung's books know how frequent are his references to the gnostics, and how often he compares our present situation with that which confronted them some two thousand years ago. It is worth while to inquire more closely, and perhaps more critically, into gnosis and gnosticism, and to ask what is to be understood by this contrast between the 'faith which is the essence of Western religions' and psychic experience and knowledge. An obstinate adherent of an 'obsolete' creed may be expected to have a somewhat different angle on the subject from that of Dr Jung, but one which may not perhaps be without some psychological and cultural importance.

The subject concerns us, I would suggest, not only for the reasons indicated by Dr Jung, but also because Jungian psychology in its later developments is itself often suspected of something very like gnosticism. 'The Zürich school of Jung', pronounces Hans Prinzhorn, 'no longer has psycho-

---

1. *Modern Man in Search of a Soul*, pp. 238, 239.

therapeutic actuality: it represents a philosophy which, for appreciation, requires esoteric association with the Master.'[1] More recently and more moderately, Dr Karl Stern has qualified his approval of much of Jung's work with the misgiving that it 'frequently leads to some sort of non-committal mysticism, a mysticism without discipline, so that in the end there remains a museum of religious experiences, with Christian, Hindu, Buddhist, etc., collector's items.'[2] Similar qualms have been expressed by Dr E. B. Strauss in his noteworthy presidential address to the Medical Section of the British Psychological Society.[3] This is not the place to examine these charges and misgivings, but they do indicate that gnosticism is by no means an issue with which we have nothing to do. However difficult the task, it may be profitable to inquire into the gnosticism of the past, and the controversies to which it gave rise, in order to see if they have anything to teach us who are confronted with similar problems to-day.

First of all, we must understand that there never was such a thing as gnosticism in the sense of a single sect, or a single coherent body of belief or practice. In *Psychological Types* and elsewhere, Dr Jung follows common usage in speaking of '*The* Gnosis'. This must not mislead us into supposing that there was only one gnosis: in fact there were almost as many gnoses as there were people who called themselves gnostics or who have been called gnostics by later historians. It should be added that these historians are by no means always agreed as to who should and who should not be called gnostics. Nevertheless there is general agreement to label as gnosticism the characteristics of a luxuriant outcrop of

1. *Psychotherapy, its Nature, its Assumptions, its Limitations*, p. 24.
2. 'Religion and Psychiatry', *The Commonweal*, N.Y., Oct. 22, 1948.
3. 'Quo Vadimus?' *British Journal of Medical Psychology*. Vol. XXI. No. 1. pp.1-11. Since this paper was written the charge of gnosticism has been laid against Jung by Martin Buber in *Merkur*, February 1952, prompting a vigorous rejoinder from Jung and a further comment from Buber in the May, 1952, number of the same review.

variegated doctrines, sects and practices which were particularly in evidence in the first two or three centuries of the
Christian era, many of which in greater or less degree
claimed to be themselves in some way Christian. But our
task of getting a clear-cut picture is still further complicated
by the fact that these sects themselves are clearly the
inheritors of ideas, myths and practices which ante-date
Christianity by several centuries; that (with modifications)
kindred ideas, myths and practices survived by many more
centuries those sects which historians are agreed to label as
gnostic; and further by the fact that the claim to gnosis,
and even to be gnostic, was by no means confined to ad-
herents of those sects. There were few more severe critics
of what we would now call gnosticism than the pagan
philosopher Plotinus or the Christian Father Clement of
Alexandria. Yet each claimed *gnosis*; and the latter, in his
Stromata, presents as the true gnostic precisely the mature
wise, contemplative, Catholic.

We must recall that the word 'gnosis' is simply a Greek
word which means knowledge: it is akin to the Sanscrit
jnana, to the Latin *cognoscere*, to the English *I know*. A
gnostic, then, is a Knowing One: one who knows, or claims
to know, things unknown (= unconscious) to the generality
of men. But that much might be said of any of the great
Greek thinkers and scientists: of Socrates, Plato or Aristotle,
none of whom would we think of as gnostics. Indeed, the
gnosis which we find in gnosticism stands in striking contrast
to that sort of 'knowledge' which had been sought by
classical Greek philosophy and science: nay further, the
success of gnosticism would seem to be largely due to the
intellectual bankruptcy and scepticism—the distrust both of
the senses and of the reason—which had been produced by
the later phases of Greek intellectualist thought. In his extensive study of the Hermetic literature and its sources, my
Dominican colleague Professor Festugière has traced that
development.[1] To the Golden Age of Greek inquiry and

---

1. A. J. Festugière, O.P. *La révelation d'Hermés Trismégiste*,
   Vol. 1. (Collection 'Études Bibliques', Paris 1944).

speculation succeeded that amorphous movement which we call Hellenism; to its search for clarity succeeded a search for mystery and a love for mystification; to its confidence in reason, a distrust of, if not a contempt for, reason, and a hankering for some sort of revelation; to its optimistic view of an ordered cosmos, a profound sense of the chaos and misery of the material world; to the classical cult of the human body, a contempt for the body and for all bodily manifestations; to the philosopher's attempt to overcome and transmute phantasy and myth into exact logical concepts and scientific thought, a reversion to myth, or rather the importation and adaptation of foreign myths and the formation of new myths. The philosophers themselves had perhaps contributed much to their own undoing. Already, in that 'Golden Age' itself, sceptics were undermining their basic postulates, and the wandering sophists were making it their business to arouse distrust for the senses and for reason among the populace. The charge of 'atheism' brought against Socrates was not altogether misplaced. Rational thought demanded the existence of God indeed; but the inferentially established God of Aristotle precisely discredited the gods of the myths and cults, and at the same time failed utterly to fulfil the psychological and social functions which they had met. The established religions themselves—the cult of the gods of Olympus, begotten in a much more primitive and less individualized culture—had become increasingly an exteriorized and perfunctory performance, a social ritual which seemed to intensify rather than to satisfy the individual's sense of loneliness, frustration and guilt, to increase his conflicts and need for personal liberation. We must leave to scholars to discuss the origin of the new cults and practices which came to try to fill the vacuum and which, transplanted to Greek soil, became what they know under the general heading of Hellenist 'mysteries'. It must suffice us here, in our own psychological terms, to see in this movement a great reaction of introversion. The psychological law of compensation teaches us that the hypertrophy of one set of functions and attitudes, and the consequent atrophy of their opposites, call forth the compulsive domination of those opposites. Thwarted in its centrifugal flow into an external world which it is unable to assimilate and integrate, the *libido* of necessity is forced to flow back, centripetally, to the interior world of the collective unconscious. We may, I suggest, be still more specific. If it may be fairly said that the heyday of Greek thought and science was characterized in the main by an unprecedented differentiation of extra-verted thinking and sensation, the revenge of introverted feeling and intuition is exactly what we should expect. And this is—speaking generally—exactly what we find. Already in the early pagan Hellenistic writings, 'to the word gnosis there always adheres the suggestion of a knowledge obtained supernaturally [i.e., by way of unconscious sources] . . . an immediate vision as contrasted with a wisdom that comes by seeking'.[1] On the other hand, some of the later 'Christian' gnostics — the Naassenes, for instance — quite explicitly claimed to continue and adapt the pagan Hellenistic mysteries, as we learn from Hippolytus. All forms of gnosti-cism display affinities with the Hellenist myths and mysteries, not only in the supreme value they attribute to immediate interior vision and enlightenment, but also in the very content and pattern of many of their visions as they have been recorded for us.

But at this point it becomes necessary to introduce a distinction between *Gnosis* and a *Gnostic* on the one hand, and *Gnosticism* and what we may call a *Gnosticist* on the other. By the latter I would understand one who, in addition to being a gnostic, makes an 'ism' of his gnosis. The distinction is of importance, if only because it is a profound mistake to suppose that, in rejecting gnosticism, the main body of the Christian Church thereby rejected gnosis or could find no room for the gnostic. It neither did—nor could. The revela-tion which the Church herself accepted, and which gave her her very *raison d'être*, was itself in its origins a gnosis.[2]

---

1. E. F. Scott, *Hastings' Encyc. of Religion and Ethics*, s.v. 'Gnosti-cism'.

2. See *supra*, VII, 'Revelation and the Unconscious', *passim*.

Clement of Alexandria, we have already remarked, claimed to be a gnostic, yet was a determined opponent of gnosticism. St Paul, we may recall, accounted gnosis among one of the most precious of the gifts of the Spirit to the Christian Church, and yet could warn Timothy against the 'godless chatter' and contradictions of what is *falsely* called *gnosis* (I Tim. 6. 20). Elsewhere St Paul passes the remark, of whose truth every analyst is aware, that gnosis 'puffeth up'. We hear Jung's own language in the Latin Vulgate translation of that text: *'scientia inflat'*—gnosis *inflates*.

In this remark we have, I would suggest, a key which will open to us the distinguishing psychological feature of all gnosticism as opposed to mere gnosis. It is customary, and certainly valid, to distinguish gnosticism by certain common characteristics of belief, certain common patterns and features of the myths, certain common practices, which will be found in greater or less degree among all or most of these gnosticist sects. First and foremost among these, though perhaps more often assumed than openly declared, is the primary, the supreme, value attributed to gnosis itself. Most authorities will agree with Professor Legge to define gnosticism as 'the belief that man's place in the next world is determined by the knowledge of it that he acquires in this'.[1] At least tacitly underlying all truly gnosticist writings, is the assumption of the possibility of liberation, not by faith, love or deeds, but primarily, even solely, by knowledge—knowledge of that kind of introverted intuition which we have seen gnosis to be, and understanding 'intuition' with Jung as 'perception by way of the unconscious'.

Closely allied to this, and its necessary consequence, is a twofold dualism. A dualism in the first place of *mankind*: there are those who do know the saving mysteries, and those who do not: there are the favoured initiates, and the rest. Gnosticism is essentially esoteric and sectarian and (in the Greek sense) aristocratic. A dualism in the second place, of *reality*: there is the domain of Spirit, the field of the gnostic's

---

1. Quoted by F. C. Burkitt, *Church and Gnosis*.

own inward-turned vision, which he expressly calls the Pleroma, the Totality, the All; and over against this the world of Matter, which lies outside the Pleroma, and which is Chaos, hostile, inherently evil. Such are the presuppositions of every gnosticist mythos: it will seek to account for the origin of the 'external world', not in terms of a creation, in which a 'good' God sees that what he has called into being is 'good', and 'very good', but in terms of a 'Fall' from the Pleroma. And indeed we have symbols on gnosticist gems and charms in which the material world is pictured as altogether *outside* the mandala. Its mythos and its praxis alike will be concerned to impart a gnosis whereby the soul may be liberated, not in and through, but *from* the 'external world' of matter.

It is not, I think, difficult for the psychologist to see in these very doctrines the expression, we may say, a rationalization, of a familiar psychological condition: indeed the symptoms of that tricky phase of inflated introversion which is a commonplace in most deep analyses, and which indeed is often stabilized in certain paranoiac psychoses. In analysis it is a critical juncture, for it is at once the moment of intensest inward vision, but also the moment of greatest danger when the very fascination of the power of that vision threatens to swallow consciousness and to alienate it from its environment. Dr Jung has written of this condition in the essay I have already quoted: 'These claims of . . . psychic life are so pressing compared to similar claims in the past, that we may be tempted to see in this a sign of decadence. Yet it may also signify a rejuvenation, for as Hölderlin says:

> Wo Gefahr ist
> Wächst das Rettende auch.
> (Danger itself
> Fosters the rescuing power).'

Elsewhere Jung has frequently explained the mechanism of this type of inflation, with its dangers and its opportunities. Ego is identified with the newly activated function of inward vision, intoxicated, overwhelmed by it; and the more perhaps the previous habitual attitude has been extraverted, the greater will be the risk of identification with the new-found, hitherto unconscious, power: with the Saviour-Hero dream-figure who often emerges at this stage to quell the inner forces of evil which had hitherto held the soul captive in its neurosis. The subject is now indeed a gnostic, a Knowing One: one who sees that 'Inner World of Man' which is hidden from Tom, Dick and Harry: nay (and here lies the danger) may fancy himself its lord and master in the very fact of consciously assimilating it; and in seeking to master and possess it he is in danger of becoming increasingly mastered and possessed *by* it.

As we read some of the records and accounts of any ancient gnosticist, we can hardly fail—I think—to recognize traces of these selfsame symptoms. His 'enlightenment', his mastery of the collective, archetypal world has mastered him completely, he is fascinated, overwhelmed, carried away by it. His sectarianism and his esotericism—his conviction that he and his like alone *know*, and that in this knowledge lies salvation—are the inevitable corollary of the identification of Ego with the inward vision. So, too, is his equation of the external material world with evil: his fear and hatred of the body and all its works, which constantly betray themselves in gnosticist tenets. The doctrine of the evil of matter is plainly, I think, a rationalization of the one-sided, introverted attitude. We have heard Dr Jung say that the gnostic teachings 'do not baulk at the shadow-side of life'. That is profoundly true if we understand it to mean that the gnosticists were intrepid explorers of that side of life which is shadow to the 'average sensual man' of to-day. Their writings show them to have been quite at home with the dark and noxious powers of the unconscious: the Serpent, for instance, was the principal cult-object of the Ophite gnostics, and all of them were on more or less familiar terms with demoniacal figures. But this is not to say that they had no 'shadow' of their own. What is light to the 'average sensual man' had become the dark of the gnosticist. The external world was clean outside his *Pleroma, his* All: hostile to it and irreconcilable with it. Absorbed in his lightsome world of phantasy, the world of fact was *his* shadow. For the gnosticist, it would seem, there was but one misfortune, and that was involvement in this material world. There was but one sin—any further involvement in this material world. There was but one repentance required, and that was to turn from the false light of the eyes to the true light of interior illumination. We shall not be surprised to find among some of the gnosticists other symptoms of inflation—if not of alienation. A private terminology, for instance, the use of foreign, preferably Oriental, languages which they plainly did not understand (one gnostic supposed that '*Eloi, Eloi lamma sabacthani?*'—'My God, my God, why hast thou forsaken me?'—was an esoteric Hebrew name for the Divinity). Neologism, also, a love for long, weird, invented words and names, high-sounding but seemingly meaningless: a thing which every alienist knows as a favourite means of asserting one's superiority. We find also in their writings bloated, grandiloquent language, of which Dr Jung has written in his diagnosis of Adolf Hitler.[1] We shall be wise to take with a pinch of salt the assertions of the unfriendly critics of gnosticism of its own time. But neither can we be altogether surprised to be told by Irenaeus that, notwithstanding the gnosticists' contempt for the body and especially for sex (we might say because of it), they had a reputation for erotomanic licentiousness. And his remark that it was chiefly among the wealthier, leisured classes that gnosticism flourished, is again very much what we might expect.

I must insist that these are all generalities. It is doubtless possible to adduce many exceptions from the literature of gnosticism: I can only indicate general trends. I must trust that I shall not be misunderstood in drawing attention to the affinities between certain symptoms of gnosticism and those of inflation and even of certain psychoses. Neither the personal sincerity of these visionaries, nor yet the genuineness or the profundity of their vision is in question. An

1. C. G. Jung. *Aufsätze zur Zeitgeschichte*, pp. 73 ff.

experienced psychologist knows better than to despise even lunatic ravings: he knows that in them he may find an insight into the interior life of the psyche seldom given to the so-called sane and 'normal'. The very concentration of the gnostic's *libido* in the activation of the interior images may make of his loss our profit. And many of the gnostics were certainly no lunatics. In the earlier part of an anonymous gnostic work called the *Pistis Sophia* we may witness, besides many of the more unhealthy features I have mentioned, a courageous process of confrontation with the archetypal mages which can arouse nothing but amazed and reverent admiration.

But it is time to leave these generalities *about* gnosticism, and to take a look at one or two of the gnostic myths themselves. One of the best known of the gnostic sects was that of Valentinus. The Valentinian *mythos*, as recorded by St Irenaeus, opens as follows:

> In invisible and ineffable heights the perfect Aeon called Bythos (Abyss) was pre-existent. Incomprehensible and invisible, eternal and unbegotten, He was throughout endless ages in serenity and quiescence. And with Him was Sigé (Silence). And Bythos conceived the idea to send forth from Himself the Origin of all and committed this Emanation, as if it were a seed, to the womb of Sigé. She then, having received this seed and becoming pregnant, gave birth to Nous (Mind). This Nous was both similar and equal to Him who had produced Him, and He alone was capable of comprehending the greatness of the Father. Along with Him, Aletheia (Truth) emanated.
>
> And Nous, perceiving for what purpose He had been produced, also Himself sent forth Logos (Reason) and Zoë (Life); He is the father of all those who come after him, and the origin and formative principle of the whole Pleroma. By the intercourse of Logos and Zoë were brought forth Anthropos (Man) and Ekklesia (Church, Community). Each of these pairs is masculo-feminine.
>
> These Aeons, having been produced to the glory of the Father, and wishing to glorify Him on their own account, set forth more Emanations in couples. Anthropos

and Ekklesia sent forth *ten* other Aeons, whose names are the following: Bythios (Deep) and Mixis (Mixture); Ageratos (Undecaying, Permanence) and Henosis (Oneness); Autophyes (Self-producing) and Hedone (Pleasure); Akinetos (Immutable) and Synkrasis (Blending); Monogenes (Only-Begotten) and Makaria (Bliss).

Anthropos also, together with Ekklesia, produced *twelve* more Aeons: Parakletos (Strengthener or Comforter) and Pistis (Faith); Patrikos (? Paternal Ancestry) and Elpis (Hope); Metrikos (? Maternal Ancestry) and Agape (Charity); Aeinous (?) and Synesis (Judgment or Conscience); Ekklesiastikos (?) and Makariotes (Blissful); Theletos (masc. proper name from *Thelo=I will*) and Sophia (fem. Wisdom).[1]

Here we have one of those preliminary accounts of the emanation of a variety of figures from an unknown and unbegotten source, in which gnostic myths abound and with which they commonly begin. These are, in all probability, the 'endless genealogies' of which we read in St Paul's First Epistle to Timothy (1, 4). It cannot be said that this example is particularly colourful or inspirational, but in fairness it should be recognized that Irenaeus is giving us only a condensed summary of a probably much more detailed and interesting story. We ourselves hardly expect inspiration from the condensed potted myths of a classical dictionary. But this example has the advantage of being comparatively simple and intelligible. An unnamable Abyss, its Silence (unconsciousness?): the emergence from both of a transcendent co-equal consciousness or *Nous*, and its feminine consort *Aletheia* or Truth. The two pairs of opposites, male and female, in their turn producing a Dekad—five more pairs of opposites, and a Dodekad—six more pairs: it is almost *too* systematic and intelligible. The names, too, are fairly intelligible Greek words; they are almost personified abstractions. Such a myth as this, it seems to me, is hardly

---

1. Irenaeus, *Adversus Haereses*, I. i. 1 and 2, adapted from translation by G. Quispel, 'The Original Doctrine of Valentine', *Vigiliae Christianae*, Vol. I. 1.

a myth at all, it is more like allegorized philosophy. We are very far indeed from the freedom and the innocence, the pure free phantasy uncontaminated by the pale cast of thought, of the primitive pre-philosophical and pre-scientific myth. We are a long way even from that world of the Old Testament or of Homer of which, in her book *On the Iliad*, Rachel Bespaloff writes: 'The ambiguous universe of demoniac forces is just receding from view; the world of rational symbols has not yet been constituted. Magic no longer possesses anything but ineffectual rites to impose on recalcitrant nature, and philosophy has still to invent its own incantations for bringing beautiful abstractions to life. At this possibly privileged moment, in the lyric preaching of the prophets of Israel and in the epic of Homer, a particular mode of thought is evolved which cannot be expressed ... in conceptual form. . . . The religion of *Fatum* and the worship of the Living God both involve a refusal to turn man's relation to the Divine into a technique or a mystical formula'.[1]

But here, in the gnosticist myth, we commonly have the very opposite of all this. The world of systematic, rational symbols has been and gone—nay, rather, has been repressed; but being repressed still exercises its sway, producing a hybrid which is neither pure imagination nor yet clear, methodical, differentiated thought. Its abstractions have been transmuted back into figures of the imagination: no longer are they the seed, but rather the fruit, of intellectual concepts. Moreover, the characteristic gnosticist attitude to transcendent powers is precisely magical as opposed to religious—in Frazer's familiar sense of both these terms—and the elaboration of a technique and a mystical formula to govern man's relation to the Divine describes exactly the gnosticist's aim. We are not surprised to learn that gnosticist *praxis* came to be concerned increasingly with a vast apparatus of charms and amulets and magical pass-words. And so far from the gnosticist 'mode of thought' being 'inexpressible

---

1. R. Bespaloff, *On the Iliad*, p. 112 (New York, Bollingen Books).

in conceptual form', the sample we have seen is almost too readily reducible to scientific concepts. The very word 'Aeon' tells us at once that we have to do with these timeless, spaceless entities which are known to us as archetypal figures of the collective unconscious (as are the 'Eternals' of William Blake). In the word 'Emanation' (another word used by Blake) we must at once recognize our own word 'Projection'. 'The masculine-feminine pair of opposites' is language very familiar to analytical psychologists.

Truly, not all the gnosticist myths of emanations are quite so simple, so rational, so schematic. At the beginning of the *Pistis Sophia* we are introduced to a far more numerous and complicated *dramatis personae*. There we find, not just a handful of Aeons distributed in sets of neatly paired males and females, but a populous Pleroma including the Treasury of the Light, the Head of the Universe, five Marks, five Helpers, three Triple Powers, twenty-four Aeons, twenty-four Invisibles, twenty-four Places, twenty-four Mysteries, three Amens, seven 'other Amens', seven Voices, and an unspecified number of Unbegottens, Self-Begottens with their Begottens, Pairs and Unpaireds, Authentics, Lords, Rulers, Archangels, Angels, Dekans, Ministers, Houses, Spheres, Guardians, as well as the 'Child of the Child' which is 'the Place of the Twin Saviour'. Here certainly we feel somewhat nearer the authentic dreamland of uncontrolled phantasy; the names, too, of these Beings are altogether less rational and more fanciful. In yet other gnosticist myths they often fail to yield any intelligible meaning whatever—though Gematria, the interpretation of names according to the numerical value of their letters, may sometimes produce significant results where dictionaries have failed.[1] But still, one has the impression of being nearer the realm of sophisticated allegory than pure myth.

But far more interesting than these 'endless genealogies', which give us little more than the *dramatis personae* of the subsequent stories—the preliminary differentiations of the

---

1. See Lee and Bond: *Materials for the Study of the Apostolic Gnosis.*

libido involved in the drama of the inner conflicts—are the subsequent stories of the 'Fall' from the Pleroma, and of the redemption of the lost and afflicted soul. In the Valentinian version 'the very latest and youngest of all the Aeons, Sophia-Acamoth [feminine Wisdom] suffers passion and desire apart from her consort'—who is Theletos, masculine controlled and controlling Will. She was, we are told, 'led astray by disordered love, which was actually *hubris*, because she did not [as could Nous alone] comprehend the all-perfect Father'—the Abyss. 'Her passion was a desire to know the Father, for she craved to grasp His greatness. Unable to realize her hope, because she aimed at the impossible, she fell into extreme agonies because of the unfathomable depth of the Father's unsearchable nature and her love for Him. Always yearning for Him, she would have been annihilated in His sweetness and dissolved into His infinite being, had she not been restricted by that power, Horos [the Limit, Finiteness], who exiled her from the Pleroma.'[1] Then, the story goes on, she finds herself imprisoned, tortured and subjected to the tyranny of the other Aeons in the material chaos, which is, we are told (and the psychological insight is breath-taking), the product of her own disordered emotions.

We may, in Freudian terms, read this story as a transparent account of the formation of an Electra complex—the impossible, forbidden passion for the Father; thus understood, the *Horos* or Limit plays the repressive function of the Freudian incest-prohibiting Censor. Or we may, penetrating more deeply, see the Freudian myth itself as a shadow of the more metaphysical yearnings of the finite for the infinite, as doubtless did Valentinus himself. The story continues:

> Left without, alone, Sophia was subject to every sort of emotion: *sorrow* she suffered because she did not obtain understanding; *fear* lest life should leave her as light had already done; moreover she was in *despair*. The root of

---

1. Irenaeus (Quispel) *op. cit.* I. ii. 1.

all this suffering was lack of inward vision (*agnosis*). Thus being bereft of the Logos who had been invisibly present within her, she strained herself to discover that light which had forsaken her, but she could not achieve her purpose because she was prevented by the Limit (*Horos*). . . . This was the origin and essence of Matter, from which this world was made: from her *longing* for the bliss of the Ideal World, the soul of the whole universe derived its origin; earth arose from her *despair*; water from the agitation caused by her *sorrow*; air from the materialization of her *fear*; while fire, causing death and destruction, was inherent in all these elements, as lack of insight (*agnosis*) lay concealed in the other three passions. . . .

When she had been expelled into the empty space devoid of insight (*gnosis*) which she had herself created by her trespass, she brought forth Jesus in remembrance of the higher world, but with a kind of shadow.[1]

Even in the condensed form of the critical Irenaeus, the story cannot be denied pathos and poignancy. We shall not, I suggest, be far wrong in equating this part of the story— the *hubris* and repression of Sophia, her persecution and agony—with the reductive phase of the analytical process. But then, we are told: 'When she had passed through every state of suffering, she raised herself timidly and supplicated the light which had forsaken her, that is Jesus.' There follows the story of her salvation by Jesus, her reintegration into the Pleroma.

In the *Pistis Sophia* (which, if not a work of a Valentinian sect, has many affinities with the Valentinian gnosis) we are told at much greater length the story of her Fall and of her rescue by Jesus. But before taking another glance at this perplexing text—one of the very few actual gnosticist texts that have been preserved for us—I want to say something about the struggle which took place between the main body of orthodox Christians and gnosticism. I do so the more readily because I believe that no more than is gnosticism itself are the issues of that conflict dead in the human psyche

---

1. Irenaeus (Quispel) *loc. cit.* I. iv. and I. xi.

of to-day. I have already suggested that every analysant is in some measure a gnostic (I do not say a gnosticist): a Knowing One who has experienced some interior vision of the archetypal, collective psyche—or at least (like the outer fringe of the old gnostic's followers) is probably involved in a transference on someone who has. And whether we profess orthodox Christianity or not, we are all in more or less conscious degree inheritors also of its distinctive values and attitudes.

Whether we share their beliefs or not, let us put ourselves in the position of those early Christians who accepted the Gospels and the Apostolic writings. Already, as Professor Buber, writing as a Jew, has said, there was a fundamental opposition between the Old Testament revelation and the fundamental assumptions and attitudes of the gnosticist.[1]

For the Christian, endeavouring to be faithful to the Gospel witness, this opposition was immeasurably increased. We cannot read the Christian Fathers of the early centuries, especially Irenaeus and Tertullian and Hippolytus, without seeing that they saw in gnosticism a very serious menace which threatened the original purity and simplicity of the Gospel message, and the tradition received from the first disciples. The gnosticists were probably not very numerous, but they were wealthy and influential. We know that Valentinus himself aspired to the chief bishopric of Christendom—the See of Rome. The case against gnosticism reduced itself to a few very simple heads which seemed to cut clean across what was believed to be the very essence of the Christian revelation. They may be briefly summarized.

In the first place there was the very sectarianism and exclusivism of the gnostic. Each gnosticist sect was a chosen, superior, favoured people, alone in possession of the saving knowledge. This cut clean across the Christian conviction that Christ's life and teaching and death and rising had been for all men, a manifestation that 'God wills all men to be saved, and come to the knowledge of the truth'; that there

---

1. See *Mamre* by Martin Buber, pp. 11 ff., also pp. 109, 142 (Melbourne University Press, 1942).

was consequently no more a particular Chosen People, but a universal, what they already called a Catholic, Church. The poor had had the Gospel preached to them, the saving message was to be proclaimed from the housetops. 'Here,' the Epistle to the Colossians had said (3. 11), 'there cannot be Greek nor Jew, circumcised nor uncircumcised, barbarian nor Scythian, slave nor free man, but Christ is All and in all.'

Yes; not only *for* all, but All and in all. The Christian faith, they believed, was '*kath holon*'—Catholic, in accord with the whole—not only because it was for *all* men, but because it was for the *whole* man, and no mere part of him. In the Valentinian gnosis (and this feature is common to gnosticism) not only was liberation not for everybody, it was not for the *whole* of each. It was only *for* the Pneuma— (the spirit, which the Valentinians expressly identified with the imagination) *from* the body and *from* the psyche. The Christian revelation of the Incarnation and the Resurrection of the flesh was a message of salvation of the whole man, in and through the flesh. One and all the Christian gnosticists were docetists: the Christ-Saviour only *appeared* to be a man, to be born of Mary, to suffer and to die. Matter was evil, the whole world of exterior sensation was repudiated in the supposed interests of its opposite, interior intuition. Christ, if not one substance with the Absolute, the Abyss, the All-Father, was certainly some divine Spirit, an Aeon from the Pleroma; but for that very reason he must 'abhor the Virgin's womb', the evil world of generation, and at most could pass through it, himself uncontaminated, as 'water through a pipe'—as Valentinus himself put it. This transcendent Entity might somehow have operated every now and again through the man Jesus; but *become* a Man, really suffer and die in fact and history, in the sphere of sensation as well as of intuition—that was unthinkable. The apostolic witness, on the contrary, was to the effect that Jesus was himself the Logos, not an inferior Aeon but the *Nous* co-equal with the All-Father, and that he was made flesh and dwelt among us in time and space—the world of fact and sensation.

The hidden mystery of existence was manifested precisely in space and time and history, and within the field of the external senses. 'That which was from the Beginning, whom we have *heard*, whom we have *looked* upon, and *touched* with our hands—this Word of Life; the Life was made *manifest*, and we *saw* it . . . that which we have *seen* and *heard* we proclaim to you also, so that you may have fellowship with us: and our fellowship is with the Father and with his son Jesus Christ. . . . And this is the message we have heard from him and proclaim to you, that God is Light, and in him there is no darkness at all.'[1]

These words from the beginning of the first Epistle of John might almost have been written—perhaps they were written—to underline the opposition of primitive Catholic and Evangelical Christianity to gnosticism. It is the opposition of those committed to the Whole to the view which would restrict the Whole to a Part. It is instructive to note in passing, that according to the Catholic Irenaeus himself, while the Catholics were antagonistic to gnosticism, the gnosticists were not antagonistic to Catholicism. They were something that Irenaeus found much more trying: they were patronizingly superior. Catholicism, they held, was all very well for *hoi polloi*, for the average Tom, Dick or Harry. The esoteric gnostic revelations were not anyhow for such as these; and they, the gnosticists, alone really *knew*—as the Catholics did not—what the Catholic beliefs and practices themselves really meant. Again we have a sidelight on gnosticism which is by no means out of date.

But the opposition cuts deeper than that; and here we touch upon Dr Jung's antinomy of gnosis and faith. Without committing Dr Jung, I think we may express this antinomy best in the words of Bacon: '*Animus ad amplitudinem Mysteriorum pro modulo suo dilatetur; non Mysteria ad angustias animi constringantur*', 'Let the conscious mind, so far as it can, be open to the fullness of the mysteries; let not the mysteries be constrained to fit the narrow

---

1. I John 1, 1-5.

confines of the mind'. In the first we have the attitude of *faith* in the Unknown; in the second the attitude, not necessarily of gnosis, but certainly of gnosticism. The first is the attitude of religion, humbly accepting a Divine revelation it knows it cannot fully comprehend; the second is essentially the attitude of magic, seeking to subject the mystery to the comprehension of Ego, and utilizing transcendent power and knowledge for its own ends and aggrandizement. The message of the Gospels and the apostolic writings was a message of salvation by *faith*; and by faith operative in *works* of *love*. Gnosticism says in effect: to know is all. The enlargement of consciousness, inward-turned to the Realm of the Mothers, the *'mysterium tremendum et fascinans'* of the archetypes, away from the chaos of the hard, cruel world of fact and human history and society: there lies salvation. Know the names and origin of the archetypes and projections of the unconscious; know their conflicts and triumphs and falls and recoveries; and you will be their master and will be saved. Not so, says Faith; that is the very *hubris* of your own Sophia-Acamoth: her lust for the impossible comprehenson of the fathomless Abyss, which imprisons her in the very matter which she despises and subjects her to the cruel tyranny of the very archetypes she would excel. Let her rather recognize the insolubility of her conflict and the impossibility of her yearning, let her be thankful for the restraint of the *Horos* who saves her from annihilation in infinite unconsciousness, let her open her mind to the mysteries and not seek to enclose the mysteries in her mind. But then she will be no longer a gnosticist *Sophia*; but perhaps she will be *Pistis Sophia—Faith-Wisdom*.

For while gnosticism has no room for faith, faith has room, indeed need, for gnosis. Gnosis cannot be a substitute for faith, but the possession of gnosis is part and parcel of the gifts to the faithful *Ecclesia*. In the Body of Christ are many members, each with their several functions: and those of the gnostic are among the most honourable. Without the intuitive understanding of what in faith she believes, the Church herself would be incomplete—uncatholic. But it is gnosis *in* faith, not in despite of faith; and it is for the benefit of the whole body and not only for the individual member. Gnosis is not supreme: it must be ruled by Faith and Hope and Charity, and the greatest of these is Charity. 'If I have prophetic powers,' writes St Paul in a famous passage, 'and understand all mysteries and all *gnosis*, and even if I have all faith, so as to move mountains, but have not love, I am nothing. . . . Love is patient and kind, love is not jealous or inflated, is not arrogant. . . . Love never ends; but as for *gnosis*, it will pass away. For our *gnosis* is imperfect, but when the perfect comes, the imperfect will pass away. . . .' (I Cor. 13). The Church also will have her introverted intuitives, her contemplatives and mystics, nay, her alchemists and cabbalists. She will have her esoterics: those with a deeper gnosis of the Divine mysteries. But never with the idea that theirs is a superior perfection denied to mankind at large. Union with God, if we may adopt the useful Sanscrit terminology, is not *only* to be attained by *Jnana* (or *Gnosis*) nor by *Jnana* without Faith and Love; but also and no less, given Faith and Love, by *Bhakti* and *Karma*. And indeed, selfless works of love and service enjoy a certain priority, for it is in the visible image of God in man that the invisible God revealed in Jesus Christ is to be worshipped and served.

I have a suspicion that in the perplexing first two documents of the *Pistis Sophia* we have a record, radically gnosticist indeed, of the titanic psychological visions and struggles of a gnosticist, probably a Valentinian, who has felt and faced the tension of his gnostic vision with the counterclaims of Catholic and Evangelical Christianity. This theory would require a paper in itself to develop; but it is a hypothesis which would solve many of the difficulties which the text has presented to scholars, and, read in this light, it may be found to be a work which many of us in our day may study with personal profit. Here the whole setting is typically gnosticist. After the introduction to the complex heavenly hierarchy, of which we have already spoken, we are shown Jesus on the Mount of Olives, eleven years after the Resurrection, talking to his disciples. They are well content with the revelation he has already made, but that had had to do only with the God of this world of change and decay, and he has more to tell them; this he does from a blinding light which terrifies them. Jesus, here, it progressively dawns upon them, is no inferior Aeon, he is one with the First Mystery which is also the twenty-fourth encompassing all others. His humanity is still, perhaps, a little misty and ethereal, but we are left in no doubt that it is also with the historical Jesus of flesh and blood that we have to do, and there is no attempt, as in regular gnosticism, to divorce the man Jesus from the celestial Saviour-Christ. He relates how he has discovered Sophia, cast out from the Pleroma by her proud lust for the Father; but she has fallen into another error, and a still greater corresponding misfortune. She has mistaken the light of the Aeons for the One True Light in which she had previously believed. It is her constant *faith* in the True Light, the Light which she rediscovers in Jesus, that saves her. She is not just Sophia— she is Pistis Sophia—Faith-Wisdom. Here we have gnosis indeed, but paradoxically it is a gnosis of salvation not *by* gnosis but by faith; one in which the perils attached to the gnosis of the Aeons are exposed, and Jesus is Saviour precisely in transcending, in conquering, and even upsetting the whole Pleroma of the gnosticists. The story is told as a dialogue between Jesus and his disciples. It is of extraordinary psychological interest, for it is a lesson not only in psychological insight into the interior world, but still more in psychological courage and patience, and perhaps most of all in its insistence that, at each stage of the successive vision, its content is to be linked up with conscious material: in this case the Psalms and the other Scriptures with which the Disciples are already consciously familiar.

I am not contending that in the *Pistis Sophia* we shall find the pure milk of the Gospels, or an unimpeachably correct statement of Catholic belief. We certainly have nothing of the sort. But if it is not, so to speak, the case history of a gnosticist whose response to his very gnosis is freeing him from gnosticism, and who is discovering the 'rescuing power' in the 'danger itself', I must join my elders and betters in agreeing that we do not know what it is all about. Towards the end of the story, even the very sectarianism and exclusiveness of gnosticism is repudiated. 'Maria the Magdalen, said she to Jesus, "My Lord. . . . Not only are we now compassionate of ourselves, but we are compassionate of all the races of mankind, that they should be delivered from all the Judgments that are cruel . . . that they should not come into the hands of the Rulers [i.e., the planetary, archetypal Forces] that are cruel, and that they should be delivered from the hands of the Receivers [presumably their passive counterparts] which are cruel in the Darkness".'

It is perhaps to be regretted that the contemporary Christian critics of gnosticism were not always better psychologists. Irenaeus obviously is striving hard to be just and not to misrepresent the gnosticists;[1] but he is no psychologist. He is a busy, conscientious diocesan bishop and pastor, mainly anxious that the flock entrusted to him be not led astray by hirelings, and, inevitably, much more concerned with *what* the gnosticists said, with what it threatened to the faith and practice of which he believed himself the guardian, than with trying to understand sympathetically *why* they said it. Even he, and still less Tertullian, commonsense men that they were, cannot restrain themselves from making fun of the gnosticist's phantasies. They are easy game. Origen and Clement of Alexandria are no less firm, but perhaps more understanding—and indeed perhaps more experienced in the labyrinthine ways of the mind and the functions of its phantasies and mysteries; we may say perhaps, in the very crooked lines whereby God sometimes writes straight. I, too, have dared to be critical, but I trust I have not mocked. There is a still greater figure in Catholic history, whose scalding, ironic words forbid me. He himself, in the course of the long and intrepid spiritual struggle which

1. See the monumental work of F. M. Sagnard, O.P., *La Gnose valentinienne et le témoignage de Saint Irenée* (Paris, 1947).

he relates in his *Confessions*, had had his gnosticist phase, and had been an adherent of the great Manichaean movement which stands in direct line of succession to the gnostic sects of earlier centuries, and which possessed many of their distinctive features. I cannot do better than conclude my notes on gnosticism with the words whereby, in later years, St Augustine prefaced some of his:

'Let those be angry with you,' he says to the gnosticists of his time, 'who do not know with how great toil truth is attained, or how difficult it is to avoid mistakes. Let those be angry with you who do not know how rare a thing it is, and how hard a thing, to be free from the phantasies which arise within us. Let those be angry with you who know not how painful is the healing of the inner eye of man if it is to behold its true Sun—not that image of the Sun in the sky which you know, but that Sun of which it is written, "The Sun of Righteousness is risen upon me", and of which the Gospel says, "This was the true Light that enlighteneth every man that comes into this world". Let those be angry with you who do not know what sighs and tears are needed if the real God is to be known—even in the tiniest degree. Lastly, let those be angry with you who have never been led astray, as you, and I, have been led astray. But for me to be angry with you, is utterly impossible. . . .

'But in order that neither may you be angry with me . . . I must beg this one favour of you. Let us, on both sides, lay aside all arrogance. Let us not, on either side, claim that we have already discovered the truth. Let us seek it together as something which is known to neither of us. For then only may we seek it, lovingly and tranquilly, if there be no bold presumption that it is already discovered and possessed. But if I may not ask so much as this of you [Knowing Ones], grant this at least that I may listen to you, and talk with you, as with people whom I, at least, do not claim to know.'[1]

---

1. *Contra Epistolam Manichaei*, cap. 3.

XII

THE DYING GOD

'IT is expedient for you that one man should die for the people, and that the whole nation perish not.' These words are attributed by the Fourth Gospel (John 11. 50) to Caiaphas, and it tells us that 'he spoke not of himself, but being the high priest for that year, he prophesied'. We are also told that it was this official utterance of the High Priest that decided the authorities to put Jesus of Nazareth to death.

This remarkable fact is nowhere mentioned, so far as I can recall, in the twelve large volumes of Sir James George Frazer's *The Golden Bough*. Yet the pronouncement of Caiaphas might well have served as a motto for the whole work. Frazer, combining encyclopaedic knowledge with rare literary grace and dramatic effect, and with much of the excitement of a detective story, set out to solve a mystery— the mystery of a haggard, hunted 'priest of the wood' by the shores of Lake Nemi long ago, a priest who had plucked a golden bough, a priest who had murdered his predecessor, and who was now sleeplessly and anxiously awaiting his own murderer. Clue leads to clue as Frazer's vast researches fan out into space and time, ransacking the annals of history, archæology, the literature of all nations, comparative religion, anthropology and folklore. Slowly there emerges the hint of a world-wide pattern of belief and practice according to which it is expedient that one should die for the people that the whole nation perish not; that the slayer and the slain should alike be some embodiment of divinity, a divine king or priest, or perhaps his son or some representative or substitute or effigy, whose death and torment is somehow necessary if the life or power which he embodies, and on which the people depend, is to survive or revive. Frazer's researches also showed the astonishing resemblances between many of the rites and ceremonies—usually associated with a New Year—which accompany this death and revival, among peoples widely separated in space and time as well as levels of culture.

Professor Frankfort has told us[1] that the facts are not actually quite so simple as Frazer—and, more conspicuously, some of Frazer's followers and codifiers—might lead us to suppose. He has brought weighty objection to our calling it a *pattern* at all, and it must be agreed that the word implies something far too rigid. But it is difficult to find another word which would describe what, we are agreed, needs to be described: namely, several similar phenomena which, in greater or less number, are commonly though not invariably found clustered together in a similar situation or context. But there can be little doubt that eagerness to find resemblances has obscured differences which, especially to the student of a particular culture, are at least equally significant. That discussion must be left to experts in that field.

But there is another question of similarities and differences to which Professor Frankfort has only alluded. He told us that, 'We can gauge the significance of such symbols as the divine child, the suffering mother, the god who passes through death to resurrection, because they recur in Christianity'. He also reminded us that Frazer and his generation claimed to see their ' "dying god" behind the figure of Christ, a totemic feast behind the Last Supper . . . a mother goddess in a primitive sense behind the Mater Dolorosa'— and (I may add) very much more in the way of impressive similarities between Christian beliefs and practices and these so-called fertility rites and cults.

Let us look briefly at a few of the facts—only a few out of a vast abundance. Frazer himself noted hundreds of parallels in the practices, beliefs, games, folklore and rituals of so-called Christian and so-called pagan peoples, all pointing to some common ancestry or inspiration in the rites of the dying

---

1. In previous talks in the series broadcast by the B.B.C.

and rising god. But he did not always distinguish beliefs, and customs found locally and unofficially in Christian countries, but many of which would hardly pretend to be specifically Christian, from those which we find are given official and universal recognition in traditional Christian creeds and liturgies. Even if we confine ourselves to the latter, the resemblances to the so-called *pattern* of the rites of Spring, is unmistakable.

Nearly all the features with which Frazer and his followers have familiarized us may be witnessed to this day during the celebration of Holy Week and Easter in any church where the ancient rites of the Eastern or Western Churches are performed in their fullness. They begin with the *rite d'entrée*, the ritual of entry into a holy place—or mood—on Palm Sunday: the solemn procession to the church, the knocking-on and opening of its doors; there 'golden boughs' of palm and olive are carried and distributed to be (as for Virgil's Aeneas) the passport to the coming mysteries. There follows the narration of the events to be re-enacted. Then, on succeeding days, there is the alternation of rejoicing and lamentation (in the Greek church it is still called the *Threnos*); mourning not only *for* the condemned, dying and dead one, but *with* him in mystical identification. There is the sacred banquet, the sacrificial communion, the setting-up of the *stauros* (the pole or cross), the solemn extinguishing and later kindling of light and fire; there are traces at least of the 'light-mindedness' or 'folly' in the banging of books at the end of the service of tenebrae—and in some southern countries where it is accompanied with fireworks and general pandemonium, it can amount to very great folly indeed. There is the recitation of the story of creation, and of previous deliveries of the people. There is the pouring of water on the earth; and though there is not the *Hierosgamos*, the sacred mating of the priest-king with the representative of the goddess, there are unmistakable resemblances to it when the flaming Paschal candle, representing Christ, is plunged into the font to the accompaniment of prayers whose references to sexual union and fertility are explicit. At Easter (and the

Venerable Bede tells us the name is that of an old goddess of dawn) there are the baptisms (the initiations or illuminations of neophytes), there is (or at least there was—it still survives in the Dominican ritual) the search for the lost and hidden life which had died: the Easter morning search for, and triumphant return of, the Bread of Life which had been hidden and ignored since Good Friday. The whole cycle of fast and feast reaches its climax in the Easter Sunday Mass, the enthronement and offering of the risen conqueror of death returned from the underworld; the partaking by the faithful of his reunited body and blood.

It may be said that these are just so many heathenish adulterations of the pure milk of the Gospel. But the matter cannot be disposed of so easily on any hypothesis. For the Catholic or Orthodox Christian who joins, for instance, in the Palm Sunday procession is not usually thinking of Nemi or Virgil or Frazer or even of the crops; he is thinking of the Gospel story of the entry of Christ into Jerusalem and his welcome with palm and olive branches; and so it is throughout the rest of the celebrations. And it is just when we turn to the Gospel stories of the Passion and Resurrection of Christ that the similarities become quite astonishing.

Frazer himself noticed this. He had a section on the 'Crucifixion of Christ' which is very striking. In his later editions he relegated it to an appendix, because, as he said, 'the hypothesis which it sets forth has not been confirmed by subsequent research, and is admittedly in a high degree speculative and uncertain'. This hypothesis was to the effect that Jesus Christ was compelled to play the actual role of victim in the cruel ritual murder of a substitute for a 'dying god'—if not by the Roman soldiers in celebration of their Saturnalia, then more probably by the soldiers of Herod and the mob in celebration of Purim, which Frazer held to be a Jewish adaption of the Asiatic equivalent of the Saturnalia, the Sacaea. His quotation from Dio Chrysostom's description of the latter is certainly impressive: 'They take one of the prisoners condemned to death, and seat him upon the king's throne, and give him the king's raiment, and let him lord it. . . . But afterwards they strip and scourge and crucify him.' Whatever is to be thought of the hypothesis, the resemblances to the Gospel story are unmistakable. And there are many more which Frazer did not mention. Not only is there the continual parallel of the Gospel narrative and the Church ritual, and of the latter with so many features of the so-called pattern of the dying god, but there are several other incidents in the Gospel to remind us of features frequent, if not universal, in the 'pattern'. There is, for instance, the *agōn* in the garden, though it is now—and this is very significant—an interior and not an external combat. We note that in fact the external combat is expressly declined when Jesus bids Peter to sheath his sword (Matt. 26. 51-52). There is also the striking of the victim by the servant of the high priest. We notice that at the Last Supper Jesus Christ not only takes the customary corn and fruit, bread and wine, it is the Passover meal to which he gives a new significance. The Old Testament had already given an added meaning to what appears to have been part of an older fertility rite; now the like meal is a 'new testament' in flesh and blood. The daughters of Sion weep for him on his way to Calvary, much as their mothers had wept there centuries before for the dying Corn-God, Tammuz—to the horror of the prophet Ezekiel. There are many parallels in the literature of the 'dying god' to the opening of tombs and the raising of the dead which, we read in St Matthew's gospel, accompanied the Crucifixion. The subsequent 'descent into hades', the underworld, of which we read, not indeed in the Gospels but in the epistles of St Peter and St Paul, is one of the more universal features of the 'pattern'. Very striking, too, is the Easter morning search of the women for the body of the dead Christ; and we notice that it is not Mary the Virgin but Mary the sinner, to whom much had been forgiven because she had loved much, who takes the lead. 'They have taken away my Lord, and I know not where they have laid him,' she says. In her language the word for 'my lord' must have been *Adoni*; and only some inhibition of mistaken reverence can prevent us from being reminded of Aphrodite, seeking and weeping for Adonis, 'for he is dead'. According to another, St Luke's, account, the woman's search is greeted with the reproachful question, 'Why seek ye the living among the dead? He is not here; he is risen.' And however it may be pictured or conceived, as a return from departed life as in Mesopotamia, as life issuing from only apparent death as in Egypt, as a rebirth of the individual *mystes* as at Eleusis, or as a final and definitive attainment of life in a new and immortal dimension as by St Paul, the answer to the search of Aphrodite or Astarte or Isis or Mary Magdalene is the same. 'The King is dead; long live the King' is the constant motif of the mysteries of the dying god in all their varieties and guises, elevations and debasements.

We have stressed—it may be thought grossly overstressed —some similarities between the Christian and pagan mysteries. Before turning to discuss their very important differences, and what a believing Christian is to make of all this, something should be said about symbols and symbolism, and about the very important contribution which the psychology of the unconscious has made to this subject in general, and to that of the dying god in particular.

Whether we are comparing the Christian and pagan mysteries, or whether we are comparing pagan 'dying gods' among themselves, we must not fail to distinguish—at least in principle—between a symbol as a bare observable or recorded fact, and the meaning or interpretation of the fact. We cannot at once argue from a similarity of fact to a similarity, let alone an identity, of meaning, as Frazer too often seemed inclined to do. Whatever a serpent on a pole 'meant' to an Israelite in the desert, or to a fourth-century Greek, it did not mean, as for us, that its bearers belong to an Army Medical Corps; but nor can I say *a priori* that those 'meanings' for different minds (and meaning is meaningless except in relation to some mind) are unrelated. All must depend on the evidence of those minds themselves. And here I would repeat and emphasize what Professor Frankfort has said so excellently: 'The appeal of religious symbols is not dependent on a correct understanding of their original meaning. Once created, their lasting forms challenge the imagination, they may be charged with a new significance which they themselves called forth, and may stimulate a new integration in alien surroundings.' Incidentally, that is a very perfect description of the functioning of what Jung calls archetypes. For these are not something fixed and immutable, uninfluenced by the stimuli that arouse them, or by the new significance which they themselves call forth. As Dr Austin Farrer, talking of our dying god or divine priest-king, has well put it: 'When human kings arose, invisible divine kings stood behind their thrones. . . . Now, if kings arose with divine support, we might suppose that the divine king was already known: for how can the human king be clothed with divine authority except by a divine king already acknowledged? But then, on the other hand, until men have seen human kings, how can they know what a divine king would be? In fact, the human king and his divine archetype arise at once; each makes the other.'[1]

Psychologists tell us that symbols are polyvalent. This means that the same symbol can have a variety of meanings —though usually interrelated meanings—for different minds, or even for the same mind. But it means also that the meaning of a true symbol is not exhausted when we have found some rational formula which will define or 'explain' it. A living symbol is very much more than a shorthand device for what can be expressed more fully and accurately. A symbol cannot only be thought about and restated conceptually, it can also be imagined, intuited, seen or heard, felt. A symbol, as we say, 'does something to us', it moves us, shifts our centre of awareness, changes our values. Whether it is just looked at or heard, acted out, painted out, written out or danced out, it arouses not only thought, but delight, fear, awe, horror and the rest. Here we touch on one of the big differences between Freud and Jung. Freud seems to have viewed the symbol *only* as a source of disguised, and usually disagreeable, information for the resisting consciousness.

---

1. Austin Farrer, *The Glass of Vision*, p. 99.

Jung saw that it was very much more than that; that it was
the very instrument which, just because it was polyvalent,
transformed consciousness itself and thereby the sick
personality. This is what Jung means when he calls the
symbol the psychological machine which transforms energy
into work, much as a turbine transforms the untamed, useless
energy of a torrent into power that can be controlled and
applied. He suggests incidentally that the so-called fertility
rites did have an actual causal effect on the crops and the
food supply; not indeed directly by sympathetic magic, but
by releasing, directing, transforming the otherwise dis-
sipated instinctive energy of primitive peoples into actual
agricultural labour, which without them would have been a
psychological impossibility.

However that may be, the analytical psychologist does
watch the actual functioning of symbols produced in dream
and phantasy by his patients, and by himself. He sees something at least of their actual causes and effects, and the role
they consciously or unconsciously play in moulding character
and behaviour for weal or woe; and he has a language or a
jargon into which to translate their 'meaning'. And he finds
this very noteworthy fact, that the old symbols and images
and rites which we associate with the dying god are still
brought forth spontaneously in the dreams of modern people,
and are still, consciously or otherwise, immensely potent in
shaping their life. The *rite d'entrée*, the plucking of the tree of
life, the quenching and kindling of light and fire, the combat,
the spilling of blood and water, the being made a fool of, the
descent into the underworld, the search for the buried
treasure—all these, in countless different guises, are regular
features of analytical healing—just as they have been found
to be regular features of the seeming gibberish of the old
alchemists. But most notably, he finds the *motif* of the central
sacrifice, the putting to death of the old ruler of the personality, the old king or divinity, or mediator with life and
divinity, the dominant psychological function of the sick
personality, whose powers have waned, whose usefulness
has been outlived, and who must die if a more robust suc-

cessor is to take his place, and healthy life is to revive. For always the priestly law holds good, in the individual as in society: It is expedient that one should die for the whole, lest the whole perish. The dying god is not just an obsolete museum-piece for the study of archæologists. Analytical psychology has limitations which we must yet consider; but at least it has shown that the dying god is not dead: he is still very active and alive in our minds.

We have drawn attention to some of the striking similarities between—on the one hand—the traditional Christian rites of Holy Week, and several incidents in the Gospel narrative of the Passion and Resurrection of Christ, and—on the other hand—the so-called pattern of the dying and rising god which emerged largely as the result of Frazer's researches in *The Golden Bough*. Fifty years or so ago it seems to have been widely supposed that these discoveries of similarity between Christian and pagan mysteries, collected by scholars like Robertson Smith and Frazer, popularized in tendentious paper-backs by writers like Grant Allen, somehow made nonsense of Christianity. And it must be admitted that they did make nonsense of a great many nineteenth-century ideas *about* Christianity; they made it impossible at least to regard it just as some sort of transcendental ethic, dropped ready-made from the sky, without roots in the earth, in history, without relevance to the basic and perennial needs of human society and the human psyche, or to the forms and forces that shape them. But I remember when, as a boy, I read one of those books published by the Rationalist Press, it had just the opposite effect on me to that intended. The Christian Scriptures and the Catholic rites to which I was accustomed, without losing their wonted sense, gained a quality and a sense of which my pastors and catechisms had told me nothing; a sense of solidarity with creation, with the processes of nature, with the cycles of the seasons. Dramatizations of the processes of vegetation they might be, but had not Christ himself drawn the analogy between the Christian self-sacrifice and the grain of wheat which must die if it is to bear fruit? Moreover, these books gave me a new sense of solidarity with humanity as a whole; whatever else I was doing when I attended Mass, or followed the Church's calendar of fast and feast, I was doing something not entirely different from what men and women of every creed and colour seemed to have been doing since the world began.

Frazer himself saw that his 'discoveries' were as patient of a Christian interpretation as of the evolutionist one which he himself favoured. He wrote: 'In the great army of martyrs who in many ages and in many lands . . . have died a cruel death in the character of gods, the devout Christian will doubtless discern types and forerunners of the Saviour—stars that heralded in the morning sky the advent of the Sun of Righteousness—earthen vessels wherein it pleased the divine wisdom to set before hungering souls the. bread of heaven. The sceptic, on the other hand, with equal confidence, will reduce Jesus of Nazareth to the level of a multitude of other victims of a barbarous superstition, and will see in him no more than a moral teacher, whom the fortunate accident of his execution invested with the crown of a god.'

However startling to our parents, these 'discoveries' of similarity between the pagan and Christian mysteries were nothing new to the Christian church. The early Christians did not indeed have a Frazer, a Robertson Smith, a Lewis Spence, a Lord Raglan, a Hocart to ransack the literature of the world for traces of the dying god, and to collect the results conveniently in books. They did not know, as we know, how agelong and widespread they are; but the rites of spring and the dying god were being enacted, one way or another, by their non-Christian neighbours on their very doorsteps, and their writers were much occupied in trying to account for the resemblances. It is noteworthy that they were, in one important respect, more sympathetic with Frazer's 'sceptic' than with Frazer's 'devout Christian': at least they were more vocal about the barbarity and superstition in the pagan rites than with talk about the types and forerunners, although this aspect did not escape them. The similarities they usually accounted for very simply; they were specious imitations and anticipations, inspired by the devil, to lure souls from the way of limitless self-sacrifice exemplified and demanded by Christ. Of course, if we regard Christianity as just one religion among many, that is a piece of gratuitous sectarian prejudice. But they did not, and could not, so regard it. With St Augustine they held that the coming of Christ had made religions, in the plural, obsolete and retrogressive. Whatever elements of truth and beauty they might have contained, along with much so manifestly false and ugly, they could now be only barriers fulfilling a diabolic purpose. For the devil, for them, was precisely the spirit which sets up the relative as a substitute for the absolute, the part for the whole, the reflexion for the reality, the shadow for the substance. 'Types and shadows have their ending, for the newer rite is here,' we still sing in a hymn translated from St Thomas Aquinas. In the Gospel story they saw the realization alike of the hope of Israel and the desire of the nations; and as St Paul, writing to the Galatians, saw something blasphemous and outmoded in continuing the rites which expressed Israel's ancient hopes now that they were fulfilled, so early Church Fathers saw something blasphemous and outmoded in the continuation of the pagan rites that expressed the world's desires.

But nowadays we need a more empirical and factual approach to the problem; and we notice that this levelling down of Jesus Christ to just one of the countless dying gods, ignores some important facts. As Professor Frankfort was telling us about the differences between the dying gods of Mesopotamia, of Egypt, and of the Greek mysteries, it occurred to me how remarkably those very differences were combined in the Gospel story and in the interpretations we find of it in the Acts and Epistles of the apostles. That opens a line of inquiry which might well be followed up and extended. But more important are the entirely new elements that the Christian story introduces into the dying god pattern, and which, I suggest, transform it completely. Remembering that we must distinguish, but cannot divorce, the symbolic fact and the symbolic meaning, we may briefly examine some of its features which, taken together, set the Christian story poles apart from the general 'dying god' pattern.

In the first place, and most obviously, it is *historical*. I am not now raising the question whether the events related in the Gospels 'really happened'. I am only concerned to point out that they are related *as if* they had really happened, and that their whole point for the writers lay in the belief that they really happened. However many features we may find in the accounts of the Passion and Resurrection which resemble those of ritual and mythology, those features are embedded in matter-of-fact historical narrative about events that take place, not in the sanctuary or the theatre, but in the workaday world of fact. It would be instructive, did time permit, to show how those very incidents which may strike us as the most poetic and mythological, which display the closest resemblances to the archetypal ritual pattern, are inextricably interwoven by the evangelists with down-to-earth existence at its most personal and individual, its most prosaic and even squalid; and it is precisely in and through this that they see the transcendent mystery. If Jesus is the victim of a ritual murder, he is still more obviously the victim of commonplace human passions and vested interests: the jealousy of the clergy, the avarice of Judas, the punctilious conservatism of the Pharisees, the disappointed fury of the revolutionary mob, the appeasement diplomacy of Pilate. If there is a sacrifice, it is now a sordid and secular execution; if there is a labyrinth, it is now the actual winding streets used by the man-in-the-street in a provincial capital; if there is a search, the searcher is now no goddess, but a very human woman called Mary of Magdala, setting about the very human task of embalming a dead human body.

All this reverses the normal process of folk-memory, which, we know, tends to mythologize history; now it is rather the mythological pattern that is realized in historical fact. It is also the very reverse of the old rites. In his stimulating little book, *The Myth of Eternal Return*,[1] the eminent Rumanian historian of religion, Mircea Eliade, sees in the old New Year rites a periodic effort to escape from the profane to the sacred, to abolish time past and utterly destroy the previous year, and to make a new start in a state of consciousness which is outside time altogether. They offered an escape from the vicissitudes and miseries of temporal existence to archetypal origins, from earth to paradise, from the uncertainties and disorder and strife of Becoming to the certainty and order and tranquillity of Being. In spite of the efforts of the higher religions and philosophies to make some sense of earthly existence and suffering—notably in India with its doctrine of *karma*—it was, he finds, only in Israel, with its new dimension of 'faith in the absurd', that it was possible for historic existence to be regarded as itself a manifestation of God and the divine purpose, in and through which deliverance and re-creation is to be found. The Christian sees the fulfilment of this in the Incarnation; his emphasis on the matter-of-factness of the Passion and Resurrection (so painful to the poet and the myth-lover to this day) is in line with his central belief that the creative Word, the divine message of healing and life, has become flesh and blood in determined units of space and time. The inner reality which the ancient rituals had expressed is now lived through. With Georges Berguer we may say, 'Jesus had incarnated in his death and resurrection an inner experience that had existed potentially for centuries in the human soul, but that had never passed beyond the sphere of the dream. He translated into life the secular dream of the peoples'.[2]

This translation into actual life of the perennial dream means—in psychological jargon—that the unconscious projection is now withdrawn: it is now interiorized, made

---

1. *Le mythe d'éternel retour* (Paris, Gallimard, 1949).
2. G. Berguer, *Some Aspects of the Life of Jesus*, p. 265, quoted R. Scott Frayn, *Revelation and the Unconscious*, p. 182.

fully conscious, and is now voluntarily *lived* out—no longer blindly, instinctively, periodically just *acted*. The Christian scriptures stress this 'interiorization'. We have already remarked how the 'agony' or combat is now an interior one fought out in sweat and tears in Gethsemane. The Gospels stress constantly the willingness with which Christ goes to his death; he *can* evade it, but he declines; he lays down his own life, no one, he says, takes it from him; inward love for his friends, not outer compulsion, leads him to the cross. Pilate, Herod and the rest are but instruments of a divine purpose; Christ freely offers himself, and 'he is offered because it is his own will'—the priest and the victim are one and the same.

With this consummation in a unique *self*-sacrifice of the old sacrifices, in which one slew another, the old multiplicity of sacrifices becomes obsolete, for the willing self-sacrifice has a universal validity. Just because it has become particularized, it is new for each and for all. 'It is expedient that one should die for the people, and the whole nation perish not,' said the last priest of the old order; and the evangelist of the new at once glosses that 'Jesus should die . . . not only for the nation, but to gather together in one *all* the dispersed children of God'.

But the self-sacrifice of Christ is not only new, it is also *final*—and this is perhaps the most startling novelty. Frazer, and still more emphatically Eliade and other writers, have drawn attention to the fact that it is of the very essence of the old dying god ritual that it should be repeated over and over again *ad infinitum*. We remember the verse from Macaulay about the priest of Nemi which Frazer quoted at the beginning of his work:

> The priest who slew the slayer,
> And shall himself be slain.

Compare that with St Paul's, 'Christ, rising from the dead, dieth now *no more*. Death shall *no more* have dominion over him. For in that he died to sin, he died *once*; but in that he liveth, he liveth unto God'. (Rom. 6. 9-10). Just because it has been lived and died out in fact and history, consciously and voluntarily, the myth is not destroyed but fulfilled; its endless repetition is broken together with its unconscious, compulsive power. Indeed, in becoming fact it ceases to be mere myth.

We are not now arguing whether these beliefs about the crucified Nazarene are true, but only recalling, in a brief and broad summary, that such was and is the significance he had, and has, for Christians. Further research and reflection may show more clearly how far these beliefs also are anticipated in pre-Christian varieties and developments of the dying god pattern. We know now, at least, that the nineteenth-century 'Quest for the Historic Jesus' was a vain illusion, if by this is meant the isolation of naked facts apart from any significance they had for Christ's own mind, or the minds of his followers: an 'historical Jesus' other than the 'Christ of faith' is a pseudo-scientific abstraction which could not have existed, and of whom there is not any historical record. Our only evidence for assessment is in the records, and (whatever historical or literary criticism may say of their provenance, date and construction), what the records record is that the Word is made flesh, the meaning is embodied in the facts, and the facts disclose the meaning.

We cannot, however, conclude without referring briefly to two questions which, these days, we can hardly evade. If the events on Golgotha put an end to the endless repetition of the rites of dying gods, why then does the Church ritual go on repeating them—as we have seen that it does? The second is more general, and more serious: if Golgotha spelt the twilight of the gods, a transmutation of religions into religion, must we not now confront a further stage in which even that must be left behind—and face a 'death of God' in the manner of Nietzsche? Has not science made Christ also obsolete and superfluous?—in particular, has not the pscyhology of the unconscious, with its study and application of psychic transformation through symbolism, outmoded also the dying God-Man of Calvary? In answering the first, perhaps we can at least point the way to the answer to the second.

Yes, it is true that the ancient Christian liturgies of Holy Week and Easter closely resemble the old rites of Spring. But their *significance* for those who take part in them is found wholly in what Christ is related to have done 'once for all': they are done in remembrance of him. But, and this is important, the Paschal ceremonies are not—with one single, significant exception—obligatory. A Catholic is quite free to attend, or stay away from, most of them: the Church does not force them on him, though she continues to make them available if he finds them helpful to the self-sacrificial following of Christ. If we try to evade that self-sacrifice by projecting that task on to him, he tells us we cannot be his disciples unless we take up our own cross and follow him. The Incarnation means that the projection must be wholly withdrawn, we may not again mythologize or ritualize the pattern that must now be lived out in fact. If the transforming power of the ancient symbols helps us to do that, they are available to that end. But the Church insists that these rites and ceremonies are what she calls optional 'sacramentals'; any efficacy they have is what theologians call *ex opere operantis*, wholly dependent, that is to say, on the response of the participant to the stimulus of the symbol. That this is the way symbols generally function has been amply confirmed by analytical psychology.

But there is one striking exception to all this: the Church insists that participation in the Easter *thysia* (or sacrifice) and *deipnon* (banquet)—the Mass and Communion—*is* indispensable and of obligation. For here, she explains, is something whose efficacy does *not* depend on our response, but is inherent in what is done—*ex opere operato*. Something is done which we cannot do for ourselves, nor do without. The sacrifice and sacrament, to be genuine at all, must be an act of God, of which we may be the instruments or the recipients, but which we cannot originate. Paganism also has sensed that the Giver, the Gift and the Receiver of Sacrifice must somehow be one, and somehow divine—

I knew that I hung on the wind-swept tree
Nine nights through,
Wounded by a spear, dedicated to Odin
I myself to myself.

Rachel Levy in her *The Gate of Horn* has indicated how already
in a Stone Age environment, sacrifice is considered to be a
giving *of* God *by* God *to* God in and through the human
priest and victim or his surrogate. St Paul sees that in the
very human death on Calvary, it is 'God in Christ who is
reconciling the world to himself', and it is on that account
that the Church dogma has insisted on the unmixed and
undiluted Godhead and manhood of her Lord. It is one of
the achievements of analytical psychology to have shown the
psychological need to which this responds. We talk loosely
of self-sacrifice, and we may mean quite heroic selflessness
and altruism. But, as C. G. Jung explains in his remarkable
work on *The Transforming Symbolism of the Mass*,[1] that is not
yet sacrifice. Self-sacrifice means whole self-giving, an
unqualified renunciation of every claim on what we possess
—and we do not possess ourselves. Indeed, the more we
advance in self-knowledge and self-possession, with or without the aid of psychology, the less we find we know, the
more we find that is beyond our dominion and control, the
more we know we are *not* our own, and therefore are
incapable of self-sacrifice. Only a Lord of all, who possesses
all, can initiate and consummate the sacrifice and impart to
us the new life which springs from death.

Psychology can tell us, in a new way, why such things
would be so, and within the limits of empirical observation,
how, why, and what the symbols work. But more than that it
cannot tell us: it cannot tell us if there be any such Lord
(even though it sometimes finds it must postulate a 'superordinated personality'), it cannot assure us that such sacrifice
really exists. As Jung puts it in the essay I have mentioned,

1. *Eranos Jahrbuch*, 1940-41. An English abstract by Monica
Curtis has been published by the Guild of Pastoral Psychology, Lecture 69.

'Psychology can deal with the matter only from the phenomenological standpoint. The truth or reality of religion lies beyond the competence of psychology.' Yet the psyche's own deepest yearning, even for its own health and sanity, is for truth and reality, whatever may be the cost of abandoning agreeable make-believe. At this very point, however, the limitations of psychology's own empirical method compel it ever to confess its ignorance, and to point elsewhere for any answer there may be. Perhaps analytical psychology itself is in danger of degenerating into a retrogressive mythology, an esoteric sect of initiates, if it fails to recognize the word made flesh, the Christian demand for the earthly realization of the symbol.

But this is not to say that analytical psychology has nothing to offer us, even those of us who call ourselves Christians. Professor Frankfort has told us how Jung's interpretations have elucidated a variety of Egyptian texts and usages which has hitherto been entirely obscure to the Egyptologist. But to many a modern man, the symbols employed by Christ and the Church have become every bit as obscure as the sarcophagus or titles of a Pharaoh. They leave him cold, because he no longer sees their significance and relevance to his own daily life. But there are many who have rediscovered that significance and relevance through analytical psychology, perhaps just by reading about it, but perhaps through experience of analysis and of their own inner life. These make some such discovery as they work through from the seemingly petty, personal, superficial problem to the collective, archetypal factors found behind it—factors so destructive when neglected or rejected, so healing when recognized and placated. But this, it is always found, can only come about by way of sacrifice; by total dispossession of what possesses us.

But we find also that, while sacrifice is indispensable, it is also impossible to the conscious ego—to you and me; that it can be possible only to a greater power within us, the power which men have called God. Jung has said that no matter how much he and his patients contribute to an analysis, they can at best only prepare the way, remove the obstacles, to healing. Healing itself, he says, always comes in some wholly unexpected way from the unknown, '*wie ein Wunder*'—like a miracle. For when the sacrifice is made, it is given back transformed and transforming. But sacrifice there must be, whether or not expressed in external ordinances; and psychology has strangely confirmed what theology has always maintained, that sacrifice can only be complete and perfect when it is the free and whole self-oblation of a dying man, who must also be the dying God.

ACKNOWLEDGMENTS

The Author and the Publishers wish to express their thanks and acknowledgments for permission to make use of copyright material to Messrs A. & C. Black Ltd., for the extract from Austin Farrer's *Glass of Vision;* to Messrs Ernest Benn Ltd., for the extracts from Ernest Jones' *Psycho-analysis;* to Messrs Jonathan Cape Ltd., for the extract from Hans Prinzhorn's *Psychotherapy;* to the Commonweal Publishing Company, for the extract from Karl Stern's article, *Religion and Psychiatry;* to Messrs Geoffrey Bles Ltd. and Dr Halliday Sutherland, for the extracts from the latter's *Lapland Journey;* to Messrs T. & T. Clark, for the extract from *Hastings' Encyclopædia of Religion and Ethics;* to Messrs G. Duckworth & Co. Ltd., for the extracts from J. C. Flugel's *A Hundred Years of Psychology;* to Messrs Faber & Faber Ltd., for the extract from Rachel Levy's *The Gate of Horn;* to Mr John Farquharson for the extract from William James' *Varieties of Religious Experience;* to Dr Edward Glover, for the extracts from his *Freud and Jung;* to Messrs B. Herder, for the extract from Father Prümmer's *Manuale Theologiæ Moralis;* to The Hogarth Press Ltd. and The Liveright Publishing Co. Inc., for the extracts from Sigmund Freud's *The Future of an Illusion,* and to The Hogarth Press Ltd. and Messrs Alfred Knopf Inc., for the extracts from the same author's *Moses and Monotheism;* to Messrs Macmillan & Co. Ltd., for the extracts from Sir J. G. Frazer's *The Golden Bough* and from William Temple's *Nature, Man and God;* to Messrs T. Nelson & Sons, for the extracts from Raymond Cattell's *Psychology and the Religious Quest;* to The Oxford University Press for the extracts from Werner Jaeger's *Aristotle;* to Messrs Pantheon Books Inc., for the extract from Rachel Bespaloff's *On the Iliad;* to Messrs Penguin Books Ltd., for the extracts from C. K. Odgen's *ABC of Psychology* and from their edition of Sigmund Freud's *Totem and Taboo;* to Messrs Rider & Co., and Professor A. N. Whitehead, for the extract from the latter's *Essays in Science and Philosophy;* to Messrs

Routledge & Kegan Paul, and the authors concerned, for the extracts from *The Psychology of C. G. Jung*, by Jolan Jacobi, from *Contributions to Analytical Psychology*, *The Integration of the Personality*, *Modern Man in Search of a Soul*, *Psychological Types*, and *The Psychology of the Unconscious*, all by C. G. Jung, from *Religion and the Cure of Souls in Jung's Psychology*, by Hans Schaer, and from *The Philosophy of the Unconscious*, *by* Eduard von Hartmann; to Messrs Williams and Norgate Ltd., for the extract from G. Berguer's *Some Aspects of the Life of Jesus*, and to The Yale University Press, for the extracts from C. G. Jung's *Psychology and Religion*.

INDEX OF BOOKS AND PERIODICALS
QUOTED FROM OR REFERRED TO.

ABC of Psychology, The (Ogden), 24
Adversus Haereses (Irenaeus), 201-202
Aion (Jung), 75n, 179n
American Journal of Religious Psychology, The, 4
Analytical Psychology and the English Mind (Baynes), 36
Analytics (Aristotle), 90
Ancient Mariner, The (Coleridge), 33
Annalen der philosophischen Geselleschaft Innerschweiz und Ostschweiz, xxxii
Année Théologique, L', xxxii
Apologia (Tertullian), 38
Aristotle (Jaeger), 82, 92, 98, 107
Aristotle: De Anima (Hicks), 90n
Art romantique et le rêve, L' (Béguin), xxix, 32-34
Asgard and the Norse Heroes (Boult), 18n

Bedeutung des Vaters, Die (Jung), 51
Belle Dame sans Merci, La (Keats), 33
Between Man and Man (Buber), 81
Blackfriars, xxxii
British Journal of Medical Psychology, The, 193

Catholic Encyclopedia, The, 185
Christian Healing (Frost), 181n
Christianity After Freud (Sanders), 45
Church and Gnosis (Burkitt), 197n
Comm. in Summa Theologica (Cajetan), 74
Commonweal, xxxii, 193
Confessions (St. Augustine), 214
Contra Epistolam Manichaei (St. Augustine), 214
Contributions to Analytical Psychology (Jung), 86, 152
Coué and St. Paul (Temple), 58n
Critique of the Practical Reason (Kant), 34
Critique of Pure Reason (Kant), 98

237

De Anima (Aristotle), 68, 81, 87-101 passim, 104
De Anima (Tertullian), 97
De Divinatione per Somnia (Aristotle), 107, 109, 110
De Malo (Aquinas), 128
De Memoria et Reminiscentia (Aristotle), 26, 89
De Sensu et Sensato (Aristotle), 89
De Sortibus (Aquinas), 122
De Testimonio Animae (Tertullian), 38-39, 179
De Trinitate (St. Augustine), 73
De Unitate Intellectus (Aquinas), 100
De Veritate (Aquinas), 99n, 108-109, 113, 114, 115, 123, 126, 128, 129, 130, 131, 132, 133, 134, 135, 137, 138
Diagnosis of Man (Walker), 160n
Dictionnaire de Théologie Catholique (Deman), 158n
Dieu Vivant, 125
Dominican Studies, xxxii, 75n

Enchiridion Symbolorum (Denzinger-Bannwart), 97n
Encyclopaedia Britannica, 28
Eranos Jahrbuch VIII, 73n, 231
            XII, 83, 90
            XIII, 6n, 17, 23
            XIV, xxxii
            XVIII, 131
Essay on Human Understanding (Locke), 34
Essays in Christian Politics, 58n
Essays in Science and Philosophy (Whitehead), 5-6
Ethics, Eudemean (Aristotle), 82
Ethics, Nicomachean (Aristotle), 82 ff.
Eudemus (Aristotle), 101

Freud and Jung (Glover), 27n, 28
Future of an Illusion, The (Freud), 4, 27, 28, 41, 42-44

Gate of Horn, The (Levy), 231
Geist der Naturwissenschaft (Schroedinger), 6n
Geist der Psychologie, Der (Jung), 17, 23, 71n
Glass of Vision, The (Farrer), 221
Gloria Dei, xxxii
Gnose Valentinienne et le témoignage de Saint Irenée, La (Sagnard), 213
God and Man (Brunner), 76-77

God and Philosophy (Gilson), 104n
Golden Bough, The (Frazer), 1, 215-220, 223
Griechische Mythen in christlicher Deutung (Rahner), 2n
Grundzüge der physiologischen Psychologie (Wundt), 96n
Guild of Pastoral Psychology Tutorial Reading Course (Wolff), 153n

Harvard Theological Review, 102n
Hastings' Encyclopaedia of Religion and Ethics, 196
Heiligkeit und Gesundheit (Goldbrunner), xxix, 71
Horizon, 27n
Hundred Years of Psychology, A (Flugel), 26, 34

Idéal religieux des Grecs et l'evangile, L' (Festugière), 101
Individuation (Goldbrunner), xxix, 71
Integration of the Personality, The (Jung), 80, 154-155
Introduction to the Psychology of Religion, An (Thouless), 4n, 67n
Ion (Plato), 110

Kinsey Report, The, 19

Lapland Journey (Sutherland), 13-14
Life of One's Own, A ("Field"), 15

Malleus Maleficarum, 175
Mamre (Buber), 207
Man in Revolt (Brunner), 76n
Man, Morals and Society (Flugel), 20, 67, 158-162
Man the Unknown (Carrel), 160n
Manuale Theologiae Moralis (Prümmer), 186-187
Materials for the Study of the Apostolic Gnosis (Lee and Bond), 204n
Merkur, 193n
Metaphysics (Aristotle), 91n, 92, 94, 96-97, 107, 110
Méthode psychoanalytique et la doctrine freudienne, La (Dalbiez), 41
Modern Man in Search of a Soul (Jung), 19, 20, 47-48, 61n, 79n, 84n, 92n, 154-155, 191-192
Moses and Monotheism (Freud), 21, 26, 27n, 28, 41, 42
Mythe de l'éternel retour, Le (Eliade), 227

Natur und Idee (Carus), 31
Nature, 126n
Nature, Man and God (Temple), 98n
Naturerklärung und Psyche, 58n
New Ways in Psychoanalysis (Horney), 20

On Prayer (Aristotle), 107
On the Iliad (Bespaloff), 203
Outline of Psychoanalysis (Freud), 26n, 36, 37

Paranormal Cognition (Bendit), 118n
Personality of Man, The (Tyrrell), 36n
Philosophy of the Unconscious (von Hartmann), 31
Physical Basis of Personality (Mottram), 160n
Pistis Sophia, 201, 204, 206, 211-213
Protagoras (Plato), 102n
Psyche (Carus), 28-31
Psycho-analysis (Jones), 36
Psychological Types (Jung), 11, 37, 85, 188
Psychologie des C. G. Carus (Bernoulli), 30
Psychologie und Alchemie (Jung), 62, 86
Psychology and Religion (Jung), 65
Psychology and the Religious Quest (Cattell), 3, 8-10
Psychology for Ministers and Social Workers (Guntripp), 64n
Psychology of C. G. Jung (Jacobi), 51n, 55n, 64, 65, 153n
Psychology of the Unconscious (Jung), 50-56, 66n
Psychopathology of Everyday Life, The (Freud), 46n
Psychotherapy, Its Nature, Its Assumptions, Its Limitations (Prinzhorn), 192-193

Rätsel der Seele, xxix, 34n, 36, 71
Religion and the Cure of Souls in Jung's Psychology (Schär), 66, 70
Religion and the Sciences of Life (MacDougall), 7, 10
Religion, Its Essence and Manifestation (van der Leeuw), 42n
Religiöse Erfahrung der Naturvölker (Radin), 67n
Revelation and the Unconscious (Scott Frayn), 70, 227n
Révélation d'Hermès Trismégiste, La (Festugière), 194
Revue des Sciences Théologiques et Philosophiques, 90
Revue Néoscolastique, 81n

St. John Climacus (Sumner), 189
Saint Thomas d'Aquin et la psychologie des profondeurs (Plé), 64n
Science News, 8n
Secret of the Golden Flower, The (Jung), 17, 21, 22, 58
Some Aspects of the Life of Jesus (Berguer), 227
Stromata (Clement of Alexandria), 194
Structure de l'ame et l'experience mystique, La (Gardeil), 106n
Successful Error, The (Allers), 48-49

Summa Theologica (Aquinas), 68, 73n, 83-84, 93n, 99n, 104-106, 107-139 *passim*
Supplément de La Vie Spirituelle, Le, 64n
Surnaturel et les dieux d'après les maladies mentales, Le (Dumas), 4n
Symbolik des Geistes (Jung), 178n

Tabula Aurea (Peter of Bergamo), 136n
Timaeus (Plato), 88
Totem and Taboo (Freud), 27, 41, 42, 44
Transforming Symbolism of the Mass, The (Jung), 231-232
Two Essays in Analytical Psychology (Jung), 48n, 50, 51n, 58, 71

Upanishads, The, 96

Varieties of Religious Experience (James), 23
Vedanta, The, 2, 74, 94
Vigiliae Christianae, 202n, 205-206

Walter Hilton: An English Spiritual Guide (White), 80n
Wandlungen und Symbole der Libido, see *Psychology of the Unconscious*
What the Cross Means to Me, 78n
World Chaos: The Responsibility of Science as Cause and Cure (MacDougall), 7, 10
Writings of Tertullian, The, 39n

Zeitschrift für Psychologie (Ach), 24-25
Zur Psychologie der Trinitätsidee (Jung), 73, 75n

INDEX OF AUTHORS QUOTED AND
OTHER PERSONS MENTIONED.

Ach, N., 24-25, 35

Adler, Alfred, 19, 47-48, 54, 154

Aeschylus, 129

Albert the Great, St., 125

Alexander, 2

Allen, Grant, 223

Allers, Rudolf, 48-49

Ammianus Marcellinus, 2n

Anthony the Hermit, St., 187

Aquinas, St. Thomas, xxxiii, 29, 31, 37, 57, 64, 68-69, 73n, 75n, 78n, 80, 81-84, 90, 98, 99, 101, 104-106, 107-139 *passim*, 157, 159, 181-185

Aristotle, xxxiii, 26, 29, 68-69, 80, 81-84, 87-103 *passim*, 104, 106, 107, 109, 110, 159, 170, 194, 195, 225

Augustine, St., 73, 214, 225

Avicenna, 182

Bacon, Roger, 209

Baynes, H. G., 36

Bede the Venerable, St., 218

Béguin, Albert, xxix, 32-34

Bendit, L. J., 118n

Berguer, Georges, 227

Bernoulli, Christoph, 30

Bespaloff, Rachel, 203

Blake, William, 33, 204

Bleuler, Eugen, 26

Boethius, 127n

Boltzmann, 6

Bond, 204n

Boult, K., 18n

Bouyer, 125

Brown, William, 144

Brunner, Emil, 76-77

Buber, Martin, 81, 193n, 207

Burkitt, F. C., 197n

Cajetan, Cardinal de Vio, 74n

Carington, Whateley, 119

Carrel, A., 160n

Carus, C. G., 28-31, 35, 83

Catherine of Siena, St., 187

Cattell, Raymond, 3, 8-10, 18, 162

Charcot, 25

Chenu, M. D., 82

Clement of Alexandria, 194, 197, 213

Coleridge, S. T., 33

Curtis, Monica, 231n

Dalbiez, Roland, 41, 45, 48, 144

Deman, T., 158n

Democritus, 88

Denzinger-Bannwart, 97n

Descartes, Réné, 26, 32, 96n, 98

Dessauer, F., 6n

Dio Chrysostom, 218-219

Dryden, John, 33

Dumas, Georges, 4

Dunne, J. W., 119

Eccles, J. C., 126n
Ehrenwald, 118n
Ehrhardt, A., 102n
Einstein, Albert, 7, 98
Eliade, Mircea, 227, 228
Empedocles, 88

Farrer, Austin, 221
Festugière, 90, 101, 194
Fichte, J. G., 31
"Field, Joanna," 15
Flugel, J. C., 20, 26, 34, 67, 158-162
Frankfort, Henry, xxxii, 216, 220-221, 225, 232
Frayn, Scott, 70, 227n
Frazer, J. G., 1, 203, 215-220, 223, 224, 227
Frege, 6
Frei, Gebhard, xxxii, 66, 71
Freud, Sigmund, xvii, xxxiii, 4, 19, 20-21, 25-28, 29, 36-37, 41-46, 47-50, 52-54, 55, 57, 59, 64, 67, 117, 143, 151-152, 154, 188, 191, 221
Frost, Evelyn, 181n

Gardeil, A., 106n
Gilson, E., 82, 104n
Glover, Edward, 27n, 28
Goldbrunner, Josef, xxix, 71
Grabmann, 82
Groethuysen, Bernhard, 81
Guntrip, H., 64n

Hamann, 34
Hegel, G. W. F., 31, 55
Heraclitus, 88, 94
Herbart, 26
Hicks, A. D., 90n
Hilton, Walter, 79, 80n
Hippolytus, 196, 207

Hitler, Adolf, 200
Hocart, 224
Hölderlin, 198
Homer, 203
Horney, Karen, 20

Irenaeus, St., 200, 201-202, 205-206, 207, 209, 213

Jacobi, Jolan, 51n, 55n, 64, 65n, 153n, 154-155, 156
Jaeger, Werner, 81-82, 92-93n, 98, 107
James, William, 23
John Climacus, St., 189
John of the Cross, St., 2
Jones, Ernest, 36
Julian the Apostate, 2

Kant, Emmanuel, 3, 34, 37, 98, 107
Keats, John, 33
Kinsey, 19

Lee, 204n
Legge, 197
Levy, Rachel, 231
Lichtenburg, G. C., 33
Liebnitz, G. W. von, 34
Locke, 34

Macaulay, Thomas, 228
MacDougall, William, 7, 10
Macmurray, 9
Mandonnet, 82
Mansion, A., 81n
Maritain, Jacques, 48, 144
Marx, Karl, 55
Mottram, V. H., 160n

Nietzsche, F. W., 229
Noldin, 187

Ogden, C. K., 24
Origen, 213
Otto, Rudolph, 65, 179

Parmenides, 94
Peter of Bergamo, 136n
Pfister, 45
Plato, 31, 82, 87, 89, 90, 91, 95,
    96, 97, 102, 104, 110, 111,
    194
Plé, A., 64n
Plotinus, 74, 194
Pope, Alexander, 33
Prümmer, 186-187
pseudo-Denys, 128
Pythagoras, 87

Quispel, G., 202n, 205n

Radin, P., 67n
Raglan, Lord, 224
Rahner, K., 2n
Robertson Smith, 28n, 223, 224
Russell, Bertrand, 6n
Ruysbroeck, 128

Sagnard, F. M., 213n
Sanders, B. G., 45
Schaer, Hans, xxix, 64, 66, 70
Schärf, Rivkah, 178n
Schelling, F. von, 30, 31, 35
Schleiermacher, 65, 107
Schmidt, K. L., 131
Schopenhauer, A., 31, 35
Schroeder, Theodore, 4
Schweitzer, A., 179
Scott, E. F., 196
Shelley, P. B., 33
Shepherd, 119
Simonides of Cos, 102n
Socrates, 194, 195
Spence, Lewis, 224

Speusippus, 102
Spiess, E., 36
Spinoza, B., 31
Stern, Karl, 193
Strauss, E. B., 193
Sumner, Oswald, 189
Sutherland, Halliday, 13-15

Temple, William, 58n, 98n
Tertullian, 38-39, 57, 97, 179,
    213
Thouless, R. H., 4n, 67n
Tyrrell, G. N. M., 36n

Valentinus, 201, 205, 207
van der Leeuw, G., 42n
Virgil, 217, 218
von Hartmann, Eduard, 31-32,
    34-35

Walker, Kenneth, 160n
White, Victor, 75n, 78n
Whitehead, A. N., 5-6
Wilhelm, R., 58n
Wili, Walter, 83, 90, 101n
Wilwoll, A., 34n
Wolff, Toni, 153n
Wundt, 96n

Zeno, 94